U.S.

v.

Crime in the Streets

U.S.
v.
Crime in the Streets

Thomas E. Cronin, Tania Z. Cronin,
and Michael E. Milakovich

INDIANA UNIVERSITY PRESS
Bloomington

Library of Congress Cataloging in Publication Data
Cronin, Thomas E.

U.S. v. crime in the streets.
Bibliography: p.
Includes index.
1. Crime and criminals—Political aspects—United
States. 2. Criminal justice, Administration of—Political aspects—United States. 3. Crime prevention—Political aspects—United States. I. Cronin, Tania Z.,
1943– . II. Milakovich, Michael E. III. Title.
HV6791.C76 364'.973 80-8842
ISBN 0-253-19017-7 AACR2
1 2 3 4 5 85 84 83 82 81

Contents

PREFACE

Politics is inevitably about power and justice. Ours is a book about power and justice *and crime*—about the politics of the national war on crime in the streets. We trace the national war on crime from its birth in the early 1960s through its troubled implementation in the 1970s to its demise in the early 1980s.

In the grand sweep of twentieth-century American history, what will probably be remembered most about the national war on crime is the emotional rhetoric calling for law and order in the 1960s and the persisting question for the later decades of why it is we have had to endure so much violent crime in a free society. Less well understood is the national response: the debates about social justice v. law and order, the countless presidential commissions and messages, a national $8 billion program of justice assistance for state and local governments and the inevitable bureaucracies at all levels this entailed, and the experiments in governing, the relegislation, and the reorganizations that went on for over twelve years in an effort to win the war on crime.

This is the story, for the most part, of a beleaguered, frustrated, and failed national effort—the kind of effort costly not only in terms of taxpayers' money and legislators' time but also to our sense of confidence in the ability of the national government to work, to solve problems, to govern.

Back around 1967, George Aiken, a respected Republican veteran U.S. senator from Vermont, came up with a novel way to end the war in Vietnam, a war America couldn't seem to win and couldn't seem to conclude: why not just declare we'd won and pull out? But, of course, we stayed on in Southeast Asia yet another five years, only to lose another thirty thousand of our own boys and probably about three or four times as many South Vietnamese, and only *then* did we pretty much do what Aiken suggested. In a sense, the Aiken solution has also been applied to the national war on crime, another war we just couldn't seem to win and couldn't seem to conclude.

National politics in presidential elections helped launch a national war on crime—the federal government, for the first time in our nation's history, became involved in helping to fight crime in the streets across the country. But in spite of billions of dollars of federal money, crime continued to spiral upwards. By 1981, as this book went to press, the number of murders per week in the U.S. rivaled the number of American boys lost per week at the height of the Vietnam War. Said critic Sen. William Proxmire (D-Wis.), "The Law Enforcement Assistance Administration (LEAA) has failed to help solve the nation's crime problem or to improve the criminal justice system. It has merely become a budgetary crutch for local law enforcement authorities."[1] So, after twelve years of the national war on crime, Congress and the president pulled out.

Throughout the war on crime, as with the war in Vietnam, there were deep questions as to whether the national government should have been involved to begin with. But in the case of crime, these questions will continue to be vitally important to every American.

We wish to state our position on several points. First, we accept as valid the assumption that violent crime did increase in the 1960s and 1970s. Further, we believe the national government *can* play a valuable role in helping to fight crime, at least in research, demonstration, and evaluation. We believe that despite all its problems, the Law Enforcement Assistance Administration did make positive contributions. All the same, however, the national war on crime was poorly conceived, ill managed, and ineffective. Putting it gently, about half the monies seem to have been wasted, another hefty quarter was eaten up by costly overhead, such as bureaucracy feeding and grant writing, and perhaps only twenty-five cents on the dollar was left as a possibly worthwhile investment. Not a complete waste, but not good enough.

We have tried to be objective, to avoid the condescending, put-down, muckraking style so often used in talking about governmental failures. The benefit of hindsight makes things that were once so complicated, untidy, and incomprehensible seem clear and simple. Instead we have tried to put ourselves—and our reader—*in the position of those who were there back then*, who, under all the political pressures, had to plan, grapple, legislate, implement, evaluate, and, in general, make tough decisions about *power* and *justice* and *crime* in America. We neither sought nor received funding from the U.S. government, from LEAA, or from any other source for this project.

We acknowledge our debt to the more than one hundred Justice Department officials, members of Congress, congressional staffers and White House aides whom we interviewed in Washington, D.C., and to the more than one hundred state and local law enforcement officials we interviewed elsewhere around the country. Quotations not otherwise noted come from these interviews. We are grateful for advice, cautions, and encouragement from Michael Couzens, Norval Morris, and James Q. Wilson. We also thank Alice Brown and Helen Lynch for their excellent typing assistance.

One last warning. Beware the great simplifiers. Beware the single solution and quick-fix folks. This is a complicated story, rich in paradoxes, ironies, and dilemmas. There were then, and there are now, no simple solutions, no easy victories—not, at least, for these complex policy questions.

U.S.

v.

Crime in the Streets

ONE

The Politics of Crime in America

> If you want to know what I think, I say the Democrats and all the experts missed the boat on the crime problem. I've got a mother who lives in New York City. She was scared to go out in the 1960s, and it's worse now in the 1980s. She's so terrified of being mugged, she's a goddamned prisoner in her apartment, and there are millions like her. You know what she says? She says the Democrats—her party—lost her on this one. She's mad at them. They thought the whole crime issue was an excuse for racism and didn't take it seriously. But they were out of touch with reality and the real concerns of average people.
> —A friend's conversation with the authors, April 1980

THIS IS THE story of how crime in the streets became a national issue and how the federal government tried, but failed, to win a war on crime. It is a kind of modern-day political fable, a tale of fear and manipulation, promises and neglect, of endless compromise, waste, and disillusionment. Most important, it is the story of a uniquely and magnificently American struggle to reconcile deeply held, competing values.

Today, increasingly, we rely on our national government to solve our society's big problems, complex, overwhelming problems like inflation, unemployment, and energy insufficiency. Yet increasingly we resent big government's regulations, we despair of its ability to make a difference, and we secretly dread that it may not really be capable of providing answers. The national war on crime, whose life history (1967–81) is essentially complete by now, offers us a chance to take a

1

careful look at what happens when we give over our expectations for policy leadership to the federal government. It offers us a chance to stand back and consider whether the solutions the presidency and Congress can provide—given their nature as political institutions—are likely to work or satisfy us. It offers a chance for us to learn, even as we struggle with other overarching social and economic problems in the last two decades of the twentieth century, about the basic governability of America.

The story of the lost war on crime is not simple, and neither are the lessons we learn from it. As perceptions become reality, who was right and who was wrong is not clear-cut. Indeed, the essence of ignorance is the denial of complexity. If ours were a simpler political system, more efficient and more centralized and less devoted to multiple checks and balances and to individual liberties, we would have far less crime on our hands to begin with—and possibly lower unemployment, less inflation, and fewer energy problems as well. No one should expect this study to provide the recipe for solving future problems. But we *can* learn about our *system's ability* to deal with complex social problems.

THE FAILED EXPERIMENT

The case for a strong government in the United States has always rested on the need to secure domestic tranquillity, to put down rebellions, and to repel invasions. Indeed, the Massachusetts rebellion led by Captain Daniel Shays in 1786–87 and the Pennsylvania Whiskey Rebellions a few years later raised the law and order banner and served to strengthen the hand of those who favored a more powerful national government. In the 1960s and 1970s, domestic tranquillity seemed shaken by a nationwide crime wave, a frightening acceleration of assaults, robberies, rapes, and murders in the streets of our cities and suburbs. For really the first time in our nation's history, the national government stepped in to help fight local street crime. What happened?

Presidents and presidential candidates inveighed mightily against a permissive society and promised an all-out war on crime. Congress established a new agency to administer federal funds. Planning agencies were organized in every state, and local police were equipped with countless tons of hardware. Eight billion dollars in federal funds was spent on local police, courts, corrections, juvenile justice, and community programs. But crime in the streets continued at an unacceptably high rate. Citizens grew more fearful and angry. Today, over 40 percent of Americans are afraid they will be murdered, raped, robbed, or assaulted if they walk alone in their own neighborhoods at night.

Two-thirds favor the death penalty for murder. "Crime, and the fear of crime have, like a dark dye, permeated the fabric of American life."[1]

Why can't our government provide its citizens freedom from the fear of being victimized, security from the likelihood of being mugged, raped, or murdered if they walk downtown at night? Did we fail because crime should never have become a national issue to begin with or because presidents should have provided stronger and more effective leadership on the issue? Were our crime control policies ineffective because money was merely pumped into the existing but inadequate criminal justice structure? Or because a series of Supreme Court rulings made it harder to prosecute criminals? Has the debate about law and order and civil liberies merely diverted attention from the economic realities of crime? Is it time to admit there are no democratic solutions to crime?

Or could it be that America has the wisdom and the wealth to solve her crime problem but lacks the commitment, is simply still unwilling to pay the higher taxes or curtail the civil liberties that might be necessary to get to the roots of crime or stop it completely? Milton Eisenhower, for one, thought so. His bitter conclusion: "It's easier to talk about attacking crime and violence than it is to do something about it." Eisenhower, younger brother of the president and former head of Johns Hopkins University, chaired the National Commission on the Causes and Prevention of Violence in 1966. He told President Nixon that we had to double the annual investment of national, state, and local governments in the criminal justice system:

> With regard to overcoming the social causes of crime at an annual cost, we felt, of about twenty billion dollars, I emphasized that most of the things we have to do in this area are already well known to the American people and most of the essential legislation has been enacted; but finances are inadequate. Better schools, better teachers, full employment at fair wages, work opportunities for youth, especially those of the criminally proven ages, a rebuilding and restoration of the tax base of our cities, better housing, reduction of dope addiction, and the ultimate elimination of the ghettoes, by both dispersion of blacks and a counter-migration of whites—all these are essential.[2]

But Eisenhower's recommendations were filed and forgotten. Neither the president nor the public wanted to spend *that* much on fighting crime. In the 1980s, faced with the grim prospect of double-digit inflation, America is more than ever reluctant to spend hundreds of billions of dollars to "cure" crime. President Reagan, even while calling for more action against crime, made the sharpest domestic budget slashes in years and made his first priority increased defense spending.

"Hard-line" and "soft-line" presidential administrations have come and gone, with little effect on soaring crime rates. Thus, many of President Johnson's Great Society programs aimed to improve the social conditions considered responsible for crime. Liberals raised the question of whether we could expect blacks and other minorities to obey a system of laws that was so obviously unfair. Said Johnson, "I feared that as long as these citizens were alienated from the rights of the American system, they would continue to consider themselves outside the obligations of that system."[3] Then President Nixon tried to direct the nation's attention and sympathy away from the festering inequalities of inner cities and toward the silently suffering, law-abiding majority. Strongly indicting society's permissiveness and disrespect for the law, he tried to strengthen the hand of law enforcement officials through legislative proposals and court appointments. But as the Federal Bureau of Investigation (FBI) crime index continued, relentlessly, to rise, critics of all political persuasions questioned whether the billions of dollars the federal government spent were justified. The national war on crime became another casualty of the quest for a balanced budget and was disbanded.

Yet even as this book went to press, there was new talk of a war on crime. Chief Justice Warren Burger said America was being held a "hostage" to crime and called for a renewed national war on crime. Liberals immediately objected that the only real cure for crime is to end poverty. In 1981, Reagan's attorney general, William French Smith, set up yet another bipartisan, blue-ribbon task force to determine whether and how the national government should be involved in helping to fight street crime. Will these new efforts be any more successful than the old? Does America just have to learn to live with crime?

CRIME—AMERICAN STYLE

The politics of the war on crime should be understood in the context of the larger political and social systems in America. Our political system, of course, is distinguished for its dispersion of powers, its checks and balances, its emphasis on individual rights and democratic procedures. Compromise is a virtue. Changes come slowly, incrementally, in small margins. We are suspicious of long-range planning and sweeping, systemwide reform, and our processes are designed to reflect this suspicion.

Our social structure is beset with the blessings and difficulties of diversity. We talk the ideology of equality yet practice economic and social discrimination. We admire rugged individualism and the self-made man while we continue to suffer high unemployment and to rely on an inadequate welfare system. We deplore and fear violent crime; yet we permit a domestic arms race. No other society tolerates—and even encourages—so many competing values.

For the voter, the issue of crime is not a spectator matter; it evokes emotional judgments about his or her personal safety and value judgments about the character of the criminal, the proper deterrents, and the role of government. Americans are divided, not only on the causes of crime, e.g., victimization by an unjust society versus inherent individual wickedness, but also about how laws should be enforced, e.g., the need for retribution and punishment versus the fear of abuses of police power, threats to privacy, and unequal justice. Americans are even uncertain about the degree of respect warranted for the law, given our continuing and pervasive class and race biases and our recent unpopular involvement in Vietnam.

Moreover, violence has had a long, if not cherished, tradition in America. The early Americans employed brutal methods to drive the American Indians westward. An every-man-for-himself mentality flourished as prospectors, adventurers, and entrepreneurs thrived. There are those who feel America's sanctioning of official violence, such as slavery or Vietnam, has been at fault:

> Violence is, so to speak, an official reality. No society exists without using force or violence and without devising sanctions for violence which are used to uphold just wars and necessary police actions. But the frequency and the manner in which official violence is used is of signal importance to the legitimation of the civic order. Any liberal democratic state is in danger of wearing away its legitimacy if it repeatedly uses violence.[4]

In the aftermath of the assassinations of John and Robert Kennedy and Martin Luther King and the attempted assassination of Ronald Reagan, many asked whether the American character was somehow peculiarly prone to habits of violence. After all, the psychiatrist Karl Menninger contended, society secretly wants crime. Perhaps American society more than others?

HOW LARGE A PROBLEM REALLY?

Precise and accurate information on the extent of crime is difficult to obtain, in part because most crimes are not reported to the police. Published crime statistics were notoriously unreliable in the 1960s and, though improved by the mid-1980s, still leave much to be desired. In the FBI's Uniform Crime Reports (UCR), which have been collected

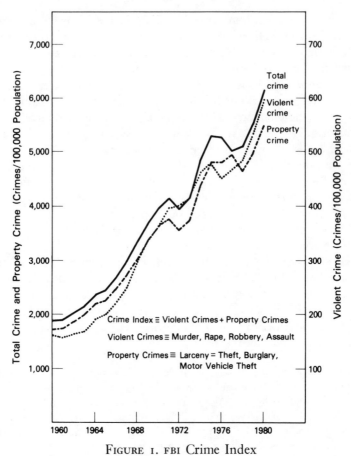

FIGURE 1. FBI Crime Index

Source: FBI, *Index of Crime, U.S.* (mimeographed) (Washington, D.C.: FBI, 1960–75) and *Uniform Crime Reports* (Washington, D.C.: FBI, 1976–79 and Jan.–June 1980).

since 1930, local police tabulate the crimes reported to them, and these lists are compiled by the FBI. Public awareness focuses almost exclusively on the FBI's index crimes: murder, rape, robbery, aggravated assault, burglary, larceny,* auto theft, and arson, which was added to the crime index in 1978. The other available national crime statistic is the National Crime Survey (NCR), or victimization survey, begun in 1973 by the Law Enforcement Assistance Administration. In victimization surveys a national sample of 132,000 members of 60,000 households is questioned as to whether and how they had been victims of a crime in the past six months. The classifications of crime in the UCR

*Since 1973 all larcenies have been counted. Earlier FBI reports included only larcenies over fifty dollars.

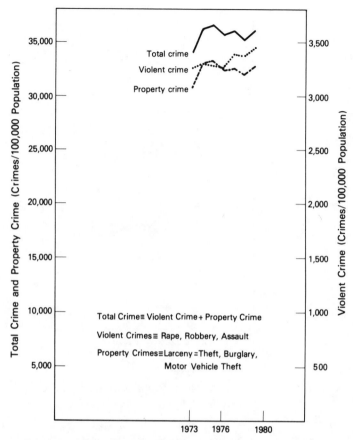

FIGURE 2. Department of Justice Victimization Surveys
Source: Bureau of Justice Statistics, *Criminal Victimization in the U.S.* (Washington, D.C.: BJS, 1980).

and the NCS are fairly similar (with the exception of murder, whose victims cannot be interviewed!, and arson, whose victim is sometimes the perpetrator).

The FBI crime index has risen rapidly in the past two decades (figure 1), but victimization studies, for the years in which they have been made, show little change in the rate of crime (figure 2). Yet surveys of victims also suggest that the FBI crime index reflects only a small fraction of the real crime rate—well under half of all crimes are reported to police (figure 3). Thus, the relatively stable crime rates indicated by victimization studies are *much higher* than the increasing FBI crime index rates.

Reconciling these statistics is complicated by the limitations inherent in both methods of data collection. Victimization surveys depend on

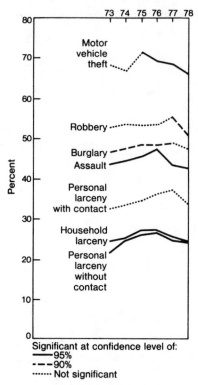

FIGURE 3. Percentage of Victimizations Reported to the Police,
by Type of Crime, 1973–78

Source: Bureau of Justice Statistics, *Criminal Victimization in the U.S.: 1973–78
Trends*, a National Crime Survey Report, NCS-N-13, NCJ-66716 (Washington,
D.C.: BJS, Dec. 1980), p. 6.

sampling techniques and the memory and good faith of the respondent;
transients, non-English speakers, and the extremely poor are more difficult to reach by questionnaire or interview. It is possible that the UCR
figures can fluctuate independently of actual crime rates. Through the
1960s and 1970s, more and more jurisdictions joined the FBI system;
today police and sheriffs' departments covering 96 percent of the nation's population file quarterly reports with the FBI. In rural areas numerous back-country police jurisdictions were persuaded by the FBI to
make their reporting more complete. In big cities centralization of
complaint handling, record automation, and the introduction of 911
emergency phone numbers have increased reported rates of crime,
sometimes dramatically. For years it has been known that some police
departments report higher crime rates when they wish to make a show
of needing more funds. When results must be shown, there is ample

room in the system to "reduce" reported crime. As one specialist put it, "Police have an obligation to protect the reputation of their cities, and when this cannot be done efficiently under existing legal and administrative machinery, it is sometimes accomplished statistically."[5]

Complicating matters has been the aggressive approach of the FBI, especially during the tenure of the late J. Edgar Hoover, persistently voicing alarm. Citing many of the common objections to UCR procedures, one expert said:

> The criticized procedures have a common denominator: they tend to increase the reported volume of crime, and the FBI, for reasons they know best, seems to believe that the nation is best served by this emphasis.... What happened was that the temptation to use the statistics they collect, for purposes of arguing the law enforcement positions they hold, has proved too strong for the FBI.[6]

Sociologist Daniel Bell argued in the 1950s, "A sober look at the problem shows that there is probably less crime today in the United States than existed a hundred, or fifty, or even twenty-five years ago, and that today the United States is a more lawful and safe country than popular opinion imagines."[7] Another specialist on crime statistics said in 1966:

> I contend that most of the sources of error [in the way Uniform Crime Reports are prepared] operate to inflate the newer figures relative to the older ones, resulting in a false picture of rapidly increasing lawlessness among the population.... 1. The errors and biasing factors affecting the Crime Index largely operate to show spurious increases, rather than decreases, in the rate. 2. The Crime Index does not provide a sound basis for determining whether criminal behavior is increasing, or decreasing, in the United States. 3. The Crime Index is highly sensitive to social developments that are almost universally regarded as improvements in the society. Thus, it is altogether possible that year-to-year increases in crime rates may be more indicative of social progress than of social decay.[8]

Even some FBI officials we talked to were reluctant to place much confidence in trends shown by early crime index data (before the 1970s).

Although no one really knows how accurate either the FBI crime index or the victimization figures are, they both point to an extraordinary rate of crime in America. We feel that the lack of reliable information about the extent of crime contains several immediate dangers. Those who would dismiss the FBI data, which show a sharp rise in the crime rate, should be careful to examine whether the flawed data are in fact manipulated or merely incomplete. Further, it would be shortsighted to use the victimization studies, which show a relatively stable crime rate, as the basis upon which to rest complacent about the high rate these figures show to start with or upon which to scoff at the very real fear of crime across the nation.

THE CRIMINAL JUSTICE NONSYSTEM

The vast array of criminal justice professionals and institutions can be called a system only because it all bears some relationship to the processing of offenders. Identifying and accusing the offender are police; prosecutors; attorneys general; specialized units, such as grand juries, strike forces, and the secret service; and, in extreme situations, the national guard and the military. Processing the accused are courts at every level of the federal system, prosecutors, public defenders, social workers, a small number of public administrators, and a few members of the medical profession. Convicted offenders are placed in the hands of local sheriffs or jailers, prison professionals, probation and parole officers, and social workers. Juveniles and addicts come under the supervision of the staff of alternative treatment centers. (Elected legislators and the higher courts define and set the parameters of processing and punishment. And of course it is the safety and liberties of the public at large that are ultimately at stake.)

But criminal justice professionals differ in their training, their values, and their vital interests. Thus the Supreme Court, under Chief Justice Earl Warren (1953–69), considerably tightened the rules for admissable evidence, restricting, according to some, the operations of police and prosecutors. In many localities, to the dismay of prosecutors and judges, police can improve their clearance rates simply by turning over suspects for prosecution, even if they *know* they have insufficient evidence to convict. In some towns police chiefs carry more weight than elected officials and run their departments autonomously. Judges, while zealously guarding the privacy of the internal workings of their courts, have been accused by others of violating the separation of powers, making laws, or playing "part-time HEW [Department of Health, Education, and Welfare] secretaries in black robes." The Federal Bureau of Prisons has difficulty obtaining adequate documentation from courts and police to accompany incoming offenders. Moreover, there are over four thousand *locally* administered jails with authority to confine adults for more than forty-eight hours. The criminal justice nonsystem, in short, is complex and fragmented. Its members more often act independently or even antagonistically towards one another than cooperatively.

IN PERSPECTIVE

As analysts have noted in other policy fields, any large-scale reform, or change in the rules of the game, produces unanticipated and frequently unwanted consequences. Changing people's behavior is always difficult, usually costly, and highly unpredictable. Moreover, the way our political system responds to new challenges is often, as in the case of the war on crime, more complicated and confused than the human mind could have imagined.

Because of our fears about national planning and the possibility of increased national regulation, we virtually backed into a set of sometimes contradictory anticrime policies not knowing much about their consequences or logic. In retrospect we wonder at our early confidence in undertaking a national war on crime. It now appears there was little consensus and much confusion about just how the national government could make our streets safe:

> In the mid-1960s, when the federal government turned toward social scientists for help in understanding and dealing with crime, there was not then in being a body of tested or even well-accepted theories as to how crime might be prevented or criminals reformed, nor was there much agreement on the causes of crime....[9]

America in the 1960s didn't yet doubt its pragmatic genius. Everything was possible if you just spent enough money!

Could we have won the war on crime? Could a national war on crime have been designed, funded, and administered in such a way as to have made our streets safe for black and white, young and old, rich and poor? There are explanations for what happened. There are lessons to be learned. But reader beware: there remain dilemmas and paradoxes.

First we should understand what kind of issue crime was in the 1960s and 1970s, who had a stake in it, and what the pressures were for an immediate response. Only by getting a sense of the fears and frustrations of the public and the motivations of national politicians can we begin to unravel the story of why our system responded as it did. How and why did our expectations for leadership in fighting crime come to be transferred from local police, courts, and prisons to presidents, Congress, and a new federal agency? The evolution of *crime as a national issue* was intimately related to the way the war on crime was conceived and born and subsequently managed and mismanaged. It is to a political history of the crime *issue* we next turn our attention.

TWO

Placing the Crime Issue on the National Agenda

EVER SINCE Franklin D. Roosevelt and the New Deal, the national government has played an increasingly activist role in promoting the economic and social well-being of all Americans. Public housing, public employment programs, welfare, and medical care for the aged and indigent are illustrative. But it was not until the mid-1960s that crime, which had been the near-exclusive responsibility of state and local governments, burst forth as a "national policy problem." Then, a series of political and social events in effect nationalized the fear of crime as a deep-seated and emotionally charged political issue.

In the mid-1960s FBI figures showed crime rates across the nation accelerating sharply. At the same time, public fears engendered by civil rights protests and the violent reactions these protests occasioned—fear of disorder, fear of riots, and fear of blacks—appear to have come to the fore in advance of the public alarm over street crime. In the minds of many people, these fears were closely related. The civil rights movement, together with the white militancy surrounding it, raised questions about the federal responsibility to guarantee law and order while promoting social justice.

THE KENNEDY ADMINISTRATION AND CIVIL RIGHTS

There is a popular impression that President John Kennedy and his brother, Attorney General Robert Kennedy, seized the civil rights

12

issue as their own and, with vigorous leadership, used all the resources of the presidency and the Justice Department to prosecute violations of civil rights laws in the South. The Kennedy civil rights program, however, was decidedly more limited than that. As Kennedy aide Theodore Sorensen noted, "John Kennedy did not start [the civil rights movement] and nothing he could have done could have stopped it."[1] In fact, Kennedy grew impatient with those on his own staff who chided him for inaction, and his chief civil rights aide resigned from the White House staff during his first year. Said another aide, "The president didn't like to be reminded of unfulfilled pledges, and he grew impatient with advocates around him, particularly advocates who wrote long memos outlining actions for which he wasn't ready." For the Kennedy administration, racial discrimination and all its political ramifications became "their major challenge, a dangerous and unpopular controversy, the nation's most critical domestic problem."[2]

In particular the freedom rides were a prelude to much that would happen in the 1960s—nonviolent black militance, white backlash, and shifting responsibilities in a federal system where local law enforcement agencies did not perform promptly, equitably, or effectively. Kennedy's response to the freedom rides was notable because the hesitation evidenced there persisted, despite the fundamental challenge to domestic tranquillity, during the Kennedy and Johnson administrations, even after riots in northern cities.

In May 1961, James Farmer, along with seven other blacks and six whites, set out in two buses from Washington, D.C., bound for New Orleans. Their purpose was to integrate the transportation system, bus depots in particular. In Rock Hill, South Carolina, they were set upon by a gang of toughs. In Anniston, Alabama, their tires were slashed, and one bus was surrounded and burned. In Birmingham, riders were dragged into an alley and beaten with iron bars. Local police knew in advance of the arrival of the buses in these cities but simply were not on hand or were strangely late to arrive as the violence unfolded. When Birmingham police chief Bull Conner was questioned, he replied that protection was not available because so many of his men were off for Mother's Day![3] To get to New Orleans from Birmingham, these first freedom riders had to fly. But symbolically, their mission was a success. More freedom rides followed immediately.

In response to the beatings visited on the freedom riders, President Kennedy urged southern governments to guarantee protection to all citizens, black and white. And he approved moderate Justice Department intervention. Yet there was continuous apprehension that the president would push too far and suffer electorally or that the course of events would overtake him. The strategy of the freedom riders was

controversial and politically precarious, involving personal risk to themselves and also to the president, who, in turn, used them as a spring-
board for urging remedies. In May 1961, Kennedy could only express
"deepest concern" and "hope,"[4] but two years later, in response to
bombings and riots in Birmingham and confronted with the specter of
uncontrollable urban disorders, Kennedy pressed for passage of his
civil rights bill. Kennedy's words in June 1963 were stronger but still
short of endorsing those who were spearheading the civil rights issues.

> The fires of frustration and discord are burning in every city, North
> and South, where legal remedies are not at hand. Redress is sought in
> the streets, in demonstrations, parades, and protests which create ten-
> sions and threaten violence and threaten lives. We face, therefore, a
> moral crisis as a country and as a people. It cannot be met by repressive
> police action. It cannot be left to increased demonstrations in the streets.
> It cannot be quieted by token moves or talk. It is a time to act in the
> Congress, in your state and local legislative body, and above all, in all
> of our daily lives.[5]

Kennedy's efforts to channel the energy of the black revolution into
support for civil rights legislation stumbled against two problems, and
the president's inability to deal with them is one of the keys to the
way presidents handled the demand for law and order in the later
1960s. First, Kennedy discovered that his powers to pass civil rights
legislation and to control abuses of police power were limited. Second,
the demand for "order" came loudest from those most resolutely set
against black demands—reactionary southern Democratic and Republican senators and congressmen. Kennedy's determination was subject
to criticism that he was rewarding lawbreakers and to profound doubts
about the leadership of the black community, what it wanted, and
what federal programs would work.

Whatever Kennedy might have wanted to achieve in the field of
civil rights was severely constrained by intense public disapproval of
what has been termed "creative disorder." In June 1961, nearly two-
thirds of a national sample who said they knew about freedom riders
disapproved of them, and about one-fifth described them as "agitators,"
"troublemakers," or "communist-inspired."[6] Later in the Kennedy administration, some 60 percent of the public felt mass demonstrations
by blacks were more likely to hurt than help their cause. In 1964, 74
percent would argue that such activities were counterproductive.[7] Kennedy's senior domestic aide gave something of the prevailing White
House view: "To provoke a bitter national controversy without achieving any gain would divide the American people at a time when the
international scene required maximum unity."[8] And, of course, foreign

policy emergencies, the Cuban missile crisis, increasing commitments in Vietnam, and confrontation at the Berlin Wall demanded the greatest share of the president's time.

By the end of the Kennedy administration a counterreaction to the civil rights movement was boiling just below the surface. Conservative columnist David Lawrence attacked some elements of the civil rights movement: "We see minority groups today pretending that they cannot express their will effectively except through marches in the streets, or 'lie-down' or 'sit-in' demonstrations which interfere forcibly with motor traffic or the carrying on of private business." He warned that the minds and hearts of the majority would not be won by "disregarding the fundamental precepts of government itself—that 'law and order' must be preserved while the facilities of debate and lawful communication are made available to all citizens, no matter how unpopular their cause may be." Moreover, he predicted the whole matter would be a major campaign issue in 1964 and criticized President Kennedy for not discouraging the civil rights march on Washington planned for late summer of 1963. "He [Kennedy] must therefore bear responsibility for any disturbance that may ensue. And the people who want 'law and order' may find they have no other recourse but to express at the polls in 1964 a protest against the coercion of our legislative or executive process by street mobs."[9] (On 28 August 1963, some three hundred thousand people marched peacefully with Martin Luther King and shared his dream of equality and freedom for all while countless other Americans looked on approvingly.)

The issue of law and order was beginning to emerge. For many, the call to restore law and order was only a publicly acceptable way of expressing racist attitudes. But increasingly the civil rights movement, and later the war on poverty, would be made a scapegoat for the much-publicized rise in crime and violence.

CRIME AND THE FEAR OF CRIME

Conflicting explanations were proposed for what, by 1964, was becoming known as the breakdown of respect for law and order. To some, the courts and especially lenient judges were responsible for increased crime; to others, the problem resulted from moral decay and lack of respect for such institutions as the church, school, and the family. Extremist groups on the left or right blamed each other: either the repressive judicial system or revolutionary ideologues were responsible for the crime wave. The debate heated up rapidly after a series of controversial Supreme Court decisions and increased mass media coverage of urban disorders.

In 1964, in the highly controversial *Escobedo* v. *Illinois* decision, the Supreme Court held that when an investigation begins to focus on an accused suspect, police must inform him or her of his or her right to remain silent and his or her right to consult with an attorney before answering any questions. For the majority, Justice Arthur Goldberg wrote, "We have learned the lessons of history, ancient and modern, that a system of criminal law enforcement which comes to depend upon the 'confession' will, in the long run, be less reliable and more subject to abuses than a system which depends on extrinsic evidence independently secured through skillful investigation."[10] In a strong dissent, Justice Byron White expressed an opinion that would become a touchstone for the crusade against crime: "I do not suggest for a moment that law enforcement will be destroyed by the rule announced today . . . but it will be crippled, and its task made a great deal more difficult—all, in my opinion, for unsound, unstated reasons which can find no home in any of the provisions of the Constitution."[11] *Escobedo* was only one of a number of Warren Court decisions aimed at protecting the constitutional rights of disadvantaged classes, of defendants, indigents, juveniles, and minorities.

These decisions generated strong emotional reactions and charges that by "handcuffing" the police the Court was encouraging crime and disorder. J. Edgar Hoover, the powerful, long-term director of the FBI, expressed his indignation: "Justice is meant for the protection of a society as a whole, not for the protection of a single individual. When you take one individual and permit him, on one pretext or another, to prey upon the public—with occasional periods of restraint—then justice is not being carried out."[12] And according to Orlando W. Wilson, then the widely respected superintendent of the Chicago Police Department, the courts shared the blame for the crime wave that was overwhelming society in 1963: "In the name of protecting individual liberties, we are permitting so many technicalities to creep into our system of justice that we are no longer convicting a sufficiently high proportion of guilty criminals." "Everybody seems to be organizing today to protect civil liberties," complained Police Chief Wilson. "I would like to organize the victims of criminal assaults who have been robbed and raped in our streets."[13]

It is difficult to determine whether, in the early 1960s, the actual increase in the crime rate was really sufficient to produce the growing atmosphere of fear and hysteria—who can say how high the crime rate must be before people begin to take notice and become fearful for their own safety?—or whether the alarm grew apace with fear rather than fact. Perhaps the public's response to the FBI increases was only a vague precognition of the stark picture to be drawn ten years later by victimization studies—that crime was in fact much higher than even FBI figures showed. Crime was probably increasing, but the perception of crime was probably increasing faster.

Doubtless the increased exposure to local television news programs added to increased fear about street safety. Yet, even before television, starting a "crime wave" once took only the work of an underpaid, underappreciated police reporter named Lincoln Steffens. In his autobiography, Steffens wrote that while he was a reporter for the *New York Post* in the 1920s, he and a friend, Jacob Riis, "started" a crime wave at the time of Theodore Roosevelt's reforming leadership of the New York Police Department. Roosevelt was the commissioner. "I enjoy crime waves. I made one once; Jake Riis helped; many reporters joined in the uplift of the rising tide of crime, and T. R. stopped it. I feel that I know something the wise men do not know about crime waves and so get a certain sense of happy superiority out of reading editorials, sermons, speeches, and learned theses on my specialty." Steffens simply began turning in stories on crimes committed; whether they were recent or not made little difference. This in turn put pressure on other newspapers to find similar stories and, finally, pressure on Roosevelt to halt the outbreak. Eventually, Roosevelt called Steffens and Riis into his office and received assurances that they would halt the stories. "When Riis and I ceased reporting robberies . . . the morning papers discovered that the fickle public were 'sick of crime' and wanted something else. The monthly magazines and the scientific quarterlies had some belated, heavy, incorrect analysis of the periodicity of lawlessness; they had no way to account for it then."[14]

The conservative press in America, while certainly not trying to create a false crime wave, felt crime was an issue that should be spotlit in the election of 1964. Readers of a national magazine, for example, learned at the time that "terrorist attacks on white persons by bands of Negroes have created an atmosphere of crisis in the city." It was reported that vigilante groups were being formed in certain neighborhoods. A New York newspaper warned that soon, even in broad daylight, persons might be forced to "travel in armed groups for self-defense." The police reported that the "Negro 'ghetto' of Harlem has become infested with anti-white gangs reportedly trained to maim and kill." A national editorial, written shortly before the 1964 Republican Nominating Convention, cried out, "Today we are in the midst of a crime wave of unprecedented proportions. . . . How long can a society endure the conditions of terror which are imposed upon it, when people fear to venture out at night?"[15] The editorial placed much of the blame on street demonstrations and the activities of some civil rights leaders.

THE GOLDWATER NOMINATION

As the Republican party met in San Francisco in mid-July 1964, its leadership sensed the growing possibilities of the law and order issue. If scandals were brewing in the Johnson administration, and if crime could somehow be connected, what an issue they would have! A breakdown in moral leadership would be responsible for the general "immorality." In a speech to the delegates at San Francisco's Cow Palace, former president Eisenhower fired the first volley in the new anticrime war. He began by stating there were many problems that were peculiarly local in character but were so serious "as to occasion a national concern, thus increasing the demand that something be done. Among these are crimes in our city streets and parks."[16]

Any contest for the Republican nomination had been eliminated several weeks earlier when Barry Goldwater edged out Nelson Rockefeller in the California primary, and at the convention the outspoken, principled conservative senator from Arizona won on the first ballot. In his acceptance speech, Goldwater sought to define clearly the political responsibility for the current crime wave.

> Tonight there is violence in our streets, corruption in our highest offices, aimlessness among our youth, anxiety among our elderly and there's a virtual despair among the many who look beyond material success toward the inner meaning of their lives.... security from domestic violence, no less than from foreign aggression, is the most elementary and fundamental purpose of any government, and a government that cannot fulfill this purpose is one that cannot long command the loyalty of its citizens. History shows us, demonstrates that nothing prepares the way for tyranny more than the failure of public officials to keep the streets safe from bullies and marauders. We Republicans seek a government that attends to its fiscal climate, encouraging a free and a competitive economy and enforcing law and order.[17]

The following day, when asked at a press conference what the major issues of the campaign would be, Goldwater cited foreign policy as the main one but crime as a close second. Citing an example of what he meant, he mentioned a story that had appeared in the evening newspaper. A young woman had used a knife to attack a rapist and was now "getting the worst of the deal, and the rapist is probably going to get the Congressional Medal of Honor, and get off scot-free. That kind of business has to stop in this country, and as the President, I'm going to do all I can to see that women can go out in the streets of this country without being scared stiff."[18]

Goldwater's remarks puzzled many of the more moderate members of the Republican party; his later and less subtle suggestions that the civil rights movement might be responsible for crime upset many of them. Congressman John V. Lindsay (R-N.Y.) said police protection was a state and local responsibility. He was disappointed by Goldwater's "refusal to acknowledge the Republican's traditional commitment to the Nation's responsibility for individual human beings in the field of equal protection of the law." This was not the last time Goldwater would disappoint the moderate wing of the Republican party.

Conservative elements of the party were concerned about the role the federal government should have in local law enforcement. Did the federal government have any business in this area at all? Goldwater stressed that the Constitution vested responsibility for law and order in the state and local communities as a protection to the individual and that he supported this decentralization of authority. He believed the federal government's police power should be used only when the states were unable or unwilling to handle the situation. Pressed further on how the federal government would stop crime, Goldwater suggested that a president should make sure the quality of judges was of the highest. *New York Times* columnist Arthur Krock pointed out a flaw in Goldwater's law and order issue: 'The federal courts, not the President, do the determining of what the law is that they enforce. And a succession of Supreme Court rulings on the rights of persons placed under arrest has very greatly hampered local police forces in getting the evidence necessary to convict for street crimes and other violence."[19] Further, Lyndon Johnson could not be held accountable for the activities of the Supreme Court because he had not appointed any of its members. Nor was there any emotional target around the office of attorney general, then held by Acting Attorney General Nicholas Katzenbach.

Still the question of law and order had strong voter appeal. Emotionally, voters could find a release for their frustrations. The suggestion that Goldwater would formulate a national attack on the problem had brought an enthusiastic response from spectators in the galleries as well as from the delegates at the nominating convention. Republican strategists hoped large percentages of the population would support the candidate who offered the more persuasive and specific programs for reestablishing local law and order. Plainly, Goldwater counted votes based on the fear of crime.

THE 1964 PRESIDENTIAL CAMPAIGN

At first the Democrats tried to ignore the whole issue of crime in the streets. Johnson simply refused to credit the law and order cry as a serious campaign issue. Responding to a question on it, he said, in mid-July of 1964, "Well, I'm against sin, I'm against lawlessness, and I'm very much opposed to violence, and I think we have to put a stop to it, and to the extent that we have the power to do so in the Federal Government we are doing so."[20] In an apparent thrust at Goldwater, he said the federal government could not take over the authority of the local and state governments.

Goldwater, however, did all he could to press the issue of law and order, and he was well attuned to the "switchblade" issue. One reporter analyzed Goldwater's speech at the Illinois State Fair in August this way: "The indirect references to disorders and riots growing out of the civil rights movement seemed to be well understood by his audience."[21] This speech incorporated the same themes Goldwater was to raise again and again. Although he defended every American's right to speak out to redress grievances, as president he would not "support or invite any American to seek redress . . . through lawlessness, violence, and hurt of his fellow man or damage of his property." Still attempting to find the key linking the Johnson administration to the increase in crime, he claimed that scandal, dishonesty, and cynicism "haunted" the federal government and set the example for the decline in national morality. But the longest applause and the loudest cheers came when he put the matter on a personal, emotional level: "Every wife and mother, yes, every woman and girl, knows what I mean, knows what I'm talking about."

In his kick-off campaign speech, given in Prescott, Arizona, in early September 1964, Goldwater hit hard at the Johnson administration. He blamed it for "the final, terrible proof of a sickness which not all the social theories of a thousand social experiments have even begun to touch." Crime was growing much faster than the population, he said, yet lawbreakers were accorded more consideration than law enforcers. Johnson cabinet member Adlai Stevenson was singled out as an example of immorality in high places. (The Bobby Baker [a former LBJ Senate aide] scandal and the Walter Jenkins [an LBJ White House aide] incident had not yet occurred.) United Nations ambassador Stevenson had made a speech at Colby College in which he had stated that "in the great struggle to advance civil human rights, even a jail sentence is no longer a dishonor but a proud achievement." Goldwater caustically responded, "Perhaps we are destined to see in this law-loving land, people running for office not on their stainless records, but on their prison records."

Although Goldwater had voted against the 1964 Civil Rights bill, he did not want to be labeled a racist. Questioned about recent rioting in Philadelphia, he said he was upset, *but*, "We all feel very strongly that we are not going to make any effort to capitalize on white resentment against Negro demonstrations." Still, he said, leadership from the White House could do a great deal to stop the rioting, "if only by the moral, persuasive power of the Presidency." Later, during a swing through the South, in St. Petersburg, Florida, Goldwater pledged that the Republican team would make sure state and local law enforcement officials got back the power to carry out their jobs. This would be accomplished through conservative appointments to the Supreme Court or through legislation and even constitutional amendment. Too often, according to the Supreme Court's logic, "a criminal defendant must be given a sporting chance to go free, even though nobody doubts in the slightest he is guilty."[22] And in Lake County, Indiana, an area where Alabama governor George Wallace had made an impressive showing in the primary election, Goldwater, speaking extemporaneously, told his listeners this election would determine the protection they and their families would have on the street, that there were areas in this country where it was safer being a criminal than a law-abiding citizen, and that he wanted a country where everyone "from the President on down" respected law and order.

Goldwater's issue was a sticky one—how to press for law and order, how to "go hunting where the ducks were," how to translate white, middle-class fears of crime into votes and still retain the unity of the Republican party and the votes of moderates and to keep the issue from exploding and branding the candidate a racist. Black leaders were intensely aware of the implications of a Goldwater victory. Roy Wilkins, president of the National Association for the Advancement of Colored People (NAACP), said he thought a Goldwater victory "would bring about a police state."[23] Wilkins said any progress in civil rights would be slowed because Goldwater's election would give power to groups hostile to blacks. Other civil rights leaders also felt this way, and a moratorium on demonstrations went into effect.

By now the White House was concerned about the Goldwater strategy, worried about a white-backlash Republican vote. As *New York Times* reporter William V. Shannon noted:

President Johnson . . . is alert and responsive to this theme, perhaps too much so. Not a week has gone by in the past two months that the White House has not announced that the President has ordered the Federal Bureau of Investigation to look into some new local situations. Sending in the FBI has become the domestic equivalent of sending in the Marines.

Although there were occasional legitimate incidents, when, for instance, local police would not respond to black complaints, "Most of this dispatching of FBI agents hither and yon is being done for political reasons to offset Goldwater's cries. . . . Once again, the political party in power is overreacting and trying to impress everyone with its vigilance and alertness."[24]

Hubert H. Humphrey, the Democratic vice-presidential candidate, responded to Goldwater's attacks by issuing a call for national unity. He said the Goldwater statements showed a sense of desperation and condemned them as "a disservice to national unity and national understanding." Refusing to be drawn into answering the charges, Humphrey said, "A presidential candidate should be saying and doing things to promote respect for the law. You don't help your country by assailing the law. . . . I would hope he would speak out for observance of the law, including the Civil Rights law, instead of charging it breeds hatred and violence."[25]

Acting Attorney General Katzenbach also joined the fray. He said Goldwater's attempt to blame the judiciary for the rising crime rate was "irresponsible and without basis in fact." The great increase in crime had been in offenses against property, he said, not against persons; much of the increase was caused by juveniles, paralleling the large increase in the population of that age group. Admitting that persons involved in street rioting were black youths, he emphasized that the "significant fact . . . is not the race of those involved. The rate of unemployment and of school dropouts among Negroes in the affected cities was two to three times greater than for whites." Although Washington, D.C., with a 54-percent black population at the time, had been frequently cited for runaway crime, Katzenbach said, "I do not recall a single reference to Phoenix, Arizona [the hometown of Senator Goldwater]—a city I pick at random—the population of which is 95 percent white and whose crime rate is a third higher than that of Washington." Katzenbach rejected charges that recent Supreme Court decisions had handcuffed police. "These assertions are uninformed, more damaging, they are irresponsible. . . . Undeniably, some decisions have created problems for state law enforcement officials. But then, so has the Bill of Rights."[26]

With the election just a month away, the GOP strategy board, which included Goldwater, Eisenhower, and the other leaders of the Republican party, met to plan the remainder of the campaign. They decided to concentrate on four major issues in the remaining weeks, including political morality and violence in the streets.

Reporting on the "curious" campaign, *Newsweek* felt that the safety-in-the-streets issue was growing,

    although far less diverse in political terms than issues of big city rioting or civil rights.... It now works slightly in Goldwater's favor, but has yet to be sharpened as a major cutting edge. Its real potency could be its close association with civil rights in the minds of many voters.... Without doubt, civil rights and street safety are the sleeper issues of the election.[27]

And further riots or racial trouble could swing votes. A Gallup poll taken shortly before the election showed that popular sentiment more closely resembled Goldwater's campaign statements than Johnson's.

Goldwater returned to the theme of crime and morality for his final speech on election eve. Repeating what he had been saying throughout the campaign, he promised to make the streets safe for our wives and all other women, attacked the failure of the Democratic social experiments to cure the problems, commended those who enforced the law, and condemned those who accorded criminals more consideration than victims. Civil rights disturbances were mentioned, and he stated that there were peaceful ways of expressing dissatisfaction. But his main blast was aimed at the self-seeking politicians who ignored riots and violence in the streets.[28]

The voters of America, who were indeed scared about rising crime rates, were still more worried about nuclear war and the man who had his finger on the trigger; they were also concerned about social security, about civil rights, about dozens of other issues on which, rightly or wrongly, they perceived Goldwater as a dangerous extremist. Although there was a growing disenchantment with the direct-action strategies of the civil rights movement, further fed by urban disorders in the summer of 1964, the sympathy that enabled the Civil Rights Act to pass was still very real in the consciousness of the American voters. Johnson was accorded a landslide victory, but fear, frustration, and reaction would continue to grow.

(Discussing the campaign in a postmortem interview in December, Goldwater concluded that many forces had combined to defeat him, including the split in his own party. In fact, he said he felt he had lost the election at the convention in July. Most political analysts would agree with him. Were the issues he raised still important? He replied with an emphatic yes and discussed each briefly—but, curiously, forgot to mention crime.[29])

DISCUSSION

The issue of crime was seized and expanded and given a national focus by candidate Goldwater. He, more than anyone else, flung down the gauntlet to Johnson and the Democrats. "To [my opponent] the way to solve a problem is to appropriate a few hundred million dollars of taxpayers' money, and see if the problem will disappear along with the money. If that doesn't happen, the next thing to do is create a new bureaucracy in the White House to meddle in the affairs of others. . . . We have heard of and seen many wars in the time of the present administration. But have we yet heard of the only needed war—the war against crime? No, not even in the city where rule lies in the hands of the federal government."[30] Goldwater offered a sharp and ringing definition of the "get-tough" position. He believed crime resulted from a decline in morals and in discipline, from the Supreme Court down to the individual family, and since no social welfare program could improve deficiencies in morals, the remedy was more police power, tougher laws, and a less permissive court system.

Johnson's response was that crime was symptomatic of other social problems, such as poverty and lack of education. "There is something mighty wrong when a candidate for the highest office bemoans violence in the streets but votes against the war on poverty, votes against the Civil Rights Act, and votes against major educational bills that have come before him as a legislator."[31] But Johnson also recognized that Goldwater's issue was potent and demanded action.

It is not enough to excoriate Goldwater (and, as discussed below, Nixon) for exacerbating public fears of crime. Certainly the implication that crime was related to the civil rights movement was a low political trick. But those who would condemn the law and order candidates should remember our friend's grandmother and other average Americans who, like her, were genuinely scared about crime and felt deserted by the Democrats on this issue.

Neither candidate's position was completely realistic. Goldwater never resolved the tension between his leave-me-alone brand of libertarianism and his call for more police and more energetic national leadership. And Johnson's grand solutions, the eradication of poverty and the establishment of equal opportunity, were not short-term prospects; even if properly embarked upon, they would take at least a generation or two before affecting the crime rate.

The battle lines over the crime issue had been drawn. The social justice advocates had won in 1964, but the law and order proponents had set out their basic ingredients: crime, the fear of crime, civil rights, and urban disorder. As the Democrats struggled in the next four years with Great Society programs and Vietnam, the law and order issue just wouldn't go away. In fact, it would return to haunt and help defeat them in 1968, 1972, and, again in perhaps a more muted way, in 1980.

THREE

A First Presidential Response

CIVIL RIGHTS and equality of opportunity were key priorities in Lyndon Johnson's Great Society, and consistent with these goals, Johnson said the best war on crime was an all-out war on poverty. Johnson was determined to prove he was not a southern bigot; he also felt a personal moral responsibility to eradicate the social conditions that he genuinely believed fed crime. Time and again he stressed that his war on poverty *was* a war against crime and disorder, his educational programs were *needed* to stamp out juvenile delinquency. But he had little objective evidence to support these propositions. And his landslide 1964 election had not really given him a mandate for this socioeconomic approach to the crime problem.

Johnson heard different interpretations from various experts. Was there, as FBI figures suggested, a crime wave sweeping the nation? Some presidential advisors claimed that the real dimensions of the crime problem were not known and that FBI figures misrepresented the true extent of crime. Prominent criminologists and sociologists, including one sociologist employed by the FBI, felt the bureau had overlooked factors that might show a reduction in the crime rate: there had been a disproportionate increase in the population of fifteen- to twenty-four-year-olds, the group responsible for 70 percent of all crime; the crime of auto theft, then classified as serious by the FBI, often just amounted to "joyriding" by juveniles; and there were no shared definitions and no shared auditing of crime reporting among local police departments.

The public, however, needed only the evidence of its own awareness and growing fear of crime. Once this fear had been injected into
the national political arena, as it had been in the 1964 election, the
finer points of statistical accuracy became less relevant. Perceptions
held the key to political success. Johnson, an avid consumer of public
opinion surveys, was aware Americans were becoming impatient with
high crime rates. Although Goldwater as a candidate had failed, that
didn't mean the American people had rejected the crime issue as un-
important. Unless crime rates were curbed, Democrats would suffer in
1966 and 1968.

The mass media tended to focus on the most extreme and squalid
stories of crime. Extensive and detailed coverage alarmed urban residents. Echoing Goldwater's campaign challenge, conservative colum-
nists began to call for a new war on crime that would produce more
effective and immediate results than the war on poverty. Lewis F.
Powell, Jr., then president of the American Bar Association (and now
an associate Supreme Court justice), added his voice. "The right of
society in general, and each individual in particular to be protected
from crime must never be subordinated to other rights." Many agreed
with him, that Supreme Court decisions were going too far in protecting the rights of criminals.[1]

The issue had other overtones as a result of the vast attention devoted to demonstrations, civil rights activities, and protest marches.
Later in the decade, Attorney General Nicholas Katzenbach would
contend there was no connection between the increase in street crime
and other forms of civil disorder. "If there had been no 'Negro revolution', no civil rights movement, no riots, no war in Vietnam, no
political furor about four-letter words, and no change in the law or
its interpretation by the Supreme Court, we would still have a serious
and growing crime problem."[2] But in 1964 and 1965 this interpretation was less than clear. Fearful of the continuing, divisive argument
between those who stressed law and order and those who emphasized
individual rights, Katzenbach warned that such a debate was "not only
profitless but damaging" to the aims of both sides. He called for positive, constructive discussions to find answers through compromise. But
the debate, which sounded much like an extension of the 1964 campaign, continued and grew in intensity.

Meanwhile, little was actually known about the effectiveness of the
primary institutions of crime control—police, prosecution, courts, and
corrections. There was no rigorous data collection anywhere about
police operations, courtroom administration, or corrections performance. Law professor and former Justice Department aide Gerald
Caplan looked back on these problems this way:

Lack of such data was reflected in the quality of the dialogue in the presidential campaign that had just been held. The candidates discussed crime in simplified terms. No attempt was made to delve into such questions as whether crime in America was the product of a large or small number of individuals; or whether it was a broad or narrow range of prescribed misbehavior; or to what extent its control would be achieved by police agencies alone, or by the whole complex of criminal justice and social service departments; or whether any new programs of promise were underway or about to be implemented. Little was said about these questions because little was known.[3]

Still, the president believed he had to act.

THE PRESIDENT'S CRIME COMMISSION

Responding to Goldwater's campaign challenge, Johnson sent his first presidential message on crime to Congress in March 1965. He called crime a "malignant enemy in America" and proposed a blue-ribbon presidential commission to probe "fully and deeply into the problems of crime in our nation" and $10 million in direct federal grants for training and education of law enforcement officials. The long-range solution, he said, was not to be found through stricter enforcement of laws, increased monies for equipment, or the appointment of commissions but through "jobs, education, and hope." Johnson wanted answers, but he needed time.

The presidential message was praised as thoughtful, restrained, and open-minded. However, it left many questions unanswered. Was $10 million enough? Or would it open the federal treasury to unlimited demands for the operational expenses of state and local criminal justice agencies? Was there any reason to suppose that this commission would be any more successful than previous study groups?

Advisory commissions were at that time neither a novel nor an especially innovative technique. National meetings to discuss possible solutions to prison reform, juvenile crime, and crowded courts had been held as early as 1870 in Cincinnati. One of the early crime commissions was created in Chicago after World War I as a result of public demands for action after the first daylight payroll robbery in the history of the city. Other cities, including Kansas City, Baltimore, Cleveland, and Los Angeles, quickly followed with their own crime commissions. In 1925, the National Crime Commission was organized in New York City, with members including Elbert H. Gary of U.S. Steel, Franklin D. Roosevelt, Chief Justice Charles Evans Hughes, and others. The commission's original purpose was to decrease crimes of violence throughout the nation by means of education and legislation, but it met with little success and much opposition and jealousy from state counterparts.

In 1929 President Herbert Hoover, who had run in part on a law and order platform, had issued a strong warning in his inaugural address: "The most malign of all these dangers today is disregard and disobedience of law. Crime is increasing. Confidence in rigid and speedy justice is decreasing."[4] Hoover proposed the creation of a federal commission to study the problems of crime and law enforcement. (Sound familiar?) In May 1929, Hoover selected eleven members to serve on the National Commission on Law Observance and Enforcement, with George W. Wickersham, who had been attorney general under President Taft, as chairman.

Two years later the Wickersham Commission's report disclosed many defects in the criminal justice system and called for major reforms in the law enforcement and judicial machinery. The courts, it found, had almost broken down under increased burdens and were simply unable to cope with the crush of cases. Quite often the dockets were cleared by "wholesale acceptance of pleas of guilty, with light punishment." There was little chance of a speedy trial and adequate punishment. Though criticizing police methods of obtaining confessions, the report advised greatly increased funds for law enforcement agencies to upgrade their efficiency, salaries, and performance. Finally, it called for prison reform, for the expansion of federal prisons, which were often outdated and overcrowded, and for the complete reorganization of parole and prison procedures. Despite its scope, clarity, and depth of analysis, the Wickersham report had little impact on the administration of criminal justice in America. Few of the proposed reforms were put into practice, and during the 1940s, 1950s, and 1960s, the problems identified in the Wickersham report only continued to get worse.

Lyndon Johnson doubtless expected more from *his* commission; he hoped it would put him in a good bargaining position, that the American people would rally behind him to support *his* kind of war on crime. Yet one might have predicted from the past that crime commissions are not prime movers. Even law enforcement officials, while welcoming the appointment of the new crime commission, were more interested in urging the Supreme Court to review its rulings.

Aides who served in the Justice Department at the time recall that Johnson's crime commission was in essence initiated by Goldwater's speeches of August and September 1964. Some of them felt Goldwater was "stealing our issue," though of course they differed with the Republican candidate's suggested remedies. Clearly, the commission was set up to steer the issue away from partisan politics and in the direction of bipartisan reform. Aides report that the Johnson White House first considered announcing the commission in September 1964 and appointing as chairman a celebrated Republican, former New York governor Thomas E. Dewey. Dewey was finally approached in May 1965 but declined, claiming he was no longer familiar enough with the problems and citing the full-time responsibilities of his law firm. In the words of a former Justice aide, "It looked too much like a political issue-stealing job."

In late July 1965 President Johnson announced the members of the Commission on Law Enforcement and Administration of Justice, with Attorney General Katzenbach as chairman. Johnson stressed that "the present wave of violence and the staggering property losses inflicted upon the nation by crime must be arrested. . . . I hope that 1965 will be regarded as the year when this country began in earnest a thorough and effective war against crime."[5] Katzenbach offered this explanation of the commission's origin:

> I felt that it was important to the country to eliminate the issue of "law and order" in the future presidential elections. I also felt that it was very important to improve the quality and efficiency of the law enforcement system in this country. What was obvious to anyone who knew anything about it—but not so obvious to the general public—was that this meant that the Federal Government had to take the lead in defining the problems, explaining the difficulties, and establishing standards of criminal justice for the states, counties and municipalities. . . .[6]

But despite generally favorable comment about those chosen to serve on the commission, many questioned whether Johnson's commission could start a real war on crime without being able to influence the Supreme Court.

During the two years the commission spent studying the problem, Johnson was able not only to refer complaints and queries to it but also to defer action in the hope that an acceptable policy would emerge. Meanwhile Johnson, beginning to make the crime issue his own and, in the process, beginning to sound somewhat more like Goldwater, personalized his concern: "I will not be satisfied until every woman and child in this Nation can walk any street, enjoy any park, drive on any highway, and live in any community at any time of the day or night without fear of being harmed."[7]

In spite of the early rhetoric, it is difficult to tell whether Johnson was then ready to commit himself to a full-scale war on crime. The White House staff had no crime experts, though several of Joseph Califano's aides would gradually become familiar with most of the main issues. The Bureau of the Budget claimed no expertise in the area of crime, an area that had a very limited national budget and hence little to warrant staff examiners. Some aides argued a war on crime would compete for funds and steal attention from the already launched but underfunded war on poverty. They felt, and apparently President Johnson agreed, that their options included funding only one domestic "war" at a time. Further, some of Johnson's advisors, both on the White House staff and in Justice, doubted that a crime wave really existed. Some mistrusted FBI statistics, others thought high crime rates were a fabrication of the opposition party. One veteran reporter covering the White House at the time said:

> Liberals there had a knee-jerk reaction against the crime issue. They saw it as a Goldwater and [George] Wallace issue. They generally underestimated the increase in crime and in drug use. And in any event, no friends of theirs were getting mugged, particularly those who were chauffered through the nice sections of Washington in White House limousines.[8]

In retrospect, former Johnson aides surmised that the president became locked into an educational and social services strategy to such an extent that a direct crime control strategy was all but preempted. Not only did Johnson and his liberal advisors really believe crime was rooted in poverty and lack of opportunity, but most of them, along with Johnson, were preoccupied with defending the Great Society legislation, both that recently passed and that still in Congress. Adequate appropriations for these programs were first priority to them.

But if Johnson was not yet ready to commit himself to a full-scale "war" at a time. Further, some of Johnson's advisors, both on the rhetoric. And *crime as a national issue* was gaining the importance that would soon force some kind of federal action.

THE FIRST STEP

In an effort to show concern about crime while awaiting the more elaborate recommendations of his crime commission, Johnson proposed, in his first crime message to Congress, a bill for $10 million for law enforcement assistance. This bill authorized the attorney general to make direct grants to local agencies to educate and train criminal justice personnel and "to collect, evaluate, publish, and disseminate information."

Abundantly aware of the fears of federal intervention, Johnson had sent Attorney General Katzenbach to testify before Congress that a massive federal subsidy program was undesirable precisely because it "would undermine the traditional division of responsibility for law enforcement among Federal, State and local jurisdictions."[9] Spokesmen for the administration stressed repeatedly that their bill was in no way a step in the direction of a federal police force, nor would it lead to any attempts to write, enforce, or interpret the laws of the states.

The legislation did not create much of a stir in Congress. It was well received and easily passed in both houses by September 1965. Fears of federal encroachment were partially allayed by the stipulation that "nothing contained in this Act shall be construed to authorize any department, agency, officer, or employee of the United States to exercise any direction, supervision, or control over the organization, administration, or personnel of any State or local police force or other law enforcement agency."[10] On signing the bill, the president again disavowed any federal incursion into local prerogatives: "We are not dealing here in subsidies. The basic responsibility for dealing with local crime and criminals is, must be, and remains local. But the Federal Government can provide an infusion of ideas and support for research, for experiments, for new programs."[11]

The administration hoped the Law Enforcement Assistance Act of 1965 would lay the groundwork for the anticipated Safe Streets bill of 1967, by which time the crime commission would have completed its report. But the 1965 act turned out instead to be an early, if unheeded, warning of the troubles to come.

At the outset, the newly established Office of Law Enforcement Assistance (OLEA) was nurtured amid compromises. The attorney general appointed a twenty-five-year veteran of the FBI to head the office, reportedly because he wanted a recognized anticrime professional, a man with a reputation known to Congress. Indeed, the plan to appoint Courtney Evans director was made known in advance of final enactment by Congress. Evans's selection was also intended to allay fears that the new office might compete with the FBI. It is reported that FBI director Hoover nevertheless felt somewhat threatened by the upstart OLEA. OLEA officials claim that Hoover complained to Katzenbach and to friends in Congress that Evans's speeches about the future of OLEA failed to praise the positive achievements of the FBI.

Congress authorized more than the administration requested but appropriated significantly less, about $7 million for each of the first three years. Top OLEA officials pointed to the opposition of Congressman John Rooney (D-N.Y.), who chaired the Appropriations Subcommittee for Justice and who was prominent among Hoover's closest friends on Capitol Hill. One Justice Department official put it this way:

Rep. John Rooney was the sole reason [that OLEA didn't prosper] in my judgment. He might have been taking orders from the FBI, though perhaps that's too rash a statement to make. He had a real bias against "soft birds." Not much was really at stake [in our appropriation] but

Rooney would keep cutting back, keeping our budget to about $7 million each year.[12]

To some extent there was a conscious effort on Capitol Hill not to repeat the performance of the Office of Economic Opportunity (OEO) in the war on poverty programs. The OEO experience was characterized by an influential Senate aide as, "to go into it too fast and learn as you were doing it, and then wind up with a program three years later that everyone was embarrassed by." And perhaps Congress wanted the war on crime to begin slowly in order to make sure that only a limited number of "liberal social engineers" were funded. Most conservative members of Congress, including strong majorities on the judiciary committees in both houses, favored federal assistance for police support and purchase of equipment, as opposed to training, research, and experimentation. "Give them the men and the tools to do the job" was a prevailing attitude.

Although OLEA was supposed to have national scope, a large share of its funds was spent to reduce crime in Washington, D.C. Johnson had been sharply criticized by Goldwater for allowing the crime rate to soar in the District, where presidential prerogatives are theoretically substantial—the president at that time appointed the mayor and nominated city council members, and the executive branch participated directly in the operations of the District government. The message from the White House to OLEA was clear: spend as much money as possible to reverse the crime rate in Washington. Said Johnson, "I want to make it clear that I want the best police force in the United States here in the capital of our nation, and I want to make it clear that we are going to have it or some fur is going to fly."[13]

Unfortunately, what the District did with OLEA money was not innovative. Its more than $2 million in grants was used to purchase 100 more police cars, to repaint a large number of old police cars, to buy motor scooters, to enlarge the police force, and to invest in better computer systems. Most of the top leadership at OLEA admit in retrospect that both the large grants to D.C. and much of what D.C. officials did with the money were mistakes and possibly even a subversion of the legislative intent. Congressman Rooney in particular disliked the "experiments" in D.C. and hammered away at OLEA officials in appropriations hearings.

Otherwise OLEA was virtually left alone by the White House and the attorney general. Little political support came from the White House, which evidently believed that until it had a major crime bill, some modest progress and the ongoing crime commission provided enough *appearance* of action to serve as a holding operation.

Because one of the guiding motivations behind the formation of OLEA was to *appear* to be doing something and to assuage the public's fear of crime, most OLEA money was spent on the most visible component of the criminal justice system, the police. Courts and corrections received only a smattering of projects. Similarly, research suffered at the expense of action projects. Little evaluation of projects was required, and the mandate to disseminate information was virtually disregarded. A survey assessment of OLEA concluded:

> As a result of an assortment of pressures, many of them from Congress and police agencies, to use its funds in a way that would demonstrate both visible and wide geographic support of law enforcement agencies, OLEA's accomplishments fell short of its goals.

> On balance, OLEA should have more aggressively sought out those individuals and agencies [prosecutors, defense attorneys, and judicial officers] in criminal justice in an effort to stimulate applications. Perhaps no funding agency should be a passive receptacle for only those applications which happen to be submitted. If priorities are properly set, and they were not in OLEA, then affirmative action to implement the priorities becomes a necessity.[14]

The inattentiveness of the White House to the implementation of the 1965 Law Enforcement Assistance Act weakened the case for legislation that called for vastly more of the same in 1967. When the Johnson administration needed all the evidence it could marshall to pass the more comprehensive Safe Streets bill in 1967, it should have been able to look to the model OLEA programs and their impact. Instead, the administration would pay a substantial price for this neglect: over a year's delay in passage and an end product that was hardly recognizable.

MIRANDA AND WHITE BACKLASH

Public attitudes towards crime in the streets began to take on a more reactionary tone. Early on Barry Goldwater had realized the political potential of connecting fears of crime and of civil rights, and by mid-1965 there was no getting around it.

Charles E. Whittaker, a retired associate justice of the Supreme Court, brought the connection into the open. Speaking to the Tennessee Bar Association in Nashville, Whittaker said he felt that much of the current rash of lawlessness was

> fostered and inflamed by the preachments of self-appointed leaders of minority groups . . . [who told their followers] . . . to obey the good

laws but to violate the bad ones. . . . [This] simply advocates the viola-
tion of the laws they do not like . . . the taking of law into their own
hands.

He further denounced the demonstrations of civil rights groups because they provided a vehicle "for infiltration by rabble-rousers, red-
hots, and Communists," resulting in the assault of police officers and
the breakdown of law and order in general. The remedy was plain—
people must insist that "our governments, state and federal, reassume
and discharge their first duty of protecting the people against lawless
invasions of their persons and property" through the "even handed,
impartial, vigorous, swift and certain enforcement of the law."[15]
Riots in Los Angeles (Watts) and Detroit in the summer of 1965
caused deep alarm in the nation's capital. One of the main fears among
politicians, especially Democrats, was of a white backlash by voters.
Johnson condemned the rioting:

A rioter with a Molotov cocktail in his hands is not fighting for civil
rights any more than a Klansman with a sheet on his back and a mask
on his face. . . . We cannot, and we must not, in one breath demand
laws to protect the rights of all our citizens and then turn our back,
or wink, and in the next breath allow laws to be broken that protect
the safety of our citizens. There just must never come the hour in this
republic when any citizen, whoever he is, can ignore the law, or break
the law with impunity.[16]

But contrary to some interpretations that he had "completely changed
his mind" on the civil rights issue, one of Johnson's major civil rights
accomplishments was still to lie ahead—the Voting Rights Act of 1965.
Yet there was a developing awareness among Johnson's political advisors that white voters would react in a backlash if black leaders continued to apply more and more pressure, especially if there were more
street demonstrations and riots in the inner cities.
The Republican party decided that perhaps now some ground could
be won. In mid-September former president Eisenhower spoke out,
condemning the "general [moral] deterioration that has been going on
since the First World War," urging every citizen to observe the "legal
and moral obligation to be a good citizen . . . and respect the law,"
and calling the Supreme Court decisions, "particularly those that inter-
fered with police methods . . . terrible."[17] Republican leaders in Washington quickly followed Eisenhower's statements by issuing a warning
to the civil rights movement that continued defiance of law and order
would severely damage the campaign for equal rights. The goal of
equal opportunity "must rest unswervingly on respect for the law—all

the law—of the land." Noting the limited success and favorable attention of their trial balloon, the Republicans prepared for the 1966 congressional campaign.

The debate was not completely one-sided, and many observers believed the whole matter of rising crime was overdrawn and distorted as a campaign issue. Criminologist Thorsten Sellin argued that "crimes against persons over the last 150 years have gone down while . . . property offenses have gone up." A Brandeis University professor concurred: "Anybody who reads the *New York Times* from the Civil War to the present sees a much improved society." David Acheson, a former chief prosecutor in Washington, D.C., observed that recent court decisions had had about as much effect on the crime rate "as aspirin on a brain tumor. Criminals simply do not read court decisions before they commit crimes." Deputy Attorney General Ramsey Clark asserted that "court rules do not cause crime. People do not commit crime because they know they cannot be questioned by police before presentment." Judge J. Skelly Wright feared that the worst by-product of the crime scare could be that "we might be entering a period similar in some respects to the McCarthy era . . . [when] the way to instant popularity . . . was to denounce Communism generally and then accuse people in high places of being soft on criminals."[18] But to people who had consumed television reports of rioting with their evening meals, to the people who were now afraid to go downtown on a hot summer midday, these reassurances had little effect.

Attacks on the civil rights movement continued. J. Edgar Hoover made headlines by branding Martin Luther King, Jr. "one of the most notorious liars in the country" after King criticized some FBI agents in the South. It was not until years afterwards that the full extent of Hoover's personal vendetta against Dr. King was revealed, in congressional hearings on the domestic surveillance activities of the FBI. Speaking in Washington in mid-October 1965, Hoover hit once again at the "Communists" and those who were their intended, yet seemingly willing, victims. He viewed civil disobedience as "a seditious slogan of gross irresponsibility." He condemned those who were leading "the impressionable minds of our youths" astray, in California and elsewhere, and he castigated the "legal mumbo-jumbo resorted to by so many of our judges."[19]

In December, the Republican party issued a policy paper reminiscent of the Goldwater campaign on law and order. In a direct attack on urban political machines, machines that were, of course, largely Democratic, the paper charged: "Administrations in some cities have really ceased to make an adequate effort to prevent crime. . . . They have, in effect, confessed that criminals, not the police, lawlessness, not the law, are in control."[20] But the white paper was not aimed so much at the central cities as at the suburbs, which were now deeply affected by crime. Suburbs were suffering from a "crisis in affluence," and, according to FBI figures, crime was rising faster there than elsewhere. Many suburbanites had moved out of the city precisely to avoid the problems of crime, as well as pollution and poor public services, only to find that now some of these same problems had followed them out. The nearby city had become a "crime-breeding ghetto," spawning delinquents who now preyed on the suburbs. Many felt beleaguered: "It's us or them." Suburbia was becoming more and more receptive to the Republican position. And, as John F. Kennedy had found in 1960 and the census now confirmed, it was these suburban votes, not the central city votes, that had become the key to election victory.

Johnson attempted to blunt the Republican inroads. In early March 1966 he delivered a second message on crime, with a weakly hopeful note that perhaps "the war against crime may be slowing its increase for the moment." In a statistical shell game (which was to be played again at other election times by Richard Nixon) Johnson seized upon the latest FBI data, which indicated a 5-percent increase for 1965 as compared to a 13-percent increase for 1964.[21]

Then in mid-June 1966 the Supreme Court announced another decision that was to become even more controversial than its previous ones —*Miranda* v. *Arizona*. In a five-to-four decision, the Court held that before interrogation a suspect must be informed of his or her right to remain silent and to have counsel.[22] Reaction was instantaneous. Police Commissioner Howard Leary of New York warned that law and order would be diminished and predicted, "It's quite possible that a great number of persons who are . . . guilty will not be successfuly prosecuted." He saw the decision as part of the development of "sophisticated law for an immature society."[23] Conservatives were outraged: previous Supreme Court decisions had had the effect, they felt, of returning rapists and killers to the streets to continue their careers of crime; the *Miranda* decision "puts immunity from punishment for crime on a wholesale basis."[24]

Many criminal justice officials had steeled themselves for the *Miranda* decision and in some regions had already inaugurated the required procedures. But though agreeing with the intent of the decision, lawyers expressed concern that the court may have acted hastily since a model station-house procedure was already being prepared for consideration by the American Bar Association. Attorney General Katzenbach conceded the decision would make law enforcement more difficult but considered it a "benefit of living in a civilized society."

The public was increasingly dissatisfied with the Supreme Court. By the late 1960s many believed that Supreme Court decisions handcuffed the police, increased crime rates, and endangered basic public safety. The Supreme Court was attacked for not sanctioning the use of wiretapping and other means of gathering evidence for prosecuting organized crime. Many observers agreed police agencies were seriously understaffed, underfinanced, undereducated, and overworked. Instead of helping, the Supreme Court had modified criminal procedure to expand the rights of the defendant, thereby policing the police. Supreme Court decisions were seen as "coddling criminals" and setting the guilty free on technicalities; the Court was especially indicted for making admissable evidence more difficult to obtain.

Members of the Supreme Court, usually hesitant to enter popular debates, were aware of the growing tide of fear and criticism. Chief Justice Earl Warren defensively acknowledged there was a tendency then to blame the Court and the rulings of the courts for the vast amount of crime. Thinking persons, he believed, and especially lawyers, knew this was not the case. They knew that crime was inseparably connected with such factors as poverty; degrading, sordid social conditions; the weakening of home ties; low standards of law enforcement; and lack of education. Warren and others who were committed to Johnson's social activist persuasion hoped the crime commission findings would support their position.

The *Miranda* decision, and the renewed violence and rioting in the urban centers of Chicago, New York, and fourteen other cities during the summer of 1966, prompted Richard Nixon to enter the debate and attack the Democratic administration. Nixon was at that time a private citizen, having been narrowly defeated by Kennedy in 1960 and then rejected by the voters of California in 1962.

> For such a deterioration of respect for law to occur in so brief a time in so great a nation, we must look for more important collaborators and auxiliaries. It is my belief that the seeds of civil anarchy would never have taken root in this nation had they not been nurtured by scores of respected Americans; public officials, educators, clergymen, civil rights leaders as well.[25]

Firing the opening salvos of his 1968 campaign, Nixon singled out two possible rivals, Sen. Robert Kennedy and Vice-President Hubert Humphrey. Senator Kennedy, he charged, had justified taking the law into one's own hands by his statement that "to the Negro the law is the enemy." Humphrey had gone even further. In a speech in New Orleans, Humphrey had said that if he lived in the degrading conditions of the slums, he "would lead a mighty good revolt"; then he had gone on to stress that the final solution was working through the law.

Nixon charged Humphrey with giving "aid and comfort to those who revolt violently in Chicago and New York."

Republicans moved throughout the fall of 1966 to give the crime issue prominence. Dwight Eisenhower said the public was "very rightly, definitely angry" about crime and violence and suggested that the Republicans take the strongest possible position and pledge to remove the cause. The Republican Coordinating Committee charged that the Johnson-Humphrey administration had "accomplished nothing of substance to date to promote public safety." Moreover, they said, certain high officials of this administration had "condoned and encouraged disregard for law and order."[26] When Congressmen Gerald Ford (R-Mich.) was asked to identify these high officials, he harked back to Humphrey's New Orleans statement.

A month before the 1966 congressional elections, Congress passed a District of Columbia crime bill, which was largely the work of the southern-dominated House Committee on District Affairs. This bill included provisions for police officers to question subjects without counsel over a several-hour period before court arraignment, for detention of material witnesses, for limited preventive detention, and for minimum mandatory sentences for first-degree burglary, robbery, and other offenses. These measures were in conflict with the 1957 *Mallory* decision, the intent of which was to prevent police officers from obtaining confessions, valid or not, by the pressure of holding suspects incommunicado and questioning them at inordinate length. Also, the District measures were out to change or at least influence the *Miranda* decision.

The Justice Department, then being led by Acting Attorney General Ramsey Clark, urged the president to veto the District crime bill, and in early November Johnson did, asserting the bill would create problems rather than solve them by provoking years of litigation. Johnson, however, did not use the occasion to speak out firmly in defense of the Supreme Court decisions, nor did he make a case, despite some evidence available at that time, that the Supreme Court rulings limiting police interrogations had *not* substantially reduced the number of confessions obtained.[27]

The Johnson administration may have missed several other opportunities to speak out in defense of protecting civil liberties because Katzenbach, who had been chairman of the crime commission, was shifted to the State Department; Ramsey Clark, the new acting attorney general, had had much less contact with the crime commission and the internal debates that went on within it, including discussions of *Miranda*. Further, Clark's leadership was tempered by the fact that he was a candidate for appointment to the attorney general post and had to be confirmed by the Senate. One observer commented about the situation:

> The Justice Department was seriously hampered in its ability to offer strong policy guidance during the winter of 1966–67 . . . because of a gap in executive leadership. For months after Katzenbach's shift to the State Department, Ramsey Clark served merely as Acting Attorney General, while Washington speculated about whether he or someone else would be appointed to head the Department. President Johnson's delay may have seemed necessary because Katzenbach was still crime commission chairman. Until after the commission completed its work, the President allowed policy-making responsibility to remain divided.[28]

In any case, the political initiative on the *Miranda* issue passed to the opposition.

The 1966 election showed distinct Republican gains, as usual for the out party in a midterm election. But the mood of the nation was changing as well. Although the Voting Rights Act was passed by Congress in 1965, support for further social reform legislation was waning. Many people believed the time had now come to respond to the needs of the white middle class. An increasing number thought the response should provide relief from what had become a primary issue —crime in the streets. Would the eagerly awaited report of Johnson's crime commission provide the answers to the crime problem and vindicate Johnson's social activist approach? Would it set out a blueprint for action and set the Democrats on the path to victory in 1968?

THE CRIME COMMISSION REPORT

Two years after the appointment of the crime commission and 19 commissioners, 63 staff members, 175 consultants, hundreds of advisors, 5 national surveys, 3 national conferences, and some $2.5 million later, the crime commission reports confirmed evidence of public anxieties as much as they contributed to a plan of action for the president.[29]

White House staff members had met often with the leadership of the crime commission, and increasingly the White House had looked to the crime commission studies as the potential basis for the 1967 Crime Message. But from the president's standpoint and from that of his top legislative aides, the crime commission's reports lacked the focus that might have led smoothly to developing a legislative reform package. Recommendations were often general and less related to crime prevention than to the protection of civil liberties. The list of recommendations did not give Johnson's 1967 Crime Message or subsequent legislative proposals a specific theme around which to sound a rallying cry, around which to "sell" a program. Now it was clear that the cost of waiting for the commission's recommendations had been high.

The final report of the crime commission was first slated for summer 1966 but was eventually completed in February 1967. The report began: "There is much crime in America, more than ever is reported, far more than ever is solved, far too much for the health of the Nation. Every American knows that. Every American is, in a sense, a victim of crime. . . ." The commission studies then demonstrated that the criminal justice system was antiquated, often invisible, and starved for funds. Poor police training, unqualified local judges, and eighteenth-century jails were documented.[30] The resulting portrait of criminal justice, as Johnson said, was extraordinary and alarming.

Basically, the commission task force studies were a taxonomy of the criminal justice "nonsystem." Special reports treated police, courts, corrections, juvenile delinquency, narcotics and drug abuse, drunkenness, organized crime, measurement of crime, and applications of technology. Although this taxonomic definition of the problem was reasonable and comprehensive, it was not necessarily related to public fears or to a national plan of action. In some cases public fears were triggered by urban riots, assassination, civil disobedience and civil rights, and antiwar militancy. In addition, the fear of crime bore a definite but poorly understood relationship to racist impulses. In some quarters the demand for "law 'n' order" was intended as a racist epithet; in others it was so perceived whether or not it was so intended. Could someone be for civil rights *and* for law and order? Could a politician applaud sit-ins *and* deplore vigilantes? Could local governments accede to demands of black militants without encouraging more disorder? Were urban riots differently motivated than piecemeal urban crime? If a former police commissioner ran for mayor with the slogan that he "meant business," was he threatening repression or lauding free enterprise? And if a federal program were started, what kinds of strings would be attached to federal anticrime monies, and who would get what? These kinds of political problems suggested that even a technically superior plan to reform the criminal justice system might not allay public fears.

Instead of a choice of key policy priorities, the commission report put forward over two hundred recommendations—a veritable laundry list of experiments to be attempted, ideals to be attained, and monies to be spent. Costs were not specified, but they would be high. In many areas specialists honestly admitted that no good solutions were at hand. Plausible crime prevention strategies either had not proved their value or cost too much. The commission had a liberal thrust, but there were recommendations for every ideological taste.

Even while the president's crime commission legitimized greater federal involvement, it plainly said the new federal role would be most difficult to define and to play. Far from settling questions, the report signaled the opening battle over the nature of the national role—major pulling and hauling over crime control policy would follow. Would the central government lead reform by establishing standards? Would it merely allocate funds? Would it stress broadened powers of prosecution and enforcement, beginning with tougher federal sanctions? Would it focus on the administration of law enforcement and criminal justice?

The president's crime commission had raised great expectations, but these expectations were to be dashed in the future political battles of the national war on crime. Five years later, the former chairman and former executive director of the commission said large numbers of their recommendations had been adopted in name but not in practice. For example, federal juvenile delinquency programs were cut back and little experimentation done in shifting from incarceration to community treatment of offenders.[31] The commission, for instance, had recommended creation of youth service bureaus at the local level to counsel and treat young people who could be diverted from the conventional juvenile court-reform school pattern. But, as Nicholas Katzenbach recalled:

> One could say that this recommendation was tremendously successful. All over the country institutions called "Youth Service Bureaus" sprang up, more than 200 of them. But if one digs into what is behind the nomenclature on this . . . one gets a very discouraging picture. Essentially, in order to get support of Federal money under LEAA, they have followed the recommendations of the Crime Commission in form, but have simply changed the names of their existing youth programs, good or bad, and have incorporated them under the caption "Youth Service Bureau." In many instances, nothing has changed, except the name.[32]

DISCUSSION

Notwithstanding the completion of the celebrated crime commission reports, President Johnson remained unsure of the kind of presidential leadership, national strategy, and specific legislation required to mount an effective and politically acceptable war on crime. Members of Johnson's own staff differed sharply on the question. Many who had invested time fighting to get the Great Society programs enacted insisted the next effort should be to secure full funding for these measures. Others on the White House staff, especially some of those who were more politically attuned to party and union leaders, urged a stronger, more direct attack on crime and lawlessness. Nearly everyone recognized that a probable outcome of the strategy debate would be a major federal subsidy program, potentially of a billion dollars. Bargaining over where and how these monies would be spent would be for high stakes.

A number of Johnson's aides early on believed that the conservatives' absorption with crime was entirely a political diversion from much-needed attention to civil rights. Others worried that Johnson's well-earned reputation as the nation's leading civil libertarian would be rejected now in favor of his becoming the nation's chief of police. Years later, one of Johnson's chief assistants in this policy area, Harry McPherson, recalled yet another factor: "I see now—there was another pressure upon him, to which he and his speech-writers accommodated; the War in Vietnam threatened to estrange the Democratic party from the President. If he was to retain the support of the national Democrats—by and large a liberal army—he would have to remain a liberal at home, talking less of stopping crime than its causes."[33]

Political uncertainties were also reflected in the White House reactions to the riots in Detroit and Newark in the summer of 1967. Certain aides recommended that the president bring in top businessmen from the big cities and urge them to hire more minorities and generate more jobs. Other aides advised Johnson to go on television and speak out forcefully to let the American people know he would establish safety and order in the streets in whatever way was required. This view was based on the belief that since Republicans would eventually blame the riots on the Democrats, the president should dramatize forcefully his opposition to civil disorder. But still other aides suggested the president not speak out on the riots at all because of the danger that he would be associated with them in the public mind—it just might underscore his limited options in the face of wide disorder.

As part of their routine program development operations, Johnson's domestic policy aides, including Joseph Califano, Lawrence Levinson, and James Gaither, set up a task force on crime in 1967. This task force was charged with pulling together specific recommendations that the president could use in a 1968 crime message as well as with giving general advice on what priorities the president should stress in pushing his legislation. The task force was chaired by Professor James Q. Wilson of Harvard University, with Deputy Attorney General Warren Christopher as vice-chair. Christopher had by this time become a stalwart ally of those White House aides who wanted to see faster progress on the president's Safe Streets bill. The task force report pointed out that most states and communities could not begin to implement the crime commission objectives because they lacked sufficient qualified personnel, and it recommended federal funds to upgrade the quality of law enforcement officials. Another recommendation was for more research and development in technology to make homes, cars, and businesses safer. Overall, however, the report urged cautious expectations, underlining that there were no magic solutions to the nation's crime problems. "If every recommendation of the Crime Commission were implemented tomorrow, it is unlikely that there would be a dramatic reduction in crime rates. There is no device, no technology, no tested program that will make the streets measurably safer in the short term."[34]

Years later, looking back on this period, Johnson admitted crime "was a more massive and profound problem than any of us had realized."[35] But despite doubts and uncertainties at that time (1967–68), President Johnson was about to commit the federal government to a war on crime. Crime as an issue was firmly fixed on the national agenda.

FOUR

Legislating for the War on Crime

THE HISTORY of the Omnibus Crime Control and Safe Streets Act of 1968 vividly suggests that national policymaking is influenced not only by activist presidents and Congress but by a variety of public expectations, pressure groups, and the political climate of the times. Lyndon Johnson liked to view himself as the nation's chief legislator and chief priority setter, but his initiatives for a war on crime were substantially amended, and in several cases completely rewritten, by conservative leaders in Congress. Some of his ideas were successfully reversed by the nation's governors. And presidential rivals Barry Goldwater, Richard Nixon, and George Wallace all had a hand in shaping the resulting legislation.

Johnson was particularly vulnerable politically when he tried to pass his war on crime legislation. During 1966 his popularity had taken a nose dive. He was now (1967–68) preoccupied with the Vietnam War, the tactics of the war itself, escalating defense budgets, and his declining national image. As a traditional liberal, who believed that mankind is essentially good and could be made better by spending money to improve its lot, he was forced to watch his Great Society programs deteriorating because of underfunding and mismanagement. Skyrocketing crime rates were especially embarrassing to his pet social and educational projects. This was the year before the 1968 presidential election, and Republicans, who had made significant advances in 1966, insisted that the president use the power and influence of his office to "do something" to remedy the breakdown of law and order. George

44

Wallace was bent on enlarging the issue of law and order to encompass riots, dissent, and other targets of public disenchantment, even the federal bureaucracy. Finally, and perhaps more directly damaging to Johnson's anticrime proposals, riots and urban disorders occurred in over one hundred cities during the summers of 1965, 1966, and 1967. The most severe came during a two-week period in July 1967 in Newark and Detroit. As a response, Johnson charged yet another new commission, the National Advisory Commission on Civil Disorders, to find out what had happened and why and how it could be prevented from happening again.[1] Johnson was on the defensive, his weakness conclusively demonstrated when, in late March 1968, midway through the congressional fight over the crime control bill, he announced he would not run for a second term.

JOHNSON'S CRIME PROPOSALS

Johnson and his Department of Justice aides tried time and again to take the crime issue out of politics, partisan and electoral. They had appointed several moderate Republicans to the crime commission. They stressed that in practice there was no Republican or Democratic way to control or fight crime—only a reasonable way to attack it at its roots. But in vain. Crime had become a hot political and partisan issue.

So Johnson began 1967 knowing he had to produce something concrete if the Democrats were to avoid being tagged as soft on crime. In his January 1967 State of the Union Address, he acknowledged that crime control needed action, not further study:

> So I will recommend to the 90th Congress the "Safe Streets and Crime Control Act of 1967." It will enable us to assist those states and cities that try to make their streets and their homes safer, and their police forces better and their correction systems more effective and their courts more efficient.[2]

Republicans did not respond immediately to Johnson's State of the Union message but waited to see his full program. They did suggest, in their own Republican State of the Union speech, that wiretapping might aid the fight against organized crime and proposed a national institute for research and training of law enforcement officers.

In early February of 1967, just before the issuance of the final report of the president's crime commission, Johnson unveiled the broad outlines of his long-awaited crime control program. He, of course, had seen advance copies of the commission's final report, and his program took its overall tone from the commission's recommendations.

Although the commission's report was generally praised as comprehensive, sophisticated, and richly detailed, the real question was whether it would have any more success than those of previous commissions in gaining the support of Congress and the public. As noted above, the report was all encompassing: it made more than two hundred specific recommendations, including suggestions for federal, state, and local programs and for the individual citizen. But as it pointed out, "The inertia of the criminal justice system is great." Most of the recommendations put forth by the Wickersham Commission in 1931 had not yet been effected; most of the same problems still existed, including the ineffective administration of justice in the lower courts because of overcrowded conditions, outdated and overcrowded prison systems, and the inefficient use of police officers to deal with crimes without victims, such as breach of peace and traffic control. The report noted that the "well founded alarm" about crime must be translated into social action, action to eradicate slums, to improve education, to provide jobs, and to make sure there is equal opportunity for all Americans: "To speak of controlling crime only in terms of the work of the police, the courts and the correctional apparatus, is to refuse to face the fact that widespread crime implies a widespread failure by society as a whole."[3] To solve many of the problems in the criminal justice system, the public must be willing to pay. Existing facilities and equipment were simply inadequate and the personnel in the system too often underpaid, undertrained, and overworked. Money alone, however, was not the answer. Research programs were also needed to assemble more knowledge about crime and justice and to generate effective operating procedures. Finally, officials of the criminal justice system had to be willing to examine their procedures openly and to try innovative ideas. Controlling crime would be slow and hard and costly, the report warned, but it could be done.[4]

Johnson proposed a system of categorical grants to state and local governments totaling $50 million the first year and $300 million the next. These grants, for reform and innovation in such areas as police training, rehabilitation, and crime education, would be administered by the Justice Department. The program was basically an extension of the old OLEA. Although the federal government would not try to dominate the grants, it would expect to impose high standards on the recipients. Johnson also called for strong gun control measures, repeated his request for unification of the federal correctional system within the Department of Justice, and proposed a right to privacy bill that would ban all wiretapping and electronic eavesdropping except in cases involving national security.

Reaction was swift in coming. Republicans, commenting through

House Minority Leader Gerald Ford, found much to criticize. Though Johnson's message focused on a number of important problem areas, it neglected some "key points," namely the Supreme Court decisions, which Ford held responsible for the "breakdown" of law and order.[5] Sen. John McClellan (D-Ark.) a conservative, a strict constructionist, and powerful chairman of the Appropriations Committee as well as of the Subcommittee on Criminal Laws and Procedures of the Judiciary Committee, felt the program deserved consideration "as a partial approach" to the extent that it strengthened law enforcement officers, "and to that extent I'll support it."[6]

Liberals, meanwhile, were enthusiastic. Aryeh Neier, executive director of the New York Civil Liberties Union, said: "When I hear a crime message I always shudder. . . . I'm always sure that another infringement on civil liberties is about to be proposed. But this time it didn't come. I found myself reading the President's speech aloud to my wife—It's a beautiful document, an astonishing document."[7] The *New York Times* reported that there was little objection to the proposal except for the ban on wiretapping: "Just about everything that criminologists, sociologists and civil libertarians have been urging for years can be found in the proposals."[8] And the *New Republic* commented, "It is a pleasure to read a 5,600 word report on crime that never once stoops to the cheap trick of blaming it all on the Supreme Court . . . [or on] criminal-coddling judges."[9]

Shortly after the crime message, the administration sent Congress several bills, the proposed war on crime contained in the one called "the Safe Streets and Crime Control Act of 1967." Basically, except for increased funding, the Safe Streets bill differed little from the experience of the past eighteen months in research, demonstration, training, and education programs under the old Law Enforcement Assistance Act. Fifty million dollars for planning grants and $300 million more for a "sweeping action program" would be made available to local law enforcement agencies as long as local governments pledged a 5-percent increase in their own spending on law enforcement. Action grants were to be given in the following *categories*: training and recruitment of police, especially police-community relations and tactical patrol squads for high-crime areas; modernization of equipment, such as two-way radios, crime laboratories, and identification systems; reorganization of personnel structures; innovative rehabilitation efforts, such as work release and community-based corrections; and crime prevention programs in schools, colleges, welfare agencies, and the like. Different amounts of matching funds for different programs would encourage local governments to spend on national priorities. For example, the federal government would pay 100 percent of the cost of contracts for research and up to 60 percent of the cost of training, equipment purchases, and crime prevention programs but only 50 percent of the cost of new construction of buildings.

Several friendly senators introduced the measure, and Congressman Emmanuel Celler (D-N.Y.) chairman of the House Judiciary Committee, and some of his colleagues introduced similar legislation in the House. Both houses began hearings on this and related anticrime measures in early March.

Acting Attorney General Ramsey Clark immediately went to the Senate and presented the administration's views before McClellan's subcommittee. But when Clark finished his brief in behalf of the Safe Streets bill, it was quite apparent that Senator McClellan, speaking for more than a few of his colleagues, was unimpressed. McClellan wondered whether Clark had anything to say about three other measures already in the Senate hopper—a confessions bill, a wiretapping bill, and a bill "outlawing the Mafia." When Clark made it clear that the administration did not want to link these Senate bills with its own bills, McClellan protested:

> I would think—I may be wrong, but I would think—that just the two
> bills you have referred to [the Safe Streets and Crime Control bill and
> the Federal Corrections Service Bill], that you have emphasized in your
> statement here, are not alone adequate to deal with the overall crime
> problem; that there are other tools and weapons that are needed in
> this law enforcement war against crime. . . . I don't think, and I am
> sure you do not, that just spending money is the answer to the crime
> problem.[10]

A week later Clark went before a subcommittee of the House Judiciary Committee. Again he presented the case for the administration's bill.

During this same month, March 1967, Johnson swore in Ramsey Clark as attorney general. Johnson took the occasion to praise his war on poverty, claiming that more than six and a half million people had been lifted from poverty levels in the last three years. He acknowledged there had been less success in making America safe. We needed to wage a war against crime and the fear crime inspires while respecting the rights of our citizens, he said. In the same mood in which he had vetoed the D.C. crime bill the previous November, he said that "the right of every American to be free from unlawful searches and forced self-incrimination must be upheld" and that the right of privacy must be inviolate in this country. In an obvious reference to conservative forces on Capitol Hill that were calling for reversals of *Mallory*, *Escobedo*, and *Miranda* and pressing for more opportunities for the police to employ wiretapping and electronic eavesdropping, Johnson argued that "innocent citizens must know that their rights will be violated neither by those who break the law—nor by those who seek to uphold it."

But Johnson's Safe Streets bill would undergo changes in Congress that would make it virtually unrecognizable.

THE CONGRESSIONAL OBSTACLE COURSE

No member of Congress, of either party, wanted to return home that year without having in hand some tangible and dramatic evidence that Congress was doing something about crime. Conservatives saw in the crime legislation before them an attempt by Johnson to take *their* issue, the issue that had been championed and pioneered by Barry Goldwater, and remold it in Johnson's own social activist image. Unlike Johnson and Ramsey Clark, they felt crime was *not* a consequence of poverty, that crime was committed more out of *greed* than *need*. Crime, they said, *does* pay—it pays too much. Punishment was necessary, and morally required, if the cities and suburbs of America were to be made safe again. Increase the cost of committing a crime, especially by increasing the likelihood of a speedy trial and harsh imprisonment, and you'll get fewer crimes, they argued.

Though leaders of House and Senate subcommittees worked closely with the White House, Republican leaders in each committee knew a vulnerable situation when they saw it and slowly but surely drove a wedge between the White House and conservative southern Democrats. Republicans began to apply pressure to take over the crime bill, preparing a crackdown on crime that went beyond what Johnson proposed. The choice they wanted in 1968 would be for Johnson either to sign a crime bill the GOP could take credit for or for him to veto it—either way benefiting them. Their strategy for 1968 was to say that the Democratic president's bill was soft, but by a united and determined effort, the Republican party in Congress got a tougher law enacted.

Republicans concentrated on passing an amendment in the House that would give control of funds to *states*, rather than to the *attorney general* or to the *cities*. Senate Republicans also worked concurrently with McClellan on getting broader wiretap powers and limiting the Supreme Court's rulings on confessions. In the end, the administration's proposals suffered in three major ways: allocation of leadership responsibilities to the states rather than to the cities, congressional emphasis on tough crime control as opposed to reforms advocated by the crime commission and Ramsey Clark, and the decreased power of the attorney general to control the operations of the new agency that was to administer the federal monies.

THE BATTLE FOR BLOCK GRANTS

Congress had been irritated by some of Johnson's early law enforcement grant programs and had grown disenchanted with the way so many other Great Society programs had been administered. Southerners in particular reacted against federal guidelines in education and poverty programs. Members of Congress were taking substantial heat from local leaders and governors regarding red tape and the arrogance of the federal bureaucracy administering categorical grants. Misgivings were sharpened by long-standing fears of anything approaching a national police state. These tangible worries help explain the many intricate arguments on federalism raised in connection with the Safe Streets Act.

Congressional opposition to applying the categorical formula to law enforcement is illustrated by a statement by Senate Judiciary Chairman James Eastland (D-Miss.):

> It has been the hallmark [of recent categorical grants] to exalt Federal power and debase the power of the States and local communities, to place high State and local officials in an inferior position to lower-ranking members of the Federal establishment. I strongly condemn this practice. It is destructive of healthy Federal-State relationships.[11]

The idea of administering the crime control program from Washington also encountered strong resistance from governors, who argued that they could not let a program of this magnitude take place within their jurisdictions without controlling how the money would be spent. An OLEA official recalled that as early as 1966 the stakes were perceived as being potentially quite high, easily in the $1 billion range, although the initial amount requested was only $100 million. The 1967 Governors' Conference passed a resolution favoring "block" grants to states, that is, federal grants that would be made directly to the states, which in turn would disemburse subgrants to law enforcement agencies in cities and counties and at the state level. The Governors' Council lobbied vigorously before congressional subcommittees.

Acknowledging that the federal government should not, and probably could not, directly influence local law enforcement, the Johnson administration still felt the federal government should provide the overall strategy, along with the financial and technical assistance, to local criminal justice agencies. National involvement was justified on the grounds that most communities were unable to provide adequate law enforcement facilities and personnel for rising populations and crime rates, important needs of local jurisdictions could not be met by local agencies alone, and crime frequently does not respect geographical boundaries. The president's crime commission had emphasized this last point as a major reason for the need for planning at the multistate or regional level.

The White House wanted a direct federal-local partnership because most states had neither the existing legal authority nor the experience to bring about the needed reforms. Attorney General Clark was aware of the effort in Congress to give funds directly to the states, but he felt it was undesirable, especially for police programs.

> Local expenditures for police exceed state expenditures many times over. I think 27 states at that time (1967) had no greater police authority than highway patrol and traffic control. No state had an office with knowledge of local law enforcement, how it performs, what the budgets are, or what its needs are.[12]

The lack of experience and the long delays in routing money through state governments had been noted under the OLEA program, limited as that program was. In part the question pitted the big cities against everyone else—the states, especially small ones, rural areas, and suburbs. Clark was seriously concerned about what Albany could tell New York City or what Sacramento could tell Los Angeles about how to deal with crime. In addition, Clark opposed block grants to states "on the grounds that more of the same would be worse than nothing, and [would] diminish the ability of the federal government to set meaningful priorities in this area." On the other hand, if funds were directed to large cities, "then money flows to the people who have the responsibility for performance and they at least tend to know what they are doing."[13]

The congressional arguments about the block grant presented an interesting irony. Conservatives favored grants to states as opposed to cities because cities were presumably politically liberal, Democratic, heavily populated with minorities. But at the same time, conservatives were advocating more money for hardware for police, and police are typically local and city—not state—agencies. Liberals, in contrast, who favored direct grants to the cities, also stressed improvements of the courts and corrections, which are mostly state agencies.

In July 1967 the House Judiciary Committee reported out a bill fairly similar to the administration's. Committee chairman Emmanuel Celler was essentially sponsoring the Johnson bill. But in August, a surprise amendment, introduced on the House floor by Congressmen William Cahill (R-N.J.) and Richard Poff (R-Va.), substituted block grants to the states in place of categorical grants to local governments. Speaking for Republicans, Gerald Ford said, "We must abandon the idea of a direct federal intervention in the cities with a federal administrator deciding arbitrarily who will get what and how much."[14] Administration lobbyists were caught off guard and outmaneuvered by the opposition. White House and Justice Department spokesmen tried to rally support to defeat the Cahill-Poff amendment. Deputy Attorney General Warren Christopher put out a blistering press release:

> They talk tough about fighting crime, but where are they when the chips are down? They are busy stalling or scuttling measures proposed by President Johnson which would make the whole country safer. With nineteenth century logic, they are cutting out the bill's heart. They are trying to rewrite it to prevent the Federal government from making direct grants which would enable local police departments to expand and modernize.[15]

But to no avail. Republican amendments also added extra safeguards to prevent a nationally controlled police force and to limit the influence of the attorney general on the operation of the proposed Law Enforcement Assistance Administration. In each case, more authority and money would devolve directly to the states. These amendments were approved by wide margins in the House.

When the administration was beaten by the surprise Republican amendment on the House floor, Justice Department aides considered compromise, but Ramsey Clark was insistent on direct grants to all cities over fifty thousand in population—the standard approach for all similar Great Society legislation. The Johnson White House staff most emphatically agreed, and Clark and his deputies for legislation decided to hold the line and seek a reversal in the Senate.

Their hope was that Senator McClellan would not permit the House block grant provision to pass in the Senate. McClellan was a hard bargainer, but the administration thought it could negotiate with him. At the time, McClellan wanted a certain candidate from the Arkansas area to be appointed to a circuit court judgeship, whereas the White House was sponsoring a different candidate. After some confusion and delay they compromised on a third person. But while McClellan allowed the administration's bill to emerge intact, with respect to categorical grants, from the Judiciary Committee, he simply sat by while Minority Leader Everett Dirksen (R-Ill.) repeated in the Senate what Cahill and Poff had done in the House. If the administration hoped that a concession on wiretapping and confessions could be traded for its desired grant formula, it was mistaken or tricked. Said one Justice Department aide, "They just ganged up on us. . . . the President had bad advice."

Senator Everett Dirksen did the same show in the Senate that Republican Judiciary Committee members had done in the House. The President might have gone to the leadership of both houses and said "Last year Detroit and Cleveland exploded, we need to get large sums of money to these big cities and fast", but he didn't—and I am not sure why—because LBJ could have won some kind of compromise and it could have had a major impact on the later effort to reduce crime.[16]

Towards the end of the congressional battles, the bill's most active spokesman was Senator McClellan. Welcoming a statement of support from candidate Nixon, he "regretted" that leaders of his own party had not come forward with such a warm endorsement. McClellan constantly remained in the public eye and pushed for support of the measure. For three weeks before the passage of the legislation he placed eighteen "crime clocks" in the Senate chamber, each pointing out a grim statistic—a serious assault occurred every two minutes, a forcible rape every twenty-one minutes, and so on. McClellan would point to the clocks and pound on his desk: "Are we going to fiddle while crime destroys America or are we going to stand up like men and vote to do something about it?"[17]

In June 1968 the Senate voted by a wide margin to accept the House amendments, with only minor changes. Even Senator McClellan finally voted on the floor for the block grant concept.

THE GET-TOUGH AMENDMENTS

Not only did Congress defeat Johnson's proposals for direct aid to cities, but they added their own emphasis on get-tough crime control. Senator McClellan spoke for many of his colleagues when he voiced his displeasure with the Supreme Court:

> The brazen criminal no longer finds it convenient or necessary to wait for darkness of night to commit his evil deeds. The prevailing conditions and existing climate permit the criminal to operate boldly, daringly, and too often successfully and with impunity against undermanned, poorly trained, and inadequately equipped police forces. And, if police do apprehend a criminal, he is unwittingly but most advantageously favored and protected by unsound and misguided Supreme Court decisions.[18]

During the hearings, dozens of witnesses advocated a get-tough view and urged changes in the Supreme Court that might lead to a reversal of its decisions (*Mallory*, *Escobedo*, and *Miranda*) that "allow criminals to roam the streets and commit vicious, depraved acts time after time after time." The flames were fanned when, in the middle of the

Senate hearings, the FBI quarterly report showed a 16-percent increase in the crime rate for 1967 as compared with the first nine months of 1966—the greatest increase since 1958. Many members of Congress reported that among their constituents anger over riots and crime overshadowed all other domestic issues and, in many cases, even the war in Vietnam.

Congress made it clear it wanted monies given to local police with no strings attached. Funds were specified for routine equipment, anti-riot equipment, and the recruitment of supplemental manpower. The message was clear: *unhandcuff* the police and give them more help and money! Better prison efficiency, equity in the courts, and experimentation in alternatives to custody were low priority. Though an institute for research and development was added to the legislation, it received little funding, and provisions for evaluation received even less attention. Observed a Senate aide:

> The Congress doesn't cotton to the research and studies approach. The thing, for example, in the area of "research" that would impress many of the senators most is a new type of bullet that would have better and more effective results, i.e., killing someone faster and more totally, that is what you have to deal with when you talk about research with Congress. They want to satisfy the hardware people and the police first, those are the people they listen to. . . .[19]

The Safe Streets Act of 1968 was definitely a policeman's program.

Other provisions were attached to make the Safe Streets bill tougher on crime control. One provision removed the federal courts' power to review state rulings that confessions were voluntarily given. This provision directly challenged the three recent Supreme Court decisions. Another provision authorized the use of wiretaps by local police under court order in a wide variety of investigations. Gun licensing restrictions were watered down and special funds provided for riot control.

Southern Democrats, with Republican support, were able to tag on a major amendment, Title II, protesting and contradicting recent Supreme Court rulings on evidence and the rights of the defendant. In the words of the committee report:

> No matter how much money is spent for upgrading police departments, for modern equipment, for research and other purposes encompassed in Title I, crime will not be effectively abated so long as criminals who have voluntarily confessed their crimes are released on mere technicalities. The traditional right of the people to have their prosecuting attorneys place in evidence before juries the voluntary confessions and incriminating statements made by defendants simply must be restored.[20]

A chief, self-proclaimed Republican contribution was emphasis on organized crime. Republicans zeroed in here by challenging the administration's ban on bugging and wiretapping. Title III, the electronic surveillance title, added in the Senate, broadened opportunities for securing information that might aid in prosecuting organized crime. Republican senators made much of Ramsey Clark's position that organized crime was a "tiny part" of the problem, and they eagerly cited that view as a major failing of the Johnson administration.

CONSTRAINING THE ATTORNEY GENERAL

Apparently much was lost in legislative skill and overall direction for the Johnson-administration bill when Katzenbach was drafted for service as under secretary of state. This shift had the unanticipated effect, according to some observers, of losing momentum generated by the productive work of the crime commission. Whereas Katzenbach was adept at administrative bargaining and at steering legislation through Congress, his successor, Ramsey Clark, encountered skepticism and antagonism.

Ramsey Clark had come to the Justice Department in 1961 at the age of thirty-four. Despite his youth, Clark had grown up with politics and the role of attorney general. His father, Tom Clark, had been attorney general in the 1940s until Truman appointed him to the Supreme Court. The family enjoyed close ties with Lyndon Johnson, dating from common roots in Texas. Ramsey was known as "Johnson's man" in the department during Kennedy's New Frontier. (Vice-President Johnson had well-placed second-tier political appointees in most cabinet departments.)

Soft-spoken, shy, and perhaps even a bit academic, Ramsey Clark was more inclined to speak in humanistic or idealistic terms than in practicalities. A former aide to both Katzenbach and Clark portrayed the latter as the "type of guy who would tell you what was right and what he felt was right, rather than what was 'doable.'" Clark strongly believed that the rise in crime was vastly exaggerated and that many whites were using the crime issue as a way of expressing racist sentiments. He was an advocate of making the criminal justice system fairer, not necessarily more hard-nosed. He was viewed in some quarters as too liberal, as an unrealistic and somewhat preachy moralist.

Unfortunately for Clark, the administration's Safe Streets bill was the captive of conservative members of Congress who were distrustful of both its kind of change and his philosophy. They used the crime bill as a chance to take a position that would appeal to their antigovernment constituency, a chance to respond to a growing sentiment that

Washington was overstepping its bounds, a chance to attack recent decisions of the Supreme Court, and a chance to criticize the attorney general. Senators and congressmen, especially from the South, could not ignore the undercurrents of the Wallace campaign. Other conservative senators, including Roman Hruska (R-Neb.), James Eastland, and Strom Thurmond (R-N.C.), also expressed strong reservations about the control of anticrime programs being vested with the attorney general in the person of Ramsey Clark. Their skepticism was reflected in an exchange between Hruska and Clark during committee hearings on the proposed legislation:

> *Senator Hruska*: Considering the vast discretionary power invested in the Attorney General in this Act and its overwhelming discretion in connection with this program, any aspect of the plan that has been submitted and approved must be OK'd by the Attorney General. Thus, if he feels it is being maladministered and not substantially complied with, he will say, "Sorry, boys, the show is over. No more money". . . . Is it not a pretty compulsive situation?

> *Attorney General Clark*: No. I think it is necessary to the integrity of the Act that its provisions be complied with and its regulations be complied with and the plans submitted be complied with! Otherwise, the very purposes of the Act fail.

> *Senator Hruska*: Exactly. As soon as control is shifted over from the local or state level, it finds its way into the Department of Justice and the purposes of this Act would fail.[21]

The heated political rhetoric and strained congressional-presidential relations over this issue may have been caused by a deeper fear that federal standards would follow federal money and that the Justice Department under Ramsey Clark would vigorously enforce other federal legislation in local criminal justice agencies. Senator McClellan, for example, believed that if Lyndon Johnson were reelected, Ramsey Clark might remain attorney general for as much as another four years. Clark seemed to him disposed to hamper the get-tough thrust of the emerging bill. Moreover, McClellan and other southerners feared that the Justice Department would use the acceptance of federal funds to allow them to uncover discriminatory hiring practices in local police departments and force the police to integrate. (Southerners and conservatives were initially successful in exempting the crime control bill from the provisions of Title VI of the 1964 Civil Rights Act, and many states interpreted this to mean that block grant funds could be allocated *without* consideration for racial balance in local law enforcement agencies.)

It was a difficult and tumultuous time in which to serve as attorney general. More riots, assassinations, and peace marches were still to come. Clark's relationship with both Congress and the White House was severely tested. When Johnson first introduced Clark as his new attorney general, just at the time the crime bill was introduced in Congress, he told a noontime audience of cabinet and congressional officials:

> I have sought, and I think I have found a man, who, as our Attorney General, will be our commander, our leader, and our general in this war on two fronts against fear. . . . Today, Ramsey becomes the lawyer for all Americans; he becomes the Nation's advocate at the bar of justice. . . . I believe that he is above all else a humble, deeply, quietly courageous man with the strength and depths of his convictions and the moral strength not only of genuine humility, but the strength and courage to carry those convictions out.[22]

But about five years later, well into retirement, Johnson told one of his old Senate aides how much Clark had disappointed him:

> You know, ol' Harry Truman said his biggest mistake was appointing Tom Clark to the Supreme Court. Well *my* biggest mistake was appointing Tom's son, Ramsey as my Attorney General. He couldn't make up his mind about a fish fry. Wanted to go around preachin' bleeding-heart stuff, but he never *did* a damn thing. I heard Dick Nixon make a campaign speech against Ramsey Clark one night and I had to sit on my hands so I wouldn't cheer it.[23]

In any event, Congress made it clear it did not want the incumbent attorney general to run the anticrime program. The administration's bill had proposed a single director of law enforcement assistance under the attorney general. But to bypass the attorney general's office, Congress decided the agency administering the money should be independent, and they contrived a "troika" leadership arrangement, with not more than two administrators of the same party. Here again in the absence of forceful presidential intervention the Justice Department was unable to appeal effectively for retaining the original design of agency leadership.

DISCUSSION

Some observers thought that in the Safe Streets legislative battles, Johnson was the victim of poor advice, poor staffing, and inept Justice Department leadership. To be sure, the White House had its Katzenbach-led crime commission. But close observers got the distinct impression nonetheless that the people over at the White House "didn't really know much about crime." They felt the view from the White House was an impaired one. There was a lot of "just postponing of the hour of decision." When the White House did intervene in congressional debates, it usually did so at the wrong time or for the wrong reason.

It has been suggested, too, that some of Johnson's political advisors and party-leader friends were indifferent to, or even counseled against, Ramsey Clark's program. To some political pros there was no political payoff for doing what Clark was urging. His reforms were devoid of glamor, difficult to effect, costly, long-term in scope, and too indirect to get excited about.

A key aide to Senate Republicans recalled the legislative history this way:

> The Administration did not really work very hard to pass its own crime legislation and I am not sure why. Perhaps it was because they favored social programs and because other programs were not funded. . . . It was clear however that Lyndon Johnson did not work hard. There was no great amount of arm twisting, etc. . . . and I might add that the bills that Congress received from the Administration in my judgment were very weak and not very effective. It was the people in the Senate who wrote in the block grants concept, the comprehensive planning component; and it was not the Administration but the Congress that put in the notion of an institute for research and development. So, there were a great number of things that were put in by the Congress and not the Administration. It was in fact a small group of determined Republicans and a few others [southern conservative Democrats] on Capitol Hill who dramatically rewrote the safe streets crime legislation. . . . The Administration doesn't deserve much credit.[24]

Perhaps Johnson's heart was not really in this legislation. By this time he was a lame-duck president and literally consumed by his other and far more major war—the one in Vietnam. Certainly, his involvement in the Safe Streets legislative battle was most unlike the show of personal concern and skill that had won him a reputation for legislative wizardry during the eighty-ninth Congress.

When the Omnibus Crime Control and Safe Streets legislation finally reached Johnson's desk in early June 1968, it was difficult to claim it as presidential legislation. The law included what Johnson advisors termed "repressive" and "obnoxious" provisions, but the president was in no position to choose. As Johnson's counsel reisgnedly told the president, "I recognize that you must sign this bill. But it is the worst bill you have signed since you took office."[25]

Johnson delayed signing. The *New York Times* and Sen. Walter Mondale (D-Minn.) urged him to veto it. The *Times* called it "one of the most vicious bills that we have seen in a good many years." Seldom had a potential law, in its view, been "so charged with sectional politics, facile solutions and clearly discernible prejudice against the ignorant and the poor."[26] Sen. Wayne Morse (D-Ohio) called it the "most shocking and damaging piece of legislation I can remember being presented to the Senate." "It was a bum bill," admitted Michigan senator Philip Hart. Still, as Hart reasoned, "When you're faced with a bill that you think is bad and yet the mood of the country is overwhelmingly for it, then a case can be made for voting for it on the ground that you're doing what the voters want you to do."[27]

Conservative leaders in Congress, Congressman Gerald Ford and Sen. Everett Dirksen, held a news conference a few days later and demanded Johnson sign it at once. "A whole week has been lost," Ford complained, a week in which over seventy thousand reported crimes had been committed. Ford declared Congress had done its "duty"; now it was time for the president to do his.[28]

A presidential veto would have supplied Republicans with considerable campaign ammunition. Besides, passage had been so lopsided in Congress (72-4 in the Senate, 368-17 in the House) that a veto would probably be easily overridden. Attorney General Clark told the president that the Safe Streets bill, as it emerged, should be vetoed on principle. He said the bill was far more a reflection of the fears, frustrations, and politics of the times than an intelligent, carefully tailored measure to help professionalize police or coordinate criminal justice. But, Clark added, "if a veto would be the moral and courageous thing to do," the mood in the country and in Congress was such that Congress might answer the veto with an even worse and more repressive bill and would surely make crime the central issue in the 1968 presidential campaign.[29]

The Democratic convention was just a few weeks away; the national elections would take place in four months. "He had to sign it, he had to even though we had lost . . . ," recalled one White House aide. Johnson's special counsel, Harry C. McPherson, underscored the fix the president was in as follows:

Safe Streets had started out as Johnson's bill, and the Congress had taken it away from him and returned it mis-shapen and abused. In an off year, Johnson might have risked a veto. In an election year, he faced the probability that Congress would override him, and the certainty that the Democratic nominee would hear about it all through the campaign.[30]

And so, on 19 June 1968, with a reluctance and resentment that can be imagined, Johnson signed into law a much different redemption of his 1965 pledge to wage a "war on crime" than he had ever envisioned.

FIVE

Law and Order in the 1968 Elections

WHILE CONGRESS was doing battle over the Safe Streets bill, the crime issue was becoming the center of loud and bitter national debate. In the 1968 campaign, presidential candidates misused, manipulated, and exacerbated the crime issue. Richard Nixon and George Wallace virtually erased the distinctions between the civil rights movement and civil disorder. And Hubert Humphrey, carrying a Vietnam albatross on his back, found it impossible to convince the nation that we could win the war on crime.

A Gallup poll conducted in February 1968 confirmed the magnitude of public fears. For the first time since scientific polling began, in the 1930s, crime and lawlessness were viewed by the public as the top domestic problems facing the nation. Over 30 percent of a national sample admitted they were afraid to go out alone at night in their own neighborhoods, and among those in larger cities the figure was over 40 percent.[1] Polls at this time also found that most Americans believed courts were "too soft" on criminals—this view was held by 48 percent in the spring of 1965 and by 63 percent by the spring of 1968. Consistent with this attitude was a poll that showed sentiment running two to one against the Supreme Court ruling restricting defendant confessions.

Whether because of hysteria or genuine concern, most Americans sided with public officials who argued that crime was an immediate, threatening problem. In fact, George Wallace's criticisms of the Su-

60

preme Court and the national government in this area appeared to be the majority position in the nation.[2]

President Johnson was a fascinated consumer of public opinion surveys and commissioned many of his own while president. Though he viewed himself as an educator and leader who was willing on occasion to move ahead of the more conservative views of the American public, the constraints of public opinion eventually dampened even his own enthusiasm for the Great Society. Gallup polls in 1964 and 1967 indicated that more than 80 percent of the public viewed poverty as a relatively permanent condition. Only one-third of those interviewed in 1966 said anti-poverty money in their area was being well spent, and one-third felt it was being poorly spent. More and more voters thought poor people should not "expect something for nothing." And still other polls suggested the Democratic administration was pushing integration too fast.[3]

By late 1967 Johnson began to decry and declaim on crime more often than he touted the successes of his war on poverty. In Johnson's last year, Nixon's bitter verbal indictments of his administration's record began to penetrate even the president's thinking. In the spring of 1968, Nixon charged that if the president genuinely accepted the proposition that a war on poverty was a war on crime, "the near 50 percent increase in the crime rate since 1964 would be adequate proof of the utter failure of the government's war on poverty."[4] To downplay the charge, the White House issued a tough anticrime letter from Johnson to Senate Majority Leader Mike Mansfield (D-Mont.). Johnson wrote, among other points, that "crimes of violence threaten to turn us into a land of fearful strangers. . . . The key to effective crime control is effective law enforcement. . . . Far too many local police are ill-paid, ill-equipped and ill-trained."[5]

Getting tough on crime was getting more and more popular.

THE CLIMATE OF CONFUSION

Events moved quickly in this election year, more quickly than anyone had anticipated. In early March, Sen. Eugene McCarthy (D-Minn.) won a surprising moral (although not literal) victory over Johnson in the New Hampshire primary, receiving 42 percent of the vote. Four days later Sen. Robert Kennedy (D-N.Y.) entered the race for the Democratic nomination. By late March, Johnson's critics were in full cry, angry over the seizure of the U.S. spy ship Pueblo by the North Koreans in January, angry about the Tet offensive in Vietnam in late January and early February.[6] On March 31, Johnson attempted to calm the country and bring peace to himself and to the world by announcing that he would not seek or accept his party's renomination for another term. Tragically, four days later on a motel balcony in Memphis, Martin Luther King, Jr., was assassinated; his murder set off a spasm of rioting in over one hundred cities that cost the lives of thirty-four persons. This was the last major rioting of the year. Then, Robert Kennèdy was struck down after he had gained impressive victories in the primary elections, and the last hope of millions of Americans vanished.

Republican campaign leaders, unsure of the meaning of these events and wary of Johnson's "retirement," attacked the administration on the theme they felt would engender the most enthusiasm: law and order. Issuing a thirty-seven-page report entitled *Crime and Delinquency—A Republican Response*, they contended the Democrats had failed to take the necessary and proper action to prevent and control crime. Noting that FBI crime statistics had increased 89 percent since the Democrats had taken office, the report outlined thirty-one steps that should be taken to combat lawlessness in America.[7]

Nixon continued to escalate his attack, charging that under the Democrats the country had become a "lawless society" and that the Johnson administration had been "lame and ineffectual" in checking the rise of crime. While campaigning in the Nebraska primary in May 1968, Nixon issued a major, six-thousand-word policy statement on crime entitled "Toward Freedom from Fear." In it he set forth his blueprint for ending the crime wave. He charged, as he had in every speech for the past six months, that the "peace forces" had been weakened and that the administration's emphasis on social conditions was a cause of crime.

Not all Republicans agreed with the hard-line law and order stance. Gov. Nelson Rockefeller of New York, an announced candidate for the Republican nomination, attempted to overcome Nixon's lead by appealing to the moderate and liberal wings of the party; he attacked Nixon's stand on the Supreme Court and strongly implied that Nixon, or some of his supporters, welcomed the support of segregationists. Discussing law and order, Rockefeller further refused to accept Nixon's charge that the Supreme Court had given the green light to crime and that efforts to reduce poverty were related to the rise in crime in America.

Alexander M. Bickel, a noted Yale Law School professor, attacked Nixon's crime program, charging that Nixon offered no new ideas and put all the blame on the Supreme Court and on "scare statistics with a political slant, and on wiretapping, which is put forward as a sovereign remedy for organized crime." Nixon, Bickel concluded, "has not yet learned how to attain a level of discourse suitable to the politics of the

American Presidency."[8] Nixon was also criticized by Andrew Young, then executive secretary of the Southern Christian Leadership Conference. Young suggested that Nixon's stand—"courting the most conservative elements of the Republican Party, appealing to the fears and prejudices of the people, and not offering creative solutions to the problem"—almost amounted to racism.[9]

Hubert Humphrey, like Johnson, sincerely believed that neglect rather than permissiveness was the primary cause of crime and that the Great Society's social programs were the best long-range strategy to solve the crime problem. But when pressed on specific programs to deal with crime, he could not point with pride to the Safe Streets Act, as it was emerging, because it was the captive of conservative and Republican interests. Moreover, he desperately needed to escape responsibility for the Vietnam quagmire. Humphrey was faced with the dilemma of just how to dissociate himself from Johnson: how could he help to bring an end to the unpopular war in Vietnam and at the same time urge more decisive action on law and order?

Nixon, on the other hand, was free to criticize the incumbent administration and could be more direct in his proposed solutions to both crime and Vietnam. He argued that the social causes of crime had been "grossly exaggerated" and suggested that certain freedoms might have to be curtailed in order to stop crime. He ignored civil rights questions, deemphasized poverty as a cause of crime, and embraced a get-tough policy. Against the political climate of frustration in the late 1960s, Nixon's explanations gained supporters as the campaign progressed.

For many people, especially those in high-crime areas, the threat of victimization was immediate and real; promises of long-range improvement were not sufficient. Many began to wonder whether social reform was indeed leading to social disorder. America was committing about seven million recorded crimes per year, fifty times as many murders as Japan, West Germany, and Great Britain combined. More and more young Americans were dying in Vietnam. A long series of urban riots and student demonstrations had so bewildered the nation that even Lyndon Johnson began to ask whether violence was a contagious phenomenon: "Is there something in the environment of American society or the structure of American Institutions that causes disrespect for law, and contempt for the rights of others?"

Charged with the task of addressing this question and studying the causes of urban rioting, the National Advisory Commission on Civil Disorders, which had been appointed by Johnson in 1967, issued its report in early March 1968. The report placed much of the responsibility for the urban riots on a century of white racism and neglect.

It further warned that unless conditions were remedied, this country would continue to move toward two separate societies, one black and one white. Most political figures attempted to disassociate themselves from the findings of the commission, chaired by former governor Otto Kerner of Illinois. Richard Nixon, continuing to establish his credentials as a law and order candidate, responded: "One of the major weaknesses of the President's Commission is that it, in effect, blames everybody for the riots. . . . I think that deficiency has to be dealt with first. Until we have order we can have no progress."[10] He felt it must be "made perfectly clear" to potential rioters that in the event of a riot the law would move in with adequate force to put down the disorder and looting. He further criticized the commission for dividing the American people, for building walls by calling America a racist society.

ORDER VERSUS CHAOS

To many in an already stunned nation, the stark contrast between the Republican and Democratic nominating conventions was proof of the Republicans' ability to maintain order versus the Democrats' disintegration into chaos.

The Republican Nominating Convention began in Miami Beach in mid-August. During the convention there were two days of rioting in the city of Miami, costing the lives of 3 black men and the arrest of 250 other persons. The National Guard was quickly mobilized and sent into the city, and although charges continued to be made that police forces had brutally suppressed the black community, the violence—and the resultant publicity—was contained.

Inside the convention, one of the liveliest topics of debate was law and order. Nixon and Ronald Reagan, governor of California, vied to see who could push the Republican party farther to the right on the issue. Nixon stressed that the right to be free from violence had become "the forgotten civil right" and lumped together the problems of racial riots, crime in the streets, and student demonstrations. "It is too late for more commissions to study violence. It is time for the government to stop it." Without specifying what actions he would take as president, he again challenged the Democratic administration to exert its "moral authority to the limit" and to marshall public opinion for a militant crusade against crime.

At the convention, as throughout the campaign, Nixon rejected the idea that *law and order* were code words for repression of blacks. Some surmised he was attempting to shore up conservative support, which was sagging under the even more right-wing attacks from governors Reagan and Wallace. Confident that he would win the nomination, Nixon was already looking ahead to November. By calling for a crusade against crime, he could appeal to conservatives, allowing more flexibility in his position on ending the war in Vietnam.

Nixon won the nomination easily and immediately outlined his plan of attack on the law and order issue. He would change the composition of the Supreme Court so it would cease weakening the peace forces. Both the courts and law enforcement officials, of course, would respect civil rights, but they must remember that "the first civil right is freedom from domestic violence." The country must have a new attorney general. And, finally, he again defended his use of the term *law and order*: "Our goal is justice—justice for every American. If we are to have respect for law in America, we must have laws that deserve respect. Just as we cannot have progress without order, we cannot have order without progress."

Nixon chose a strong law and order running mate—Gov. Spiro T. Agnew of Maryland. Agnew's selection stunned many people, including Agnew himself, and brought charges that a deal had been made with the Old South. Liberal Republicans were angered by the selection because of Agnew's record on civil rights. In his election as governor, Agnew had defeated a racist opponent, but once in office he, at one point, had condoned the police shooting of suspected looters who had failed to halt when commanded, denounced the Poor People's Campaign, called the Kerner Commission report an incitement to further rioting, and roughly handled peaceful demonstrators from a black college who had sat in at the Maryland statehouse. However, Nixon was firmly in control of the convention, and an incipient revolt against Agnew by delegates was quickly put down. The Republican convention ended on a note of optimism and apparent unity.

Columnist James Reston of the *New York Times* felt Nixon had outlined a winning strategy but also warned of the possible consequences of such a victory. Nixon, he wrote, "undoubtedly will emphasize 'order' in the cities, for that is his best issue. . . . He thinks he can tame the ghettos and then reconstruct them, and he may very well make reconciliation with the Negro community impossible in the process."[11] Even leading Democrats began to admit privately that Nixon might have devised a campaign strategy that would be hard to beat.

Soon after Nixon's nomination the Democrats held their convention in Chicago. Threats of peace demonstrations and protest marches had led the city to overprepare. The convention site, the International Amphitheatre on the south side of the city, took on the atmosphere of an armed camp, enclosed by a chain-link and barbed-wire fence. A twelve-thousand man police force was placed on twelve-hour shifts, and it was supplemented by a fifty-six-hundred-man force of National Guardsmen as well as seventy-five hundred army troops.

The convention itself had been in doubt through the month of August because of recurring strikes and the fear that the hall would not be ready. Communications workers had been on strike throughout the city for several weeks, and cab drivers walked out just two weeks before the convention. The threat of no telephones, no transportation, and a multitude of pickets at the convention site brought calls for moving the convention to another city. But just before the opening session, Mayor Richard J. Daley received assurances the phones would be put in, the convention hall ready, and the cab strike settled. The threat of demonstrations remained. Severe restrictions were placed on the news media both on and off the convention floor. A vigorous security system, which hassled and hampered delegates, was installed, and thousands of young, white antiwar demonstrators massed in the city.

During the week of the convention, there were sporadic and sometimes spectacular clashes between the demonstrators and police. The confrontations reached a climax the night Humphrey was nominated. Mobile television units on Michigan and Balboa avenues captured demonstrators being manhandled and clubbed—episodes the Walker Commission report would later characterize as a police riot. The scenes radicalized some and polarized most people in America. For some the bitterness over the system that had led us into Vietnam was now combined with the outrage over Chicago. Others turned in disgust to the Republican party, which promised, and looked like it could deliver, a return to law and order.

Meanwhile, inside the convention hall, Humphrey used his acceptance speech to hit hard on the issue of law and order. He said a president must employ every resource available "to end once and for all the fear that is in our cities," that "rioting, burning, sniping, mugging, traffic in narcotics and disregard for law are the advance guard of anarchy, and they must end, and they will be stopped." There was no solution to be found by attacking the courts or the attorney general, he said; rather, the answer was in "reasoned, effective action by state, local and federal authorities."[12] The Democratic platform was, in fact, quite similar to the Republican on the law and order issue—with one major exception. The Democrats still stressed the importance of the underlying social roots of crime. In addition, the Democratic platform was felt by many to be superior because it avoided a demogogic attack on the courts, pledged effective gun control laws, and called attention to the need for rehabilitating criminal offenders.

But many could not believe that Humphrey could provide the leadership to restore law and order when he could not contain disruptions at his own convention (just as many could not believe he could end the war in Vietnam when he could not dissociate himself from Johnson's position). Humphrey would spend much of the early part of his campaign trying to overcome this credibility gap. Moreover, many were persuaded that crime, rioting, the civil rights movement, and protest demonstrations were all part of the same picture. Middle-class, white voters were especially susceptible to Nixon's subliminal implications that black demands for equality and student protest demonstrations were somehow connected with crime. Expectations created during the Kennedy-Johnson years, opposition to the war, the "yippie movement," challenges to traditional morals, obscenity, drugs, and violence: all these tensions erupted at the Chicago convention and were linked with the Democrats. It was a bitter and tragic affair, and it may have been that Hubert Humphrey lost the election there.

THE RHETORIC OF LAW AND ORDER

Fully rested, and kept from public view during the Democratic convention, Nixon was greeted by an enthusiastic crowd when he formally launched his campaign in Chicago in early September. He declined comment on the disorder at the Democratic convention but, in a statewide television interview, commended President Johnson for appointing a commission to look into the matter. Pressed on the issue of law and order, he offered a moderate and tempered definition: "I have often said that you cannot have order unless you have justice. Because if you stifle dissent, if you just stifle the progress, you're going to have an explosion and you're going to have disorder. On the other hand, you can't have progress without order, because when you have disorder and revolution you destroy all the progress that you have."[13]

Regardless of this diplomatic answer, the phrase *law 'n' order* continued to concern some of his advisors, friends, and campaign staff, Republican senator Edward Brooke of Massachusetts in particular. Denying rumors that he was about to abandon the Nixon camp, Brooke persuaded himself that he had succeeded in changing Nixon's approach to key issues that were "of immense symbolic value to the Negro community." His success, however, was in persuading Nixon to stop talking about "law and order" and start talking about "law and order with justice," a variation that had been introduced early in the campaign by Sen. George McGovern (D-S.Dak.).

Nixon could now afford to play down the crime theme because his running mate had taken the field and quickly embraced it as his own. Agnew proved to be an able and more-than-willing surrogate. He commented on the issue this way: "George Wallace uses the term law and order as a hatchet. We know that. We can feel that. Hubert Humphrey uses the term as a shield against criticism of the sluggish Administration of which he is part. But Nixon uses the term as a pledge. Not maliciously. Not defensively. But as a commitment to logic and as a commitment to America."[14] At one point in the campaign, however, Agnew went too far. Responding to Humphrey's description of Nixon as the "Cold Warrior," Agnew in turn attacked Humphrey as one who had been "soft on inflation, soft on Communism and soft on law and order over the years." He also said the Nixon administration was "not going to be squishy soft as this Administration had been on the question of crime and 'knowing your enemies.' "

Democrats were understandably outraged. Lawrence O'Brien, the Democratic national chairman, replied, "It is apparent that Agnew has been delegated by Mr. Nixon to travel the low road—and with the tradition of Nixon campaigns, the low road is rock bottom. . . . [Agnew] has been charged with the task . . . to show Wallace supporters that they can feel comfortable with Mr. Nixon and Agnew."[15] Agnew's remarks also brought a hurried reaction from the Republican leadership. Gerald Ford and Everett Dirksen said the statement was ill timed and that the Republicans, with a wide variety of first-class issues, such as inflation, crime, and lack of leadership, didn't have to push this way. Further, they were unaware of any evidence that Humphrey was soft on Communism.

Willing to drop the communist issue for the remainder of the campaign, Agnew remained critical of civil disobedience, which he opposed even in the most passive form, such as the sit-ins that had been used in the South in the late 1950s and early 1960s to desegregate lunch counters. Agnew said that if the demonstrators had expended the same amount of energy in other ways, "using the good old American know-how to dramatize their idea," they could have achieved the same goal through the courts or the ballot box. Civil disobedience threatened the rights of the majority, he said, and he claimed *he* would not disobey a law that might ban him from swimming in a public pool, eating at a lunch counter, or drinking from a public fountain. When asked if preaching disobedience against unjust laws was not in the spirit of Jesus, Mahatma Gandhi, Martin Luther King, and Henry Thoreau, he replied that "the people you have mentioned did not operate in a free society."[16]

Agnew hit over and over at the Democrats, charging that they had attempted to whitewash the crime crisis and had remained complacent in the face of a soaring crime wave. The Democrats, he said, were simply unable to create a climate "conducive to law."

Public opinion polls found that although Vietnam was still more important, Republicans possessed fertile ground in the crime issue and had evoked widespread agreement with their campaign positions. A Harris poll, taken before the Democratic convention and released in early September, found that 81 percent of the voters agreed that law and order had broken down in this country and 84 percent felt that a strong president could make a difference in preserving it. Organized crime, "Negroes who start riots," and communists were blamed equally for the breakdown. In another Harris poll released about the same time, voters reported that they felt Nixon was the one candidate who could best preserve law and order, rating him 38 percent to Humphrey's 26 percent, with Wallace following with 21 percent. The poll also disclosed that "more than half the voters—54 percent—felt personally uneasy on the streets today."[17]

Still weary from the Chicago convention, Hubert Humphrey launched his campaign with a march down Fifth Avenue in New York in early September. He was faced with the major task of pulling his party together and healing wounds before he and vice-presidential nominee Sen. Edmund S. Muskie of Maine could attempt to defeat Nixon. He began by immediately attacking the Republican strategy on law and order. Nixon and the Republican party, he said, "have chosen this year to join forces with the most reactionary elements in American Society," having adopted a southern strategy very similar to Mr. Goldwater's. And Humphrey claimed Nixon was naïve and simplistic about the problem of crime.

Humphrey had a problem with the crime issue. He was "considered, rightly or wrongly, something of a Johnny-come-lately, since his two principal opponents . . . Nixon . . . and Wallace . . . have long been known as hardliners," said one newspaper. H. L. Mencken had said it in other words: "In politics, the first candidate who grabs an issue always gets the best of it. The plain people distrust the tailer, particularly if his vacillations have been made public, and their distrust has a sound instinct under it."[18]

To establish his credentials on the issue, Humphrey issued what he called a "serious, practical blueprint" for dealing with crime, largely through a massive federal program of direct aid to state and local police, courts, and correctional institutions. This aid could amount to more than $1 billion within a few years, and the effort would be accompanied by expanding programs against poverty and other social problems that contributed to crime. And Humphrey's campaign manager, Lawrence O'Brien, tried to tighten up the campaign organization and enlarge television coverage in the hope that the voters would begin to respond.

Humphrey's crowds slowly began to grow, but he still found himself faced with the problem of being heard. Although hecklers and antiwar demonstrators were beginning to appear at the Nixon rallies, Humphrey was constantly faced with a determined group of war opponents who often gained more attention than did his own speeches. To Humphrey's dismay these protesters merely confirmed in the minds of many the need for a stronger law and order candidate.

Humphrey's running mate, Sen. Edmund Muskie (D-Me.), had more success in being heard, and he also hit the Republicans hard on the crime issue, accusing Nixon of misleading the public. Muskie claimed that states with Democratic governors had much lower crime rates than did those with Republican ones. When asked if this meant the Democrats were better crime fighters, he said no, that it meant party labels were simply irrelevant when it came to crime, that there were no simple answers. But such candor did not help the Democratic ticket; Muskie was unable to persuade voters with this honesty.

The unknown factor in the campaign was still George Wallace, Democratic governor of Alabama, now running for president as the candidate of the American Independent party. Ignored early on, he showed little strength in the polls until the murder of Robert Kennedy, when his support jumped considerably. By mid-September, he showed yet more strength in the two major polls, outside as well as inside the South. His support had a reasonably broad base of middle- and lower-middle-income voters, including rank-and-file labor union members as well as rural farm workers. A Wallace rally was never a dull affair, and the press covered the event for what might happen as well as for what the candidate might say. Law and order was always among his chief themes, and he liked to warn protestors and demonstrators that they had better not lie down in front of *his* car. He also called the Kerner Commission report absurd; "the country's not sick, the Supreme Court is sick," he would say. His praise continually went to the police, and he wanted the courts to unhandcuff them.[19]

Wallace was asked if law and order wasn't simply a code phrase for putting blacks in their place; he replied that wasn't the way he meant it. He insisted the overwhelming majority of all races in the country were against the breakdown of law and order. But he had trouble convincing many Americans. His campaign continued to generate support; however, his choice of Curtis LeMay, a decidedly hawkish and controversial retired air force general, as his running mate apparently damaged his campaign as much as his pugnacious rhetoric did.

Nixon attempted to ignore Governor Wallace while using nearly the same appeal. He expended considerable effort blaming Johnson's attorney general, Ramsey Clark, for practically encouraging crime. Time and again he exclaimed that to restore order and respect for law in this country there was only one place to begin. And then he would raise the Ramsey Clark issue: we were going to have a new attorney general of the United States of America. In a campaign tour through the South, Nixon hit at Clark as the symbol of "unprecedented lawlessness." He denounced the Supreme Court and the U.S. Office of Education for their efforts to enforce integration, and he called for the support of all law enforcement officials.

In large part because of Wallace, Nixon could attack along the law and order line without being branded an out-and-out racist in the minds of the general public. Wallace, who had blocked the doorway to exclude blacks from the University of Alabama years before, carried the racist label for him. Wallace realized what Nixon was doing and countercharged that Nixon was courting the South under the guise of law and order while quietly maintaining ties with the eastern establishment and, worse, supporting civil rights legislation.

Humphrey, more vulnerable than Nixon to losing traditionally Democratic votes to Wallace, tried to link Nixon and Wallace. In a tour through the South, Humphrey bitterly rounded on Wallace, accusing him of a calculated campaign to bring the nation to the brink of broad-scale disorder. He attacked Wallace as "the creature of the most reactionary underground forces in American life," a charlatan and a demagogue, whose promises to restore law and order through a national police force were "as phony as a three-dollar bill." He said Nixon appealed to the same passions and the same frustrations: the Wallace tactics, he charged, were also found "in the perfumed, deodorized campaign of my Republican opponent—a man who had deliberately courted the most radical extremist elements in his own party— who continues this appeal in his speeches—and who will be fully in their debt should he win the Presidency." He further charged that Nixon's campaign against the Court and against the attorney general would inevitably set "group against group and race against race."[20]

The debate on law and order had one casualty early in the campaign. Supreme Court Chief Justice Earl Warren had notified Johnson that he wished to retire as soon as a replacement could be found, and Johnson had chosen as his replacement Associate Justice Abraham ("Abe") Fortas. Fortas was a southerner, but he had served in government or practiced law in Washington, D.C., since the mid-1930s and was better known as a long-time crony of LBJ's. His nomination ran into serious opposition from Republicans and southern Democrats. Fortas became a campaign issue when Humphrey challenged Nixon to deny that he had made a deal with Sen. Strom Thurmond of South Carolina to block the nomination in return for promised southern support. The blocking action continued until late September, when a filibuster against the confirmation was begun in the Senate. An attempt at cloture in early October failed by fourteen votes, and Fortas asked that his name be withdrawn. In a letter to Johnson he said that he would continue as associate justice but that the long and bitter debate and attacks on the Court would be especially inappropriate and harmful to the nation if they continued while the Court was in session. In an unprecedented move, Johnson withdrew Fortas's name and announced he would not make a second nomination, leaving the chief justice appointment to his successor.

The law and order debate began to wind down at the end of September. Nixon made one last major radio address, offering general programs to curb crime. They included the establishment of a cabinet-level national law enforcement council (to be similar to the National Security Council or the Council on Economic Advisors), which would coordinate federal policy against crime; the promotion of nationwide town-hall conferences on crime prevention and control; and the establishment of a national academy of law enforcement, which would provide local police with modern training and techniques. Nixon also supported the block grant approach, which had become the formula for the Safe Streets bill, and encouraged expanded use of wiretapping.

Columnist Tom Wicker said Nixon was taking dangerous political advantage of the country's concern about crime and that the net effect "could be to present his erstwhile new Administration with a far more serious problem than the one Nixon speaks about so forcefully—and which is, to some extent, imaginary." Nixon had created a climate, Wicker felt, such that if were elected, every "heavy-handed policeman" in the country would take it as a license to beat up somebody— and "probably somebody poor, black, or young, and preferably all three."[21]

Late in the campaign, Ramsey Clark also began speaking out more forcefully, contending that Nixon was appealing to "fleeting prejudices of the majority by fabricating false issues on law and order." In an attempt to counter Nixon's personal attacks, he asked, "Can a man who deliberately misleads be trusted to lead?", accusing Nixon of appealing to "fear and hatred and emotionalism by using trigger words and misstatements on the crime issue."

By the end of the campaign Humphrey and Muskie had almost managed to pull their party together and had made tremendous gains on Nixon. If, many felt, the election had been held two or three weeks later, the Democrats might have won. But the Republican party was more or less united and its appeal widespread. Nixon pledged not only safe streets but peace with honor in Vietnam. His approach to the crime issue appeared to many voters to be pragmatic and action oriented—and in 1968 voters wanted action. Nixon had the crime issue first and molded his campaign rhetoric for maximum political advantage. He managed to spark the hope that *he* could restore order to troubled cities. His policies favored professionals, white-collar workers, farmers, older persons, and WASPS, and they voted for him overwhelmingly. Rather than voting for Nixon, many voted against the Democratic party and against Johnson and Humphrey, whom they blamed for escalating the war and failing to reduce crime. Democratic voters —blacks, urban residents, blue-collar workers, and young persons— split their votes between Wallace and Humphrey. Nixon won by half a million of the more than sixty-three million votes cast.

GETTING TOUGH ON CRIME

Why did Richard Nixon succeed in 1968, where Barry Goldwater had failed in 1964, in making successful use of the law and order issue? In addition to the party split arising from the Chicago nominating convention, Democrats were torn between different approaches to the crime issue. At the same time that public opinion polls suggested tough-minded anti-social-welfare attitudes prevailed, Humphrey and Muskie were locked into Johnson's liberal long-term socioeconomic strategy. The Republican party, on the other hand, was more cohesive. And Nixon had targets, plenty of them—Ramsey Clark, Earl Warren, Abe Fortas, and Lyndon Johnson and his protégé, Hubert Humphrey. Neither party knew how to deal effectively with crime, but the Democrats exposed their indecisiveness.

The ideological deadlock between the social justice model and the get-tough school explains a good part of Johnson's inability to organize his war on crime and Humphrey's failure to benefit electorally from it. According to Nicholas Katzenbach, the debate was a basic conflict between two contrasting value systems, and Katzenbach was as firmly committed to one as he was opposed to the other.

> . . . This country faces a choice . . . which I don't think is well understood by American people. That is, that with the increase in crime, as it goes on, we are either going to put the resources of intelligence and hard work into incorporating the kind of recommendations that this report [the president's crime commission] has to improve police, to improve the courts, to improve the correctional process and to make it work, or we are going to have more and more in the way of repression.

Katzenbach gave a passionate defense of the social justice model at a 1971 Senate hearing:

Senator Edward Kennedy: Aren't there those who say what you are really recommending is "coddling" the criminals and who ask what difference it really makes in crime levels, unless you have decent housing, job opportunities, quality education for your children? How do you respond to those who say "let's get rid of tough criminals and teach them a lesson and then they won't commit so many crimes in the future." —How should we respond to that argument?

Mr. Katzenbach: I think the only response I know is that if that is the kind of society that one wants to live in . . . where police make indiscriminate arrests, where they have "search and seizure" without bothering to get warrants, and where people can be held in jail without being convicted of crimes and held for long periods of time—then I think if you want to live in that kind of society it is perhaps possible to control crime in that kind of a way. I don't want to live in that kind of society.[22]

Katzenbach's perspective had much to do with the initial Johnson-administration response.

Several commentators, among them political analysts Richard Scammon and Ben Wattenberg and Professor James Q. Wilson of Harvard, had begun to suggest that the Democrats not shy away from the crime issue. They said the rise in the rate of street crime was real and painful, not a statistical artifact or an FBI public relations trick. To be tough on criminals was not the same as to favor the police over the poor. Poor people, including a high proportion of blacks, had a much higher rate of victimization and therefore a common interest in curbing street crime. Moreover, in Wilson's words,

the increase [in street crimes] came concurrently with a general rise in the standard of living and thus could not be explained by worsening social conditions . . . [and] though continued improvements in prosperity and in ending discrimination may ultimately be the best remedies for crime, in the short term (anything less than the next decade or two) society's efforts must be aimed at improving the criminal justice system as a mechanism for just and effective social control.[23]

But even though Johnson grew more impatient with his own social programs, his attorney general persisted as a staunch advocate of the social justice approach to crime. As an earnest civil libertarian, Clark was very firm in his beliefs. In his own quiet way, he, along with two or three liberal White House staff lawyers, counseled for a course of reform, experimentation, research, and programs to upgrade corrections.

Clark and Johnson's more liberal advisors held to the view that crime as a *problem* should be distinguished from crime as an *issue*. The best response to one, they implied, might not be the best response to the other. Crime as an *issue* was at least partially a rhetorical refuge for all manner of fears, antiblack sentiments, and reactions to war protesters. Liberals in the late 1960s felt cornered in such a way that their response to crime as an issue was as understandable as it was electorally deficient.

Crime is one of several areas where popular opinion divides and clusters in consonance with emotion-charged symbols, symbols that can and often do conflict with the findings of empirical investigators, with the consensus of specialists, and with technical considerations that are difficult to communicate to the broad public. In 1968 people were confused and frustrated about crime, impatient with the president's crime commission, angry at the Supreme Court, and deeply fearful of not only crime but the civil rights movement, antiwar protests, riots, and assassinations. These were the symbols that won the votes.

Thus, poll after poll in the late 1960s showed that the greatest citizen complaint about the quality of justice was that "convicted criminals are let off too easily." The practical argument was made that prisons and parole, as presently constituted, are drearily reliable in their ability to encourage recidivism and even careers in crime. But conservatives, and increasingly moderates as well, could not be convinced by arguments for bail reform, rehabilitation efforts, and decent prison conditions. The impulse for retribution, and its collateral assumption that retribution deters others, are very ancient tenets in Anglo-American law and reflect deeply held sentiments. Debates continue on this matter today, with scholars, lawyers, politicians, and even Supreme Court justices arguing about whether severe penalties deter crime. Still others claim society must pragmatically arrange its sanctions so crime does not pay or offer economic advantages, as it apparently does at present for so many.[24] Nowadays analysts argue that whether or not harsh sentences deter others or discourage recidivism, incapacitating convicted criminals at least means they cannot commit more crimes while in prison. (This is the reasoning behind the idea of mandatory prison sentences.)

It is only fair to note that however mistaken might have been the public's view of the Supreme Court's decisions, however mistaken might have been the urge to support harsh prison sentences or preventive detention, the situation was not one in which the "right solution" was neglected or rejected—because *no one knew in 1968*, and *no one knows today*, what the right solution to the crime problem is. Moreover, mistaken solutions must not be assumed to be the monopoly of conservatives or even of the uneducated public. For instance, the liberals' assumption that police, prisons, and courts were amenable to immediate improvement just by an infusion of federal funds proved to be naïve (as we shall see in later chapters).

Yet presidential candidates failed, despite the thousands of words of debate on crime, to talk about just what the national role in reducing crime should be, failed to address key issues that would later affect policy implementation in the war on crime. Candidates failed, for instance, to discuss the consequences of distributing massive amounts of federal funds to local police departments at a time when civil rights groups, antiwar protesters and college students were demonstrating against U.S. involvement in Vietnam. They failed to discuss reform ideas for police departments, where money would be most efficiently spent to make streets safe, the opportunity costs of spending money one way or the other, or the strengths and weaknesses of state and city governments in administering funds.

Voters in 1968 tended to choose on the basis of their frustrations and fears. Nixon played to these frustrations and fears and succeeded. Looking back on Nixon's contribution to our understanding of crime, John Dean, who was at the time a young lawyer working for Republicans on the House Judiciary Committee, put it this way: "I was cranking out that bullshit on Nixon's crime policy before he was elected. And it was bullshit, too. We knew it. The Nixon campaign didn't call for anything about crime problems that Ramsey Clark wasn't already doing under LBJ. We just made more noise."[25] But Nixon made the kind of noise the public wanted to hear. The crime issue, in substantial part, had won the presidency for Richard Nixon.

DISCUSSION

Actually doing something about crime was, of course, considerably harder than just talking about it. Nixon sounded tough (and spoke in a tone remarkably similar to that President Ronald Reagan would use eight years later) when he spoke about governmental programs: "We have been deluged by government programs for the unemployed, programs for the cities, programs for the poor, and we have reaped from these programs an ugly harvest of frustrations, violence and failure across the land. . . . I say it's time to quit pouring billions of dollars into programs that have failed."[26] But now the embryonic federal war on crime was a *Republican* program, and it would be the *Nixon* administration that would begin to pour billions of dollars into it. Could a law and order administration stop crime?

SIX

Launching the War on Crime

NATIONAL POLICYMAKING for the war on crime had only begun with the passage of the Safe Streets Act and the election of a law and order president in 1968. For the next twelve years political controversies that had plagued early efforts to legislate for safe streets would continue. Conceptual difficulties, stemming from the way the crime issue was nationalized, would continue to hamper the war on crime throughout its abbreviated lifetime. Yet substantive improvements, in either reducing the crime rate or accumulating knowledge about how to reduce crime, proved elusive. If ever there was a case of a political response to a problem being inadequate, such was the case with the national war on crime.

In the Safe Streets Act, Congress acknowledged that "crime is essentially a local problem that must be dealt with by state and local governments if it is to be controlled effectively." Most street crimes—that is, homicide, rape, assault, and burglary—are, of course, not under federal jurisdiction, and because control of these crimes is not delegated to the federal government, it is constitutionally reserved to the states. A strong tradition of local control and a suspicion of a national police force also support this principle. Still, national policymakers, presidents and congressmen alike, conservatives and liberals alike, plainly felt—and some helped to create—political pressures to respond at the national level.

Is it fair to say that throwing out national funds to the states and letting them handle the problem was merely an expedient way of defusing political pressures?[1] Or a skillful means of assuming credit but avoiding responsibility for an unmanageable problem? Or just a knee-jerk reaction of legislators conditioned to big-spending social programs? Now that anticrime policy was in the national ball park, would national policymakers really assume responsibility for the policy they designed?

The extenuating facts are that little was then known (and little still is) about how actually to reduce crime, and there was little direct experience at that time with the block grant mechanism. These were severe policymaking handicaps. It has even been suggested that crime was perceived to a large extent as a problem of unemployed urban black juvenile males, but addressing the issue in such specific terms was too hot to handle politically, so ambiguities were purposely written into the legislation.[2] But it is also true that despite early difficulties with the block grants and a growing suspicion that even high levels of funding might not help (given our lack of systematic knowledge), national policymakers kept pouring more and more money into a program they knew was severely troubled. Political pressures on presidents and congressmen only increased as negative feedback on the war on crime started coming in and the FBI crime index continued to soar.

The Safe Streets Act was amended five times, basically each time it came up for reauthorization (until finally planning and action funds were totally cut out of the budget, reducing the Law Enforcement Assistance Administration to a skeletal administrative operation in 1981). The general thrust of the earlier amendments can be described as "creeping categorization,"[3] a disease in which the block grant was successively restricted until it became more and more like a categorical grant. The amendments also dealt with structural rearrangements in the administering agency, the distribution of funds between cities and states, and the centralization of standards. Revisions were made in an unsystematic and "Band-Aid" manner (until the final amendments in 1979, which completely reorganized the agency but which were followed by no appropriations for LEAA grants). All kinds of changes—new categories of high-priority crime areas, structural rearrangements in the bureaucracies administering the grants, formulas for the allocation of funds between cities and states, and new ideas about centralizing crime measurement and crime control accounting—were scattered throughout the amendments, throughout administrative guidelines, throughout new laws and Executive Office decisions.

National policymakers primarily concentrated on distributive niceties—exactly who got exactly what—of the block grant. For the most part they did not resolve the tensions in the original legislation, tensions that severely constrained the implementation of the war on crime. Too many and ill-defined goals and ambiguities in the control of funds persisted throughout numerous amendments. The multitude of goals included not only reducing or preventing violent street crimes, at various times emphasizing various specific crimes, but also strengthening the criminal justice capabilities of the states, strengthening the state and local units of general government, and pioneering a new method of distributing federal funds. Ambiguities in the control of funds arose because the block grant, a hybrid between categorical grants and revenue sharing, was extremely susceptible to interpretation and modification by recipient state and local governments.

THE BLOCK GRANT MECHANISM

The Safe Streets Act of 1968 set up a new federal agency, the Law Enforcement Assistance Administration, in the Department of Justice to administer federal anticrime funds. Small planning grants were given out to each state to establish state planning agencies, each of which was asked to prepare a yearly comprehensive plan for all law enforcement and criminal justice activity within the state. Once this plan was approved by LEAA, the state planning agency would receive larger action grants, which it in turn would distribute to law enforcement and criminal justice agencies within the state, according to the comprehensive plan. Eighty-five percent of the total action grant monies were to be block grants, that is, given out to different states according to their populations. The other 15 percent of action monies were called discretionary grants, given out directly to law enforcement and criminal justice agencies by LEAA. (The act also established the National Institute of Law Enforcement and Criminal Justice, with a relatively modest budget for research and training programs.)

The block grant mechanism, as the vehicle for the largest proportion of funds, rapidly became a source of dissatisfaction on all sides. Created as a compromise, it emerged as a paradox: increased centralized funding and continued decentralized administration. Conceived as the mechanism by which national funds would be used to help state and local governments, it contained ambiguities that were readily exploited by policymakers and state recipients.

The hitch in the block grant mechanism was that block grants were *not quite* free gifts to the states. They were to be authorized only after LEAA had reviewed and approved the comprehensive plan prepared by the state planning agency. LEAA guidelines for the state plans, which were revised annually and frequently changed in the middle of a planning cycle, became a source of considerable friction. Additional, special conditions were attached to federal funds when states did not meet the LEAA guidelines. Then, too, the priorities of national policymakers, emphasizing special areas of crime control, were reflected in different percentages of the action grants available or in different matching requirements of state to federal money. Action funds in the initial 1968 authorization, for example, were restricted to seven categories: equipment, recruiting and training law enforcement personnel, education about crime prevention, construction, special law enforcement units to combat organized crime, riot control, and recruiting and training community service officers. Limits were placed on the amount of federal money that could be used for salaries. Also, as advocates for cities and states continued to compromise, Congress kept refining exactly how money was to be given out; there resulted some very detailed "pass-through" requirements (the percentage of federal money the state planning agency must give to cities and localities) and "buy-in" requirements (the percentage of the cities' matching money that must be contributed by states).

From the local point of view, block grants were far from satisfactory. Although an attempt was made in the original legislation to protect cities, the statutory language, that the comprehensive state plan should "adequately take into account the needs and requests of the units of general local government . . . and provide for an appropriately balanced allocation of funds between the state and the units of general local government," was vague and open to abuse. Real power rested in the state planning agencies, which in effect made categorical grants to cities and localities.

Another hitch in the block grant mechanism was that states not only had to set up new planning agencies and design new programs but deal with a new federal bureaucracy, whose congressional mandate was far from clear. LEAA's role was initially conceived to be primarily advisory: after consulting with state and local officials, it was to set guidelines for the state plans, evaluate projects funded by action grants, and "cooperate with and render technical assistance to the states." This was a difficult dual role: to be helper to the states and at the same time to serve as judge of their plans and evaluator of their programs. As discussed in later chapters, some LEAA administrators felt their role was merely to pass on funds to states, whereas others felt they were responsible for seeing that federal money was wisely spent and thus became more involved in the planning and monitoring processes. Congress, reluctant for political reasons to withhold any money but reluctant as a policymaker not to direct how that money should be spent, had merely passed this dilemma on to LEAA.

THE NEW FEDERALISM

In adopting the block grant as the delivery system for the 1968 Safe Streets Act, Congress opted for a functionally broader and administratively more decentralized crime control strategy than had been present until then in a variety of specialized anticrime bills. The flexibility of the states was increased, pleasing Republicans, and the influence of national administrators was reduced, also pleasing Republicans, as well as an increasing number of moderates.

During the 1960s, recognizing the inability of most state governments to assume leadership in solving major urban and social problems, Democratic administrations had used categorical grants-in-aid, which dealt with specific and often very narrowly defined areas of national policy, required compliance with numerous national conditions (thirty-three separate procedural requirements) and generally granted considerable influence to federal administrators. But now there was a growing awareness, especially among policy analysts and public administrators, that although federal funds might be desperately needed by hard-pressed states and localities, federal strategies for solving national problems might actually be weakening state discretion. As political analyst James Sundquist observed, "The more the states were excluded the more they lagged in developing competence and so the circle progressed."[4] The block grant was designed to be a remedial enterprise, to upgrade responsibility in state executive branches.

The block grant approach also appeared philosophically akin to an idea that kept resurfacing during the 1960s as an alternative to categorical grants, namely, revenue sharing. Revenue sharing meant a certain percentage of personal taxable income would be returned to the states and localities, to be used at their discretion. In 1964 revenue sharing was strongly endorsed by Walter Heller, who was chairman of the Council of Economic Advisors under Kennedy and Johnson. The Heller-Pechman plan (with Joseph Pechman of the Brookings Institution), which emerged from LBJ's 1964 task forces, advocated revenue sharing as a means of sharing surplus federal funds. The plan, however, was at first shelved and then postponed by Johnson as the Vietnam War and Great Society programs sharply depleted federal resources.

But revenue sharing, as a means of providing fiscal aid to states, was especially appealing to Senate Republicans since most of the state governors were Republicans. A wide variety of revenue-sharing bills were repeatedly introduced in Congress; the idea was endorsed by the liberal Republican Ripon Society, by the bipartisan Advisory Commission on Intergovernmental Relations (ACIR), and by both party platforms in 1968. Young staff aides to those Republican and conservative southern congressmen who had changed the Johnson Safe Streets bill to the block grant formula were also feeding to candidate Nixon, for use in his white papers and speeches, the idea of federal monies going directly to states. President Nixon's transition task force advocated revenue sharing.

In a television address in August 1969, Nixon outlined the new administration's philosophy as the New Federalism. The key to New Federalism, according to former Nixon White House aide Richard Nathan, was "a single idea—the need to sort out and rearrange responsibilities among the various levels and types of government in American federalism including federal, state, local, and private groups."[5] Thus some policy areas, such as crime control, were to be more decentralized but others more tightly controlled at the federal level. But the primary thrust of New Federalism was in reaction to the expansion of the federal government's powers during the 1960s. Its basic principles included decentralizing power, reorganizing and strengthening federal field offices, granting greater discretion to states, reducing bureaucracy at all levels of government, clarifying the responsibility for grant administration, and shifting the responsibility for planning to the local level. The goals of New Federalism were to be achieved through a strategy of revenue sharing, reducing categorical grants, and strengthening the management capability of general-purpose state and local governments. The 1968 Safe Streets legislation, and the block grant concept in particular, fit in nicely with the philosophy of New Federalism. In 1970 Richard Velde, LEAA assistant administrator, called LEAA "the cutting edge of the New Federalism—putting the responsibility where the problem is, and then putting the money where the responsibility is."[6]

Nixon followed up his New Federalism address with a message to Congress on revenue sharing, and in September 1969 the administration's first revenue-sharing bill was introduced in the Senate. But no hearings were held that year in either the Senate Finance Committee or the House Ways and Means Committee, perhaps because of the lack of interest of the chairmen of those committees, Sen. Russell Long (D-La.) and Congressman Wilbur Mills (D-Ark.), respectively, and because of the fact that the Nixon administration gave higher priority to its welfare reform and family assistance proposals. But the idea of revenue sharing continued to incubate and gain importance as part of the political environment in which the 1968 Safe Streets Act was relegislated during the coming years.

THE LAW AND ORDER PRESIDENCY

After the strong rhetoric of the 1968 campaign, the incoming Nixon administration thought it had a mandate to get tough on crime. Egil

Krogh, Jr., Nixon's Domestic Council aide for crime policy, recalled that Nixon viewed law and order as his principal domestic issue. Attorney General John Mitchell was on record as saying that no issue was more important than crime for the Justice Department and that no administration program had higher priority than LEAA as the chief federal tool to aid law enforcement efforts. (Twelve years later, after the demise of LEAA, Attorney General William French Smith would make virtually the same statement, that crime would be his department's top priority.) A few days after his inauguration, Nixon fairly summed up his administration's philosophy about the crime issue:

> I recognize . . . that in the long run crime itself also requires much more far-reaching and subtle approaches. But the rapidly mounting urgency of the crime crisis . . . marks immediate, direct anticrime measures as the first priority task.[7]

However, during the transition of White House administrations, LEAA was by and large left alone by the White House. With Mitchell so close to President Nixon, no one in the White House was in a position to lobby for or monitor Justice Department activities. Attorney General Mitchell, sensitive to the potential political value of LEAA's discretionary money, immediately told the holdover Johnson appointees that all discretionary grants would have to be approved by Deputy Attorney General Richard Kleindienst—this in spite of Senator McClellan and others' expressed desire that LEAA be independent from the attorney general's office.

Soon after his election, Nixon let it be known that he would replace the Johnson LEAA administrators and that his appointments would be calculated to please conservative southerners and northern Republicans in Congress. In February 1969, Nixon appointed Charles Rogovin, a nominal Democrat who had been director of the Organized Crime Task Force of the crime commission, as LEAA administrator. The task force had the reputation of being more "hawkish" than other areas of the crime commission, and Rogovin appeared, at least at first, to agree with the Republican administration's emphasis on a limited federal role and block grants favoring states. In his Senate confirmation hearings, Rogovin stated his interpretation that LEAA could rule on the "comprehensiveness" of state plans but not on the specific projects within a state plan.[8] The two associate administrators of LEAA were Republicans Richard ("Pete") Velde, who, as legislative assistant to Senator Hruska, had been a central figure in writing the LEAA legislation, and Clarence Coster, the police chief of Bloomington, Minnesota, home district of conservative Republican House member Clark MacGregor.

The Nixon-appointed triumvirate could not agree on administrative matters. Rogovin and others felt there was no support or policy guidance from the White House or Justice Department. When Rogovin resigned in June 1970, the Nixon administration left the position of LEAA administrator vacant for nine months. In the absence of strong presidential or cabinet leadership, state and local interest groups and their representatives in Congress assumed more importance. Indeed, the pressures exerted by state and local interest groups tended to moderate the positions of both Democrats and Republicans responsible for administering LEAA.

The attention of the Nixon White House during the first year was concentrated less on the functioning of LEAA than on the designing of new law enforcement legislation. Four major bills were sent to Congress by the Nixon White House: in April 1969, the Organized Crime Control bill, building on proposals by Senator McClellan; in July, the Drug Abuse Prevention and Control bill and the District of Columbia Crime Control bill; and in February 1970, the amendments to the 1968 Omnibus Crime Control and Safe Streets Act. About this series of "political law and order bills" one White House aide frankly acknowledged, "It was my view that while these bills would suggest a tough law and order demeanor by the Administration, the legislation itself did not provide an enhanced ability to the police departments or to the courts to reduce crime. . . ."

The most controversial of these bills was the District of Columbia Crime Control bill, heralded by John Mitchell as a "model anti-crime package," a prototype for other cities, and containing the famous no-knock and preventive detention provisions. No-knock meant police could enter a home or other building without knocking or announcing themselves if by knocking or announcing themselves they would endanger their lives or lose criminal evidence. Preventive detention provided that a defendant could be detained without bail for up to sixty days before his or her trial if he or she would endanger the community. The D.C. Crime Control bill also granted wide wiretap powers to police, eliminated jury trials for juveniles, and provided that a thrice-convicted felon could be sentenced to life imprisonment regardless of what the third felony was. Sen. Sam Ervin (D-N.C.), a strict constructionist, strenuously opposed the D.C. Crime Control bill, claiming it was repressive and unconstitutional and calling it a "blueprint for a police state." But 1970 was an election year, and despite vigorous opposition, the bill was passed by Congress in July.

Congressional critics of the proposed Nixon-Mitchell D.C. crime control legislation, led by Congressman Emmanuel Celler in the House Judiciary Committee, were also disturbed by Nixon's Organized Crime Control bill, which gave the federal government extensive new powers in gathering evidence, such as limiting challenges to evidence obtained by illegal electronic surveillance. Despite the committee's feeling that parts of the bill contained the "seeds of official repression," the bill finally passed in October 1970.

By some accounts, the Nixon administration and Attorney General Mitchell in particular were more interested in cultivating their get-tough image than concerned with accusations of being repressive.[9] Crime continued as the number-one national problem, according to a Gallup poll in the spring of 1970. The mood of the public was hard-line, anxious, and punitive. The 1968 electoral victory had vindicated the strategy of appearing to crack down on criminals. Candidate Nixon had repeatedly castigated Attorney General Ramsey Clark as "soft on crime" and "coddling criminals" and accused the Warren Court of hamstringing law enforcement officials. Well, Nixon's new attorney general would be "Mr. Law and Order" himself, and Nixon's first-year appointees to the Supreme Court, Chief Justice Warren Burger and Associate Justice Harry Blackmun, were judicial conservatives who had expressed their belief that the court should not "make" laws. (Blackmun later became more moderate on some issues.) Nixon took a particularly hard line on left-wing student movements and peace demonstrators, whom he labeled "bums" and classed together with political extremists and terrorists.

As part of this get-tough-image tending, the White House generated an early feeling of optimism about the war on crime. Nixon, in signing the Organized Crime Control Act in October 1970, declared that the government "will win" the war against organized crime. He confidently claimed that the crime rate would be lowered by 1972:

> Crime has gone up 150 percent in the past eight years, but it is now finally beginning to go back down. . . . We have a remarkable record on the law-and-order issue, with crime legislation, obscenity and narcotics bills. We now have the most effective program to deal with crime.[10]

Attorney General Mitchell, who had already made increased use of the wiretapping and electronic surveillance provisions of the 1968 Safe Streets Act, cited the new powers available in the 1970 Organized Crime bill as the means by which the Justice Department had set up successful strike forces in several cities. He touted FBI statistics for the first half of 1970 that showed that the violent crime rate was increasing more slowly than in 1969. (One in-house dissent came from White House aide and Harvard professor Daniel Patrick Moynihan, later Democratic senator from New York, who warned that not enough research on crime was being done.) It was with the new Nixon admin-

istration taking this hard-line, confident position that Congress began
the task of fine tuning the Safe Streets Act.

EARMARKING FOR CORRECTIONS

The 1968 Safe Streets Act had been authorized for two years, so
reauthorization hearings began in February and March of 1970 in subcommittees of the House and Senate judiciary committees. These hearings served as a forum for initial evaluations of the block grant and
LEAA's performance and also as a second chance for those liberals who
felt the cities had been cheated by the 1968 Safe Streets Act.

Evaluating how well the 1968 act worked depended on one's perspective. The FBI Uniform Crime Report indicated a 12-percent increase in the nation's violent crime rate in 1969 (and would later indi-
cate an 11-percent increase for 1970). Congress, though fully aware
of the political expediency to themselves of defusing a hot issue like
crime by passing the responsibility on to the states, had also expected
at least *some* results from generous federal funding; moreover, 1970
was an election year for them. But everyone agreed that the administrative birth pangs of LEAA and the state planning agencies made it
much harder for all involved to reduce crime rates immediately. (The
many administrative difficulties of LEAA are discussed in chapter 8; in
brief, delays in the appointments of LEAA administrators, first under
Johnson and then under Nixon, led to delays in developing guidelines
for state plans and cut down on the time available for states to draw
up their plans. Comprehensive plans became primarily shopping lists of
police requests rather than coordinative blueprints for innovation. Further, the Nixon-appointed triumvirate of administrators could not
achieve consensus, thus stalemating many LEAA decisions.)

The National League of Cities/U.S. Conference of Mayors published a detailed report contending the states hadn't focused block
grant monies on the major urban areas that had the highest crime
rates and instead were distributing funds on a shotgun basis, in many
grants too small to have an effect. The report claimed the block grant
imposed two new levels of bureaucracy, state planning agencies and
substate regional offices, and thus created delays in getting federal
funds for LEAA to the cities. These difficulties were considered a result
primarily of the original legislation and the fact the states just did not
listen to LEAA directives.

But the National Governors' Conference, not surprisingly, thought
the block grant formula was working well. Delays, they said, had been
caused by federal, not state, inaction, and states had indeed passed a
high percentage of their block grant funds on to the cities. The gov-

ernors opposed the idea of setting aside a certain percentage of funds for courts or corrections. Another study group, the prestigious, bipartisan Advisory Commission on Intergovernmental Relations, found that only about half the states passed on to their largest cities the same proportion of funds that those cities contributed to the total state-local budget for law enforcement. Yet the commission recommended that no changes be made in the block grant, perhaps because of the principle that the block grant, as an experimental form of intergovernmental relations, should be unadulterated during its trial run.

The Nixon administration's bill arrived a day before the House hearings and was introduced by conservative Congressman William McCulloch (R-Ohio) and other cosponsors, including Gerald Ford, as minority leader in the House, and, in the Senate, Roman Hruska, LEAA's most active and influential congressional sponsor. The most significant amendment in the administration bill was a new part E, a grant program for constructing and renovating correctional facilities, which are primarily state run. Stimulus for paying special attention to corrections came mostly from within LEAA itself, which was responding to outside critics. Top administrators at LEAA agreed the whole criminal justice system was in need of improvement. Having noted that most of the first-year funds went for police equipment and communication systems, LEAA administrators viewed the new part E as a "block grant within a block grant," that is, as a means of expressing national priorities without interfering with the states' planning responsibilities.

Democrats proposed several amendments to change the original block grant formula and make it more favorable to their urban constituencies. For example, Sen. Philip Hart (D-Mich.) proposed that 60 percent (instead of 15 percent) of action funds be distributed by LEAA as discretionary grants and that of these discretionary grants, 75 percent go directly to large cities. Another bill, sponsored by Sen. Vance Hartke (D-Ind.) and Congressman Jonathan Bingham (D-N.Y.), suggested 50 percent of action funds be discretionary funds, without any matching requirements. Sen. Edward Kennedy favored writing in block grants to the cities, in addition to the block grants to the states.

Former attorney general Ramsey Clark testified, "We do not need more of the same. We need essentially different qualities in the process of criminal justice." He urged the House subcommittee to reconsider the block grant and to ensure an allocation formula based on the incidence of crime and not solely on population:

> I think several States have already indicated that they are going to do what the Congress itself, in a sense, did on the State level: distribute according to population. . . . If we did that in some other

programs, . . . it would mean funds for boll weevil eradication in Bedford-Stuyvesant. It just doesn't make sense.[11]

There followed a battery of governors who argued, predictably, for keeping the block grant and a barrage of mayors who complained, predictably, that the cities weren't getting enough LEAA funds and were not well enough represented on state planning agencies.

Strong testimony in defense of the existing block grant formula came from Attorney General John Mitchell, who claimed LEAA was achieving "unprecedented goals" in the war against crime and was "building the optimism and the hope of success" against crime. He said the mayors were wrong and that the "cities have fared extremely well" under the present system. "The nation's 411 cities of 50,000 have less than 40% of the total population and have 62% of the serious crime. It is our initial estimate that these cities have been granted 60% of all action funds."[12] Mitchell offered other statistics to show that block grants were actually generous to the cities when compared to the amount cities contributed to the total state-local budgets for law enforcement and criminal justice.

The battle of statistics in the House and Senate hearings was a confusing one. For instance, arguing directly against Mitchell's statistics was an ACIR report: "In 33 states the 5 largest cities had received a share of financial assistance significantly below their burden of the crime in their States." The problem was that no agreement existed on how to determine what was *a fair share* for the cities: population rates, crime rates, the total local police expenditure, or the local portion of the total state-local police expenditure. Big-city mayors claimed that crime rates per capita increased with population and that the widespread fear of crime was primarily generated by city street crime. But some legislators pointed out that if money were given out according to crime rates, some police departments might inflate their reported crime rates. The large, old cities were financially most pressed for funds because traditionally their populations provided the weakest tax base and required the most expensive services. Was it really fair, then, to deny federal money to those who needed it the most? And deciding what proportion states and cities contributed to total law enforcement budgets was complicated by the fact that cities benefited indirectly from state-run courts and correctional systems. One could also draw different interpretations according to whether one examined the fifteen large cities with the highest crime rates, the five largest cities in each state, all cities above fifty thousand in population, or all nonstate jurisdictions, including counties. The block grant was evaluated according to everyone's different perspective—mayor or governor, urban member of Congress or states-rights senator, planning director or police chief.

To make matters worse, by the time hearings began in the Senate, Charles Rogovin, the LEAA administrator, had resigned because of the unworkable troika arrangement. Yet both Mitchell and the two associate administrators, Richard Velde and Clarence Coster, still supported the troika arrangement. Arguing against the Democratic amendments, Velde (who later became LEAA administrator himself) gave an eloquent defense of the block grant:

> A direct grant program to cities would make Washington a dictator over every anti-crime program in the country. It would also, by necessity, spawn an enormous federal bureaucracy to evaluate these programs, and would undermine the whole concept of a federal-state cooperative partnership which this Administration has attempted to establish.[13]

LEAA friends, such as Senator Hruska, were inclined to be patient with the states and to look forward to system improvement:

> It is well known and anyone who has studied that program for four hours will know that the first two years have been devoted almost entirely to planning grants. . . . This year for the first time we are going to get into action grants as opposed to planning grants.[14]

Liberals, such as Edward Kennedy and Philip Hart, felt that LEAA's task was to reduce crime and that the problem of crime could not wait.

> While we are trying to experiment to see whether block grants to the states are the best way and means of providing resources, we find hundreds of the major cities of this country who are willing and able to spend money in fighting crime. . . .[15]

> We cannot wait a few more years for the distributive channels of the Safe Streets program to be improved. . . . The Safe Streets Act must include some provision to give the cities an extra shot in the arm.[16]

In the end, both the House and Senate bills kept the original formula of 85 percent block grant to 15 percent discretionary grant and accepted earmarking funds for corrections. In the Senate, conservative southerners and Republicans still dominated much of the discussion. In general the House went a little further than the Senate in meeting the demands of the cities.[17] But the House Judiciary Committee, under Emmanuel Celler, had a conservative cast, so in conference committee the Senate version prevailed easily.

The final bill was passed by both houses in December 1970 and signed into law by President Nixon in early January 1971. On balance it was a victory for the Nixon administration and for the states. Yet, as with most legislative battles, the victory was founded on compromise. Congress, by earmarking funds for corrections and imposing more restrictions on the grant-making procedures, increased its control. This in turn required more elaborate guidelines from LEAA. The cities were given only minor concessions in comparison with the states' retaining discretion over the largest segment of funds.[18] Yet everyone got more money because appropriations, which had jumped dramatically each year from the original $63 million in 1968, were now set at $529 million for fiscal year 1971 and were expected to rise even beyond that.

THE MONAGEN HEARINGS

The spring of 1971 seemed to be a time when LEAA might get its second wind. Congress had just finished authorizing LEAA, generously, for another three years. Finally, after the nine months during which the chief leadership slot at LEAA had been left vacant, Nixon appointed as LEAA administrator Jerris Leonard, a friend of John Mitchell. Leonard, who had a reputation for being a strong administrator and someone who could be trusted politically, immediately set about reorganizing LEAA.

But as LEAA entered the big leagues financially, criticisms also intensified. Press reports around the country now highlighted waste and misuse of Safe Streets funds: "Government Squanders $2.3 Million of Your Money on New Police Cars that are Too Small for Most Cops"; "Indiana Governor Used Plane Bought with U.S. Crime Fund." *Time* magazine's indictment in 1971 was typical: "The handling of the program has been extraordinarily inept. The history of the LEAA has been one of waste and mismanagement."[19]

In June and October of 1971, using press reports as a launching pad, Congressman John Monagen (D-Conn.) held public oversight hearings of his subcommittee of the House Committee on Government Operations. The hearings revealed serious conflict-of-interest and illegal expenditures in some states, such as Alabama, California, Florida, Indiana, New Mexico, and Wisconsin, and raised doubts about LEAA's deferring to the states. Alabama's attorney general, for instance, charged that

> what had appeared to be a law enforcement officer's dream for badly needed help was becoming merely a politician's dream for the biggest pork barrel of them all. . . . politics was the primary and sometimes sole consideration.[20]

A former administrator of the Florida planning agency testified that the governor's office pressured the agency to exploit LEAA funds for political motives, often in direct defiance of sensible planning efforts. He urged that strong federal guidelines be strictly enforced.

A senior official of the General Accounting Office (GAO), the congressional watchdog agency, testified that of the 1970 funds, only about 37 percent had been transferred from state planning agencies to state and local agencies and cited several instances of LEAA monies spent on antipoverty or educational programs that were not directly related to criminal justice. Although couching his criticisms in mild bureaucratic language, the GAO official chided LEAA for not providing adequate technical assistance to the states, for approving inadequate state plans and permitting innovative programs to be shelved in favor of financing old programs under new labels, and for not even knowing what its money was being used for!

Former LEAA administrator Charles Rogovin suggested that until LEAA established goals and standards, Congress should freeze its funds at the 1972 level. LEAA goals should be more narrowly and realistically defined, he said, and funds should be earmarked and directed at critical needs rather than "let loose for the politically strongest agencies to grab." He expressed his disappointment with the lack of policy direction in the legislation and lack of interest on the part of the White House and attorney general:

> too much money has become available too quickly for action projects. . . . the LEAA has been compelled by the sheer availability of money to spend less than judiciously. The pressure in a field like this in which there is so much intense public and political interest, to spend has led to massive dispensing of money without careful analysis either before or after the money is spent. . . . And indeed, most shocking of all, there is not even a knowledge of what LEAA funds are being spent on.[21]

Privately, two domestic advisors to President Nixon admitted many of these criticisms were valid:

> When we went in and looked at LEAA's activities, we found that next to no understanding existed as to where the money was going, what the money was being spent for, etc. . . . , and it turned out that there is no understanding of optimal use of funds, very little work has been done on a carefully devised information system. . . . they need a lot of help and need important assistance!
>
> We have had a great deal of problems with LEAA. Their auditing was terrible, they just didn't keep records and couldn't trace what they were doing. . . . The red tape was great, there were conflicting

purposes, and conflicts among the chief administrators. People at
LEAA were all new to the area, mostly unskilled in this new federal
grant area, and they had little experience with the block-grant concept.[22]

But the new LEAA administrator, Jerris Leonard, denied the charges
of the Monagen hearings. He said discretionary grants—the only ones
over which LEAA had substantive jurisdiction—already carried an evaluation component and that evaluation programs were in fact required
of the states. Already on record against cutting off funds to achieve
civil rights compliance, Leonard cited other reforms and innovations
he had already begun: concentration of discretionary funds on "high-
impact" grants to a few cities (see below); the creation of the National
Advisory Commission on Criminal Justice Standards and Goals, to be
headed by Delaware governor Russell Peterson; and the expansion of
LEAA's auditing staff and the establishment of a training program for
state auditors. Leonard thought Monagen and the GAO were unfair in
zeroing in on the few states that were doing the worst job. He coun-
terattacked by suggesting that LEAA was being used "as a whipping
boy for those people who oppose special revenue-sharing."

The concept of special revenue sharing was a modification of general revenue sharing: federal funds would be returned to states and
localities for use at their discretion *within a given functional area.*
Special revenue sharing was very similar to the block grant concept,
so LEAA's early administrative and policy failures probably did con-
tribute to discrediting special revenue sharing when it was proposed
by Nixon in his 1971 and 1972 State of the Union messages. On the
other hand, because there was so little difference between the two
methods of distributing funds for law enforcement assistance, there
was little reason for Congress, which had just completed lengthy action on the Crime Control Act of 1970, to consider changing the legislation so soon. Moreover, the direction of the 1970 act was opposite
to the direction of special revenue sharing; i.e., Congress wanted more,
not less, control over how federal funds were spent. The Monagen
hearings were important, not so much because they anticipated congressional opposition to special revenue sharing, but because they underscored that LEAA's performance would be viewed as a test of
whether Nixon had succeeded in realizing two of his major domestic
priorities—reducing crime and increasing local control of federal
funds. The Monagen committee's Democratic majority issued its report
in May 1972, charging that although LEAA had spent $1.4 billion,
"there has been no visible impact on the incidence of crime in the
U.S." The committee majority claimed the administration's efforts to

curb crime were beset by waste, inefficiency, and corruption. Congressman Monagen accused LEAA of "relying on public relations rather than a solid achievement in crime control." In putting Nixon on the defensive, the Monagen hearings helped set the climate for the 1972 election, an election in which Nixon knew he would be called to account for his law and order promises.

PREPARING FOR THE 1972 ELECTION

From the beginning of his first term, President Nixon showed a personal interest in lowering the crime rate in Washington, D.C., a city he had labeled "the crime capital of the U.S." in the 1968 campaign. The District crime rate was strategically important: as the only city in which the federal government had direct responsibility for street crime, the District would certainly be read in 1972 as Nixon's record of accomplishment or failure in the war on crime; as a convenient showcase for his personal commitment to law and order, the District could be used to highlight the hard-line image of the administration—that is, if crime could actually be reduced there.

District police chief Jerry Wilson, appointed by Nixon in August 1969, became an enthusiastic lobbyist for the Nixon administration's controversial D.C. crime bill, with the no-knock and preventive detention provisions. Wilson recalled that

> in January, 1970, the personal commitment of the President to crime reduction in the District of Columbia was translated into direct instructions from the White House to the city government to develop a list of whatever programs were necessary to reduce both the number of serious crimes in D.C. and also the fear of crime within the city. . . . unless significant improvements were achieved, all city government officials responsible for law enforcement should expect to be replaced.[23]

In response, federal funds were poured in—for more police, more prosecutors, high-intensity street lighting, and narcotics treatment programs. As one White House staffer said, "We did everything possible and squeezed out every ounce of money for the District of Columbia."[24]

LEAA involvement in the District was described by LEAA associate administrator Richard Velde this way:

> It's fair to say that we have been treating D.C. in a different way [from other state LEAA programs]: it began earlier, it's a crash program, we have had to resort less to reforming institutions here than

pouring a lot of money into police and narcotics. And there is pressure to produce results here. We have put in over $6 million of LEAA funds in the past few years, this is only part of the federal budget of $80 million or more. Washington now has the largest percent of police per capita in the world, I guess. It is not the right way to do it properly, and we are not getting at the root causes of crime, but that is what we are doing and results may come.[25]

The initial results indicated the District was able to show an immediate, slight decrease in its 1970 crime index and a 13-percent decrease in 1971. But crime statistics rapidly became a focus of contention in the preliminary election skirmishing. Attorney General John Mitchell claimed the U.S. had "turned the corner" on crime in 1970: nationally, the *rate of increase* in the crime index had slowed, and this, he said, would be the beginning of further reductions that would continue throughout Nixon's next term. Mitchell said the crime index had actually decreased in the District of Columbia and in twenty-one other cities with populations greater than one hundred thousand. And he generously praised LEAA as the chief tool of the federal government in fighting street crime. "Fear is being swept from the streets of some—though not all—American cities," he asserted.[26] The Justice Department announced that in 1971 the increase in the nationwide crime rate (the FBI crime index) continued to slow down and that crime had actually decreased in fifty-three large cities. Nixon proudly called Washington "one of the safest cities in America." Police Chief Wilson reciprocated, loudly crediting the president with building police morale by the president's visiting police headquarters, writing personal letters, and inviting members of the police department to the White House.

Critics charged that while Mr. Nixon was "wrapping himself in blue" and having a "public love affair with the police," he was actually deceiving the American public with his statistics.[27] Scholar Michael Couzens noted that the decrease in crime in certain cities was primarily a result of a decrease in property crime (burglaries, larcenies, and auto thefts) and that violent crimes were still increasing. And in Washington, D.C., the decrease in property crime had been helped by downgrading the value of stolen items, thus diminishing the number of larcenies reported.[28] Further, in spite of small decreases in some cities, crime and the fear of crime were still increasing across the nation, and crime in the suburbs, in particular, had soared. The *Washington Post* summed up the case in an editorial in 1971:

> [Mr. Mitchell's] claim is based on the undisputed fact that the *rate of increase in serious crime* was 11.3 percent in 1970—a rate lower than

the rate of increase in 1969, 1968, 1967, 1966, and 1964. But . . . it is equally fair to write that the *numerical increase in serious crime* in 1970 over 1969 was the second highest in the nation's history. . . .[29]

Despite the official optimism from the White House, the Justice Department, and the new LEAA administrator, some LEAA officials were more cautious in their assessment of the crime situation. One senior bureaucrat questioned the D.C. crime statistics:

> The situation in D.C. is a fantastic manipulation of reality. With such an infusion of manpower, with more police making more arrests, the D.C. crime rate should be going *up* and *then* curving off. They are clearly being deceptive. I think it all stems from Chief Jerry Wilson's order to his captains last year to reduce crime in your districts or lose your job—and they responded with a lowering of the crime rate![30]

LEAA inquiries in cities where serious crime declined failed to produce persuasive evidence that LEAA and federal assistance were significant factors. For every city in which the crime rate slowed, there were others where it kept rising. So few were the cities with declining rates and, with a few exceptions, such as Seattle and Washington, D.C., so marginal their rate of decline that no statistically acceptable generalizations favorable to LEAA could be drawn. As one LEAA official explained:

> Some cities [in the twenty-three cities Mitchell claimed had lower crime rates in 1970] received no LEAA money; others would not admit that LEAA has contributed. But both they and we won't refute Attorney General Mitchell because they want more LEAA funds and don't want to risk getting cut off.[31]

Though there was a growing pessimistic in-house research atmosphere in LEAA about the inability of federal strategies to lower crime rates, the political pressures to reduce the crime rate only increased. The White House, stung by the extremely negative publicity surrounding the Monagen hearings and privately feeling some of the charges to be valid, was running out of patience with LEAA. The thinking was that since the public's fear of crime reflected the FBI crime index in an exaggerated way, even a small decrease in crime rates might produce a considerable surge of public confidence, which would be important for the 1972 elections. By 1971, several aides in both the White House and the Office of Management and Budget (OMB) were regularly prodding LEAA to move faster to provide concrete evidence of a federal impact on crime rates.

LEAA statisticians in the National Institute of Law Enforcement and

Criminal Justice set to work to show positive results by the 1972 elections. Said one senior-level former LEAA administrator:

> The statisticians and my staff were working on ideas of how they might show positive results by the '72 elections. Actually we called it the biennial report. It turns out that of all violent crimes, robbery is by far the biggest volume crime on the FBI index—one half of violent crimes are robberies. One is 40 times more likely to be robbed in big cities than in rural areas. And *ten cities* accounted for one half of the robberies. So we figured out that if we really saturated these ten cities we might reduce the robbery rate by 9 or 10 percent, thereby getting the national crime rate down by 2 percent or so, rather than having it go up 11 percent a year. There are two approaches being considered: what was used in Washington, D.C., sheer saturation of manpower where you just double the police force; and identifying hard core repeaters and tracking them down and keeping them in jail for longer periods.

> But to do this in these 10 cities we figured it might cost $300 million this next fiscal year. Now LEAA's budget for FY 1972 is about $800 million, but $600 milion of this is action monies, and when research, etc. is taken out. . .[32]

In January 1972, after three months of planning, Vice-President Agnew, along with Attorney General Mitchell and LEAA administrator Leonard, announced, with great fanfare, a variation of this idea, called the High Impact Anti-Crime (Impact Cities) Program. As LEAA's most ambitious project to date, the Impact Cities program would concentrate $160 million of LEAA's discretionary funds on helping eight medium-to-large cities—Atlanta, Baltimore, Cleveland, Dallas, Denver, Newark, Portland, and St. Louis—reduce certain high-volume crimes. The target date had been shifted, more realistically, to 1976 and the largest cities excluded, presumably because their public safety budgets were so massive that even an average of $20 million per city would still be a drop in the bucket.

From the beginning, the Impact Cities program was a political creature, designed not only to reduce street crime but to maintain the Nixon administration's image of a massive assault on crime, even if no significant reductions could actually be made, and, incidentally, to "make a name" for the National Institute of Criminal Justice and Law Enforcement, which had planned the program. The program suffered from many of the same symptoms, such as ambiguous goals and decentralized administration, that its parent agency, LEAA, exhibited. The first announced goals of the Impact Cities program were to reduce stranger-to-stranger person crimes—murder, rape, assault, and robbery

—and the property crime of burglary by 5 percent in the first two years and by 20 percent in five years. However, this quantification of goals appears to have been casual at best:

> When asked where the figures came from, Martin Danziger, the official who planned the program, said, "I just made them up. It sounded good. . . . It got attention and people are impressed with what you actually do. They needed the 20 percent goal for sex appeal. It was an educated guess and it was important to start setting quantified goals in the criminal justice system."[33]

A second major goal of the program was a research goal, as distinct from the first, action-oriented goal of reducing crime. Impact cities were to use a Crime-Oriented Planning Implementation and Evaluation (copie) cycle in their programs. This concept, strongly supported by Jerris Leonard, involved concentrating resources of different agencies on crime-specific programs. Each city was to recruit a special Crime Analysis Team (cat) to prepare a master plan and collect data for evaluation of the program. But the pressures from the White House to produce programs fast, in time for the '72 election, made serious planning difficult. (Only one city, Denver, was evidently able to resist these time pressures.)

Another conflict was that although the Impact Cities program was supposed to help the president politically, it still had to partake of the New Federalism philosophy—impact cities would use funds according to their own priorities, the program would be administered by leaa regional offices and the state planning agencies, and leaa agreed not to impose any mandatory evaluation designs on the states.

The creation of the Impact Cities program marked a new perspective on leaa. The Nixon administration was in a bind: Nixon had campaigned in 1968 on the platform of reducing street crime, and now leaa was *his* administration's program. Criticisms, such as the well-publicized Monagen hearings, and charges that leaa was doing nothing to reduce crime hurt. Yet when it came to using leaa, it turned out that most of the action monies were tied up in block grants that filtered down to mayors and local officials. And even the White House recognized that leaa lacked leadership.

What was the White House to do to reduce crime? Nixon White House aide Egil Krogh explained the predicament this way:

> The President had campaigned on his desire to reduce crime, to reduce crime nationwide. Crime had to be stopped. I don't think as a matter of intelligent politics he could have been in office for one year and then said, "I've discovered that the federal government has little

jurisdiction over street crime in the cities, towns, and counties; and
therefore it is a matter for the states to handle. Good luck!"

We realized that having an impact between 1968 and 1972 was going
to be hard to achieve, but to publicly disavow responsibility at the
federal level and extend it to the states would have been perceived as
a cop-out—and something that was directly inconsistent with what he
had campaigned on.

We didn't have the luxury to do nothing or to conclude that because
the problem was so complex and seemingly intransigent nothing should
be done. . . .[34]

The Impact Cities program appeared to be one solution to this dilemma—concentrate available discretionary funds where they would do
the most good.

There was another alternative the White House *could* have tried:
to learn the intricacies of bureaucratic politics within LEAA, to mediate
the day-to-day management problems of the agency, and to offer policy leadership by close consultation with the Justice Department. But
implementation leadership is the least glamorous and most tedious of
presidential responsibilities, and the loyalist Nixon White House already leaned toward circumventing balky bureaucracies and taking the
reins of management into their own hands.

At this point, LEAA had a big and growing budget, and the political
usefulness of its discretionary funds began to merit attention, especially
from John Mitchell's politicized Justice Department. As Egil Krogh
later explained:

Whatever discretionary money there was . . . in many cases would
come directly to the White House, and be addressed there by Mr.
Erlichman, by my staff, and in some cases the president directly. In
terms of developing [LEAA] programs, my office felt, first, yes, there
is something that must be done as a policy proposition, but it is also
something that must be done to make a political record in 1972.[35]

LEAA discretionary monies were used to fund projects for which it
might be awkward or time-consuming to seek congressional authorization. For instance, in order to win the support of hard-line mayor and
former police chief Frank Rizzo of Philadelphia, Nixon sent a White
House staff assistant to Philadelphia to prepare the city's plans for a
large discretionary grant and ordered that the check for $1 million be
put through three days later.[36] Or when the Office of Drug Abuse and
Law Enforcement conducted a strike force, LEAA discretionary money
could be given to local police chiefs who cooperated.[37] LEAA funds
were also channeled to Governor Rockefeller of New York for nar-

cotics treatment programs in that state, to Miami for added police protection during the nominating conventions, and to Nixon's San Clemente estate after he resigned from the presidency.

Thus, whereas the discretionary portion of LEAA's budget had originally been a lever for congressional liberals to get more money to their constituents in the cities, it was now a tool of the Republican administration to advance its own interests in the 1972 elections. It is ironic to note that less than two years after Democrats had called for greatly expanding the discretionary portion of LEAA funds, these funds were being used at the discretion of the Nixon White House.

To the extent that crime was an issue in the 1972 election, Nixon apparently still had the best of it. He still had a "get-tough" image and claimed credit for a slight downturn in national crime rates, a decrease that, though very marginal and ephemeral, was at least timely. George Wallace, Nixon's threat from the right, was lying paralyzed in a hospital, the victim of an assassination attempt. The Democratic nominee, George McGovern, was struggling under the reverberation of his own campaign pledges: to "go on his knees to Hanoi" in order to end the Vietnam War immediately, to back Tom Eagleton 1,000 percent, to give every person a $1,000 tax rebate. McGovern just didn't have a piece of the law and order issue. Moreover, Nixon had made successful election-year trips to the Soviet Union and China, and although the Cambodian invasion backfired, at least most American boys were now home from Indochina, and Henry Kissinger said "peace was at hand." In November, despite some continuing press reports about an attempted break-in at the Democratic Party National Headquarters, located in a posh Washington apartment and office complex called Watergate, the law and order president was reelected by a landslide.

REJECTING SPECIAL REVENUE SHARING

During Nixon's first term, the White House had made repeated attempts to get revenue-sharing legislation through Congress. In his 1971 and 1972 State of the Union messages, Nixon had called for greatly expanded funds for general revenue sharing, arguing that the federal government was "so strong it grows muscle-bound" while the states and localities "approach impotence." General revenue sharing was perceived as a fiscal issue and an issue of federalism. Liberals liked the fact that as a substitute for cutting the income tax, it also provided a net increase in public expenditures. Conservatives liked the fact that the money had no federal strings attached and much of it would go to Republican governors. The Treasury Department released mouth-watering statistics showing how much each city and state might be expected to receive if the Nixon revenue-sharing plan passed. Even with this incentive, general revenue sharing took two years to get through Congress and was finally passed just before the 1972 election.

Nixon also asked Congress to organize existing grants in six areas— law enforcement, education, transportation, job training, urban development, and rural development—into special revenue-sharing programs. Special revenue sharing, however, represented more of a challenge to client groups that already had vested interests in each area. During 1971 and 1972 Congress held no hearings and took no action on the administration's proposals to convert LEAA to special revenue sharing, largely because neither House Judiciary Committee chairman Celler nor Senate Judiciary Subcommittee chairman McClellan was at all interested. The Nixon White House was determined to try again, and since the authorizing legislation for LEAA ran out at the end of fiscal year 1973, this was the time.

The overwhelming mandate Nixon received in November 1972 gave new confidence to White House efforts to extend the philosophy of revenue sharing and to reorganize the bureaucracy (and, incidentally, move loyal Nixon lieutenants into key spots in the departments and agencies). But these management innovations were quickly overshadowed by the imbroglio of the Watergate cover-ups. By February and March of 1973, new and damaging Watergate revelations began cascading into the public domain, and the struggle to contain this damage was rapidly becoming the chief preoccupation of the White House.

The early White House posture with respect to Watergate was to tough it out, or, in the soon-to-be-famous phrase, "stonewall" it. Yet, even as Nixon was wrapping himself in blanket denials and citing executive privilege to prevent his staff from testifying before Congress, he was still nurturing his hard-line anticrime image. In a March 1973 State of the Union massage to Congress he proclaimed that "the only way to attack crime in America is the way crime attacks our people— without pity." He took credit for vastly expanded LEAA programs (even though Congress had appropriated more money than the administration requested), called for reinstituting the death penalty, and again urged special revenue sharing for LEAA. In a companion radio address he delivered a particularly ironic defense of his now-precarious position as the "law and order president":

> There are those who say that law and order are just code words for repression and bigotry. That is dangerous nonsense. Law and order are code words for goodness and decency in America. . . . There is nothing disgraceful, nothing to be ashamed of, about Americans wanting to live in a law-abiding country. . . . I intend to do everything in my

power to see that the American people get all the law and order they are paying for. . . .[38]

The administration's special-revenue-sharing bill would have removed the last apron strings still tying Safe Streets funds to LEAA control: it would have merged grants for planning, action, and corrections into one annual payment to each state, substituted a "planning process" for the state planning agencies, and removed the requirement that LEAA approve state plans before states could spend their money. It also would have removed matching requirements, limitations on personnel salary and maintenance of effort, and the fixed percentage of spending for correction. The bill would also have given control of LEAA to a single administrator.

Yet the administration's proposal for special revenue sharing would not have altered the 85:15-percent ratio of block grant to discretionary money or the pass-through formula for money going from states to cities. There was considerable feeling, both on Capitol Hill and in LEAA, that the bill would not represent much of a change from the status quo. Passing the bill almost represented just doing the administration a favor. The House sponsor, Congressman Edward Hutchinson (R-Mich.), said, "Special revenue sharing is just this Administration's phraseology for block grants."[39] The sentiments of Paul Woodward, LEAA counsel and self-proclaimed house (LEAA) liberal, were shared by others throughout Congress and the Nixon administration:

> Special revenue sharing is a dishonest concept. I don't think more than a dozen states could use it effectively and honestly at the present. We have had to go along with the White House on revenue-sharing (even though they could have stayed away from us since we were more there than most federal programs) because there are those people over at the White House who are committed to revenue-sharing as an experiment. But we have worked with them and it won't change our efforts all that much. Actually if we passed special revenue sharing we wouldn't change much from what we have.[40]

Or, as LEAA's associate administrator, Velde, expressed it: "What would pass if Congress would pass it, won't be much of a change from what we are doing. We are very much like a special revenue program now and I don't think there is need for too much more change from what we are doing."[41] LEAA had in fact been patiently inching its way toward revenue sharing. Jerris Leonard, in his year and a half as LEAA administrator, had decentralized the approval of state plans to ten regional offices and expressed the opinion that "philosophically, our job is to work ourselves out of business, so that eventually LEAA will con-

sist of no more than an administrator, a check writer and 100 auditors."[42] Leonard had also moved to eliminate some of the political
abuses of funds that had been so well publicized in the 1971 Monagen
hearings. In Congress, the excitement of those critical hearings had
died down as attention shifted to the possibility of Watergate investigations.

The major alternative to the administration's special-revenue-sharing
proposal was to send funds directly to the cities. In one version, introduced by congressmen James Stanton (D-Ohio), Charles Sandman (R-
N.J.), and John Seiberling (D-Ohio), block grants would be made
directly to cities of over two hundred fifty thousand in population. In
another version, introduced by Sen. John Tunney (D-Calif.), state
plans would have to undergo a standard evaluation, and local governments would be reimbursed for innovative proposals; then funds would
be sent directly to large cities. Senator Kennedy also offered an amendment for block grants to large cities.

By March 1973, when reauthorization hearings were initiated in a
subcommittee of the House Judiciary Committee, the cast of policymakers involved with LEAA's future had changed considerably. With
the defeat of Emmanuel Celler of Brooklyn, Peter Rodino, a Democrat
from Newark, New Jersey, had taken on the chairmanship of both the
subcommittee and the Judiciary Committee, a role that would become
extremely significant when impeachment hearings were announced in
January 1974. Richard Kleindienst, a Goldwater conservative, had succeeded Attorney General Mitchell when Mitchell left to direct Nixon's
1972 reelection campaign. LEAA had a new administrator, Donald Santarelli, an eloquent, conservative debater who had been in charge of
the Justice Department's efforts to clean up crime in Washington,
D.C., and who had written the controversial no-knock provision of the
administration's D.C. crime bill. And state planning directors across the
country had newly organized to form the National Conference of
State Criminal Justice Planning Administrators.

Testifying before the House subcommittee, Attorney General Kleindienst praised LEAA's small staff. Not unexpectedly, the spokesman
for the planning directors claimed that bottlenecks arose not because
of state planning agencies but because local governments couldn't
spend money on subgrant projects fast enough. If Congress gave funds
directly to cities, the planning directors predicted, the program would
be "more of a police act than it is today."[43] Not surprisingly, the National League of Cities/U.S. Conference of Mayors, as well as Congressman Stanton, argued for decentralization to the cities: "We are
ill-equipped in Washington to do anything about crime in the streets
. . . and the governor doesn't know any more about fighting crime

than you or I do."[44] By the time the Senate subcommittee, under Senator McClellan, held two days of hearings in June, events were proceeding even more furiously in the Watergate investigation. Nixon had fired Robert Haldeman and John Erlichman; Kleindienst, resigning under a cloud, was replaced as attorney general by Boston Brahmin Elliot Richardson, and Archibald Cox, of Harvard Law School, had been appointed special prosecutor; Sen. Sam Ervin was holding televised hearings of his Ethics Committee. As in the spring of 1968, when Lyndon Johnson announced he would not run for a second term, the White House, now in deep trouble, was unable to offer its crime proposals serious guidance through Congress. An in-house memorandum, written for the Office of Management and Budget and leaked to the press, perhaps best summed up the shaky administration's position. The memo said that though LEAA was considered a forerunner of revenue sharing,

> this similarity has been elevated to a guiding principle by LEAA and has been misinterpreted and misapplied as a justification for the exercise of minimum management responsibility for the funds which it administers. . . . LEAA doesn't know what is happening, evaluation is impossible, and attacks on a defenseless program are encouraged.[45]

Changing LEAA from its present block grant structure to a revenue-sharing format would have been a welcome chance to scrap the present bureaucratic morass in LEAA and start afresh.

Congress, however, still felt a general skepticism about revenue sharing and was reluctant to give up all control over anticrime funds. In the face of proposals both to increase and to decrease federal control of these funds, Congress basically opted for the status quo. The House committee and the Senate rejected both the administration's proposal to convert block grants to special revenue sharing and the Stanton-Seiberling and Tunney proposals to give block grants directly to the cities. The Senate basically agreed to most of the House bill; the major compromise was over the length of the authorizing legislation. The House, more pessimistic in its assessment of LEAA's performance, provided for only two years' authorization, whereas the Senate wanted five years'. The conference committee agreed to a compromise of three years before LEAA would come up for reexamination. The Senate, under the prodding of Birch Bayh (D-Ind.), would also have stipulated that 20 percent of LEAA funds be spent on juvenile delinquency programs in the next fiscal year and 30 percent in the subsequent years. The conference committee merely substituted the requirement that each state plan include a program for the improvement of juvenile justice; this was not viewed as a significant rebuff, however, because new legislation in this area was expected shortly.[46]

The final bill was cleared by conference committee two days after LEAA's previous authorization had technically expired, and the Crime Control Act of 1973 was signed into law by President Nixon on August 6. Although Senator Hruska, who had introduced the administration's bill, considered the final bill so similar to the administration's proposal that he called it the "prototype" of special revenue sharing, the final bill was, in fact, a defeat for Nixon and for special revenue sharing and a victory for LEAA and the block grant mechanism. "The exercise of Federal responsibility [was] emphasized by focussing on [LEAA] approval of state plans,"[47] which were still required, as was the fixed 20-percent spending for corrections and the new obligation to include juvenile justice in state plans.

Another real victory for LEAA was the elimination of the troika system of leadership, which had been a severe administrative handicap. All policy and administrative authority was now vested in a single administrator, who would be responsible to the president (not to the attorney general) and who would be assisted by two deputy administrators. A number of other, more minor modifications were also made in response to the cities' complaints.[48]

DISCUSSION

In the year after the signing of the Crime Control Act of 1973, pressures on the Nixon White House stemming from Watergate grew steadily. In the "Saturday Night Massacre," Nixon fired Special Prosecutor Cox, and, in protest, Attorney General Richardson and Deputy Attorney General William Ruckleshaus resigned; Haldeman, Erlichman, Mitchell, Dean, and others were indicted, and the president was named by a grand jury as an unindicted coconspirator. In January 1974, Congressman Peter Rodino began impeachment hearings in the House Judiciary Committee. During the spring of 1974, juvenile justice legislation was also being debated in Congress; this legislation would eventually categorize LEAA even further, by placing a new, separately funded Office for Juvenile Justice and Delinquency Prevention under LEAA. The besieged White House, preoccupied with the president's fight for survival, apparently offered few or no suggestions for this legislation. Nixon was forced to resign on August 9, and it was President Gerald Ford who, on September 7, signed the Juvenile Justice Act of 1974 into law. (This act is discussed in the next chapter.)

The Watergate cover-ups were a supreme irony for a management-oriented law and order president. It is hard to imagine a more convincing demonstration of the impossibility of Nixon's campaign promises to reduce crime or a worse backfiring of the hard-line, friend-of-the-police image Nixon cultivated. Was the use of crime as a political issue involved in developing the atmosphere that made Watergate possible? Did the manipulation of the public's fear of crime teach only too well the lesson that manipulation of reality pays, and was this belief behind the initial decision to cover up White House involvement in the Watergate burglary attempt? By promising more than he could deliver, or than any federal program could deliver, on crime control, did Nixon force his strategists to bypass Congress and the bureaucracy, and did this habit expand into a distrust of everyone outside the White House? Did nurturing a hard-line, repressive image on crime set the stage for a series of stonewalling cover-ups, the series of lies that, even more than the initial burglary attempt, were responsible for Nixon's downfall? In true irony, such as this, the developments are neither completely causal nor purely coincidental. In his compelling narrative of the Watergate period, journalist Theodore White concluded about the law and order president, "The myth he broke was critical—that somewhere in American life there is at least one man who stands for law, the president."[49]

Whatever future judgment is made about the magnitude of the Watergate scandals, they certainly served to distract attention from the ongoing national war on crime. For all Nixon's law and order rhetoric, his real contributions to the workings of LEAA were his development of the New Federalism and his constant advocacy of revenue sharing. But even revenue sharing came in for some hard knocks. One critical political scientist felt, "Revenue sharing is thus a cop-out rather than a panacea as far as the responsibility of the national government to make real judgments of its own in response to its own analysis of domestic needs is concerned."[50] These critics, and most of Congress, in 1971 and again in 1973, still wanted federal guidelines to accompany federal monies. A 1974 MITRE report nicely summarized what New Federalism and special revenue sharing meant to LEAA: "Just as New Federalism is a major help to LEAA in its relationship with OMB, so it weighs heavily once again in the bureau's relationship with Congress, where—on the contrary—it is a hindrance."[51]

Nixon was also accused of preferred special revenue sharing for its political usefulness in protecting him from criticism. As one political scientist put it, it was as if revenue sharing were "a bone thrown to cities and towns with a warning attached that if the bone should taste bad or if indigestion should ensue they have no one to blame but themselves."[52] Whether Nixon actually believed special revenue sharing would be best for LEAA because it would help produce better results, that is, it would reduce crime and strengthen the criminal justice system, is not clear. At the very least, it is fair to say that Nixon's desire to reduce crime was most evident right before the 1972 election and that he then turned not to LEAA's block grant formula but to the discretionary funds, which could be directed by the White House.

During Nixon's presidency, LEAA was exploited, categorized, and neglected. Crime rates across the nation continued to rise, rebounding dramatically after their small hesitation in 1972. Evidently, making the war on crime work was too hard a job even for the law and order president.

SEVEN

The Decline of LEAA

DURING ITS formative years, LEAA had struggled to reduce crime and to respond to changing presidential and congressional priorities while managing a rapidly expanding budget. But by the mid-1970s, as the FBI crime index kept accelerating and complaints and criticisms of LEAA also continued unabated, inflation-conscious presidents began submitting reduced budget requests for LEAA. Inflation was roaring away at the beginning of the 1980s, and even though the crime index had also jumped to a new high, LEAA was given practically zero funding for 1981. (At the same time, renewed calls for a national war on crime began to be heard.)

During the period of lowered expectations for the war on crime, policy thinking was hemmed in by the same old problems as before—lack of substantive knowledge of what to do about crime;[1] battles between cities and states for funds; attention focused sporadically on police, communities, the courts, or corrections; and a lingering suspicion that crime would never be significantly reduced until social conditions, employment in particular, were improved. The character of crime as a national issue changed, however. The old condemn-and-promise rhetoric that was so expedient in the sixties and early seventies gave way to the political necessity of not upsetting LEAA's constituencies. Despite the fact that the Safe Streets grant programs were charged with inefficiency, mismanagement, and ineffectiveness, despite the fact that they had not been shown to reduce crime, LEAA monies had be-

107

come an accepted part of the budgets of countless police chiefs, mayors, and governors, who now felt entitled to these funds.

Even as LEAA took on a life of its own, it became the unwanted child of the national government. It had become apparent even to politicians that no president could make a promise to end crime and keep that promise. As national policymakers continued to tinker with formulas and priorities, the surrounding atmosphere became one of defeatism or, in a more fashionable phrase, lowered expectations. A new rationale developed among national policymakers: one shouldn't really expect great results from Safe Streets monies since they constituted only about *5 percent* of total state and local budgets for criminal justice and law enforcement. After all, crime might be even worse if federal monies had *not* been spent. As late as November 1978, for instance, LEAA acting administrator Henry ("Hank") Dogin was still scaling down expectations on his agency. "There is no way," he told a news conference, that LEAA alone "can reduce crime."[2] As lowered expectations became policy, LEAA's funding was sharply reduced until the agency was killed off.

THE FIRST BUDGET CUTS

Though America let out a sigh of relief when Mr.-Nice-Guy-President Gerald Ford proclaimed that the "long national nightmare" of Watergate was over, the new administration was in many respects a solidly Republican continuation of the old. The new president's personality—his obvious affability, his straightforwardness and candor—stood in sharp contrast to that of his predecessor. But some of his domestic policy positions, in particular his support of the New Federalism and his hard line on crime, sounded much the same.

Ford firmly believed in a limited federal role in social welfare programs. As a member of Congress, he had been a loyal supporter of Nixon's policies. Back in the sixties, when Great Society categorical grants had been in vogue, Ford had been among the first to propose revenue sharing with the states. In a 1971 speech, he reiterated the New Federalism rhetoric:

> Federal revenue sharing is a continuing financial transfusion that can save our federal system and bring new strength of government at the grassroots level. Money is power, and the idea is to put more of the money where more of the power ought to be—at the local level.[3]

Ford had also supported such hard-line policies as wiretapping and the controversial preventive detention and no-knock provisions of the Washington, D.C., crime bill.

Ford's tough line on crime fit the country's growing "lock-'em-up" mood. FBI crime index figures showed that serious crime had soared by 17 percent in 1974; this was the sharpest annual increase since nationwide statistics were first collected. At the same time, LEAA victimization studies, in which selected samples of households in five large cities were interviewed, indicated that only about half the crimes committed were ever reported to the police, so presumably the real crime rate was twice as high as the FBI figures indicated. A Gallup poll taken in October 1975 showed that the public viewed crime as their communities' most pressing problem and that half of the people were afraid to go out in their own neighborhoods at night.[4] More and more states were debating new death penalty provisions, mandatory fixed sentencing, and gun control legislation.

The question was, once again, what could a *president* actually do about reducing crime in the streets? Ford could, and did try to, restore the image of integrity to the highest office in the land, but his credibility was badly damaged by his pardon of Nixon. He could appoint a new attorney general, former University of Chicago president Edward H. Levi, to take the politics out of the Justice Department, but Levi was *so* apolitical he did not help the president's hard-line image: "Levi did not like all the rhetoric of a war on crime, and promises to reduce crime. He didn't believe it, and wasn't that kind of person."[5] Moreover, Levi had to deal with an ongoing congressional investigation of the FBI and bureaucratic warfare within LEAA. Ford could talk tough about crime, but his first priority was to fight inflation, and that meant cutting the budget.

In a bitterly ironic episode in September 1975, as Ford was en route to California to address the state legislature on crime, a young woman pointed a loaded revolver at him from just two feet away. Ford went on to call for a nationwide effort to curb crime and "the abandonment of partisanship on a scale comparable to closing ranks in war time against an external enemy."[6] Less than three weeks later, in San Francisco, another woman fired a shot at him. The incidents prompted concern on Capitol Hill for gun control and protection of likely presidential candidates but no renewed examination of LEAA.

If any hopes remained that LEAA could actually reduce crime, they were rapidly extinguished by a number of damning assessments. The General Accounting Office finished up a year-and-a-half-long series of studies that criticized LEAA: "LEAA and the States have established no standards or criteria by which some indication of success or failure . . . can be determined. . . . Although LEAA encouraged states to evaluate their projects, LEAA did not take steps to make sure comparable data was collected."[7] The GAO said LEAA did not attempt to find out what approaches should be tried and did not prod the states to continue projects started with LEAA funds. An Office of Management and Budget study, reviewing LEAA's budget for fiscal year 1976, also roundly criticized LEAA for lack of evaluation, for funding projects unrelated to improving the criminal justice system, and for funding the purchase of "interesting but unnecessary equipment." The independent Twentieth Century Fund, in New York, pointed out political misuse of LEAA discretionary funds and called for clarifying LEAA's legislative mandate and for dismantling LEAA's regional offices. Another group, the Lawyers' Committee for Civil Rights Under Law, in Washington, D.C., said LEAA had become a "federal relief program" reinforcing existing deficiencies in the criminal justice system and that it should concentrate on research. Yet another report, from the Center for National Security Studies, in Washington, D.C., charged that LEAA had failed to reduce street crimes and should be abolished. A frustrated research analyst for one of these groups complained in a December 1976 interview that "LEAA is a real bust. It should be abolished, and some altogether new effort begun all over again. Its impact is very little. Except for a very few people, they are all idiots over there. Most of our studies show it has very little or no effectiveness in reducing crime."[8]

Most White House and Justice Department opinions of LEAA's capabilities were no less pessimistic. Former attorney general William Saxbe concluded that LEAA had been "a dismal failure," and then–attorney general Levi acknowledged, "Certainly the crime rate *is* going up. It's shocking." A Justice Department aide, who said he inherited LEAA oversight responsibilities because Levi was largely uninterested, explained: "Levi viewed the Department of Justice like many attorney generals have, as running a big law firm, with LEAA outside it. He viewed LEAA, and others in the Department of Justice hierarchy did also, as a 'wounded animal.' Nobody in the Department of Justice knew anything, or wanted to know anything about LEAA."[9]

A Justice Department task force made eighteen proposals for changing LEAA's status, including eliminating all discretionary programs and certain controversial corrections programs, but these suggestions were for the most part rejected by Levi and Ford. Apparently, the idea of seriously altering LEAA did not receive much attention from the White House staff. A White House staff member said: "The essential premises of the program were not challenged in the presentation to the President. I don't know of anyone at the White House who is dissatisfied with the essentials of the LEAA program. . . ."[10]

Why didn't Ford consider a major overhaul of an agency so widely perceived as a failure? The partisan view was to point to a lack of leadership capability. A more rational assessment, however, must include the relative inexperience of the new Domestic Council, Ford's strong agreement with the block grant concept and his higher priority of cutting the budget, and Attorney General Levi's desire not to jeopardize gun control legislation by antagonizing congressional interests. A mood of lowered expectations for LEAA was beginning to emerge among Washington policymakers. The new LEAA administrator, Richard ("Pete") Velde, felt this was what Congress had wanted all along. Velde had replaced administrator Donald E. Santarelli in February 1975 after Santarelli had been quoted as favoring the resignation of then-president Richard Nixon. Richard Velde had been an associate administrator since the early days of LEAA and before that an aide to LEAA's Senate "godfather," Roman Hruska, and he consistently said Congress wanted LEAA to play a limited role, showing the way, *but not dictating*, to states and cities. From Velde's perspective, "There is a maturity in the politics of crime control which moves away from the rhetoric of 'safe streets.' President Ford is interested in setting priorities but he is not setting goals too high and beyond what can be achieved."[11]

With the country's fear of economic disaster breathing hard down his neck, Ford slashed LEAA budget requests. In fiscal year 1976 he requested 14 percent less than Congress had authorized the previous year, and in fiscal year '77 he asked for another 13-percent cut. These were the first severe budget cuts in LEAA's history, and although Congress made smaller reductions in appropriations than Ford had recommended, these cuts marked the beginning of the end of unlimited optimism and budgeting for LEAA (figure 4). A mood of fiscal conservatism and the coming taxpayers' revolt were beginning to intersect with the national policymakers' panic to pour more money into crime programs.

EARMARKING FOR JUVENILE JUSTICE: THE 1974 AMENDMENTS

One of Ford's first actions as president was to sign into law a measure that had long been simmering on the congressional burner, namely, the decision to coordinate all federal juvenile justice and delinquency prevention programs under LEAA. Although he signed the bill, Ford indicated he would seek no funding for it, making it clear that holding the line on federal expenses was simply more important than launching another federal program against crime.

Though most of the amendments to the 1968 Safe Streets Act were initiated in order to improve the block grant structure or the functioning of the agency, the 1974 juvenile justice legislation had a separate

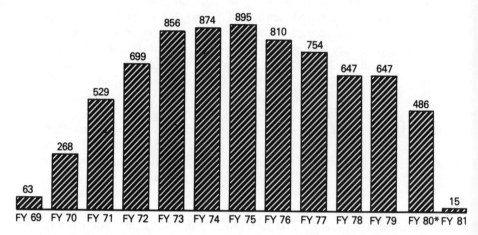

FIGURE 4. LEAA Budget History (in $ Millions)

*The Justice Systems Improvement Act of December 1979 reorganized LEAA (see text).
Source: Adapted from Department of Justice, *General Briefing, LEAA.*

history. The first national attention to juvenile delinquency had begun in 1961 with HEW-administered categorical grants for limited pilot programs. Although the issue of juvenile delinquency ranked high in public opinion polls, President John Kennedy had been only moderately interested, and Congress had provided relatively low funding for the act and its subsequent reauthorizations.

Studies of crime rates in the early sixties showed that more than half the crime was committed by persons under twenty-one and that the average age of persons charged with serious crime was steadily decreasing. Johnson requested and Congress enacted the Juvenile Delinquency Prevention and Control Act of 1968, which provided block grants to the states, as well as discretionary grants, to be administered by HEW. Meanwhile, the Safe Streets Act, passed in the same year, also provided block grants to states that could be used by juvenile justice programs.

In the early Nixon years, juvenile justice and youth services programs within HEW and the Office of Economic Opportunity became viewed with distrust as "liberal" social programs. Nixon officials saw the holdover Johnson appointees in the social welfare bureaucracies as hostile to their goals. Distrust on both sides may explain why HEW requested only $49 million of its $150 million congressional authorization for juvenile justice from 1968 to 1971. In contrast, LEAA, under New

Federalism, was outspending HEW for juvenile justice almost eight to one by 1971. LEAA's role kept increasing—in 1974 LEAA created a juvenile delinquency division within the National Institute for Law Enforcement and Criminal Justice.

The overlap between HEW and LEAA jurisdictions in juvenile justice was only part of a larger picture of confusion, inconsistency, and duplication. The field of juvenile justice had long been plagued by the need to deal with "status offenses"—those acts, such as running away or drinking, that are illegal only because the offender is underage—and as a result, a mélange of various state laws and informal adjudicatory procedures had developed. The national effort against juvenile delinquency was notably uncoordinated. Among the agencies administering programs designed to help young people were cabinet departments: Agriculture, Commerce, HUD, HEW, Interior, Justice, and Labor; dozens of sub-cabinet-level bureaus, divisions, and offices, such as LEAA's Juvenile Delinquency Division, HEW's Office of Education, Youth Development, and Human Development, ACTION, the Federal Bureau of Prisons; and thousands of federally subsidized youth service programs administered by state and local governments. Often, programs were duplicative, boundaries of responsibility blurred. One state agency, for example, might receive HEW funds to support young persons *placed* in institutions; another agency in the same jurisdiction might receive funds on the basis of how many youths were *diverted* from such institutions.

The HEW program was small and its record disappointing; on the other hand, LEAA, while outspending HEW, didn't have a particularly successful history of juvenile justice programs either. By 1974, when the Juvenile Delinquency Prevention and Control Act came up for reauthorization, the question of which agency should manage the federal juvenile justice programs was at the core of the debate.

The champion of juvenile justice legislation was undoubtedly Sen. Birch Bayh, who, as chairman of the then liberal Subcommittee to Investigate Juvenile Delinquency, drafted most of the legislation. Bayh had persistently offered amendments to Safe Streets legislation trying to require states to set aside a fixed percentage of funds for juvenile delinquency prevention, and he had been holding hearings on the subject since 1971. In 1972 he proposed a comprehensive bill that placed all responsibilities for federal juvenile justice efforts under an office of juvenile justice in the Executive Office of the President. After reintroducing the legislation in 1973, Bayh changed his mind and placed the office in HEW.

However, by the spring of 1974, Bayh's bill got into full Judiciary Committee, where it met up with senators Hruska, McClellan, Eastland, and Thurmond and other conservative friends of LEAA. They said LEAA, not HEW, was the logical place for an office of juvenile justice because LEAA's grant and planning mechanisms were similar to those proposed for juvenile justice and, moreover, the administrative machinery had already become established in LEAA. That the existing machinery was not operating successfully was a point politely ignored: in this case, political "logic" was in reality a demonstration of how strong LEAA's congressional friends were. LEAA administrators themselves, along with administration spokesmen, said the new law was unnecessary since by 1972 LEAA was already spending almost $140 million for juvenile justice programs. (However, when pressed by Senator Bayh, LEAA administrator Velde could not account for more than $120 million, and the next year the actual expenditure for juvenile justice was revealed to be $112 million.)

In any case, conservatives had a clear majority on the Judiciary Committee and could promise more money for Juvenile Justice if it were to be placed in LEAA, so they won out easily. The Senate bill amended the Safe Streets Act with a new part for juvenile justice. Bayh also wanted three times more funding for what he called "special emphasis" programs—basically discretionary grants—but the Judiciary Committee reversed this balance. Hruska may have been opposed to limiting the states' discretion by targeting or earmarking LEAA funds, but by putting juvenile justice in LEAA, he could make sure that most of the funds went out as block grants and not categorical grants. Bayh did win a maintenance-of-effort, or "hold-harmless," provision that ensured that, in addition to separate authorizations for the new Office of Juvenile Justice, LEAA would not spend any less of its regular monies on juvenile justice than it had in 1972. This was, in effect, a new categorization of LEAA funds.

The House reached a conclusion different from the Senate's: the "logical" place for the Office of Juvenile Justice was in HEW. LEAA's approach was considered to be too much in narrow terms of crime and punishment, whereas HEW had the broad-ranging human resource programs needed for an in-depth, coordinated attack. Just as the Senate report ignored criticisms of LEAA, so the House report ignored complaints leveled at HEW programs.

In conference committee, the Senate version prevailed, and the Office of Juvenile Justice was placed within LEAA, with separate but parallel funding. The final legislation was free-standing; although it amended the Safe Streets Act, funds were authorized separately. LEAA won an unwanted victory over HEW, but not without incurring the permanent battle scar of further categorization.

However, a new challenge lay ahead for juvenile justice: President

Ford did not want the program funded. The Ford administration requested only a nominal $25 million or so per year for the program. Senator Bayh held oversight hearings, angrily entitled "Ford Administration Stifles Juvenile Justice Program." But the Ford administration continued to block additional funding.

FINDING EXCUSES—
1976 REAUTHORIZATION

LEAA itself came up for reauthorization in the middle of a period of conflicting pressures. Crime was still intolerably high, but so were inflation and unemployment, and there was a real threat of recession. Though there was increasing pessimism about LEAA's effectiveness in the war on crime, the agency by now had a strong constituency receiving its funds, and it still had powerful congressional friends. In June 1975, President Ford sent a crime message to Congress stressing that "America has been far from successful in dealing with the sort of crime that obsesses America day and night—I mean street crime" and calling for a generous, five-year reauthorization of LEAA. Meanwhile, Ford would soon be slashing LEAA's budget.

Hearings of the Subcommittee on Criminal Laws and Procedures of the Senate Judiciary Committee were begun in October 1975. Senator Hruska, who introduced the administration's bill and was due to retire the next year, set the tone as defending champion of LEAA: "I say to the critics of this program—let us put our effort against crime into proper perspective: the short space of 7 years and some $4.0 billion should not reasonably be expected to cure all the problems inherent in our ancient system of law enforcement."[12] He also said LEAA programs were not the "federal government's direct response to the rising crime problem" since LEAA's function was only to *help* state and local governments, which bore the *direct* responsibility, and, furthermore, LEAA funds amounted to only 5 percent of the total outlay for law enforcement. Seconding Hruska's defense of LEAA, Attorney General Levi called, in his own inimitably eloquent style, for patience: "When Congress votes money for an effort of this kind, the Congress must take into account that the very success of this kind of an effort is going to be accomplished by recognizing that, as it proceeds, errors are inevitably made because we are operating in an area where we have to discover new ways of doing things."[13]

Liberal Sen. Edward Kennedy, rapidly moving up in seniority in the Judiciary Committee and also beginning an extensive revision of the criminal code, cast himself in the role of challenger to LEAA: "Surely it is too late in the day to say that the mistakes by the agency are the result of growing pains." He cited rising crime rates as a *"prima facie* case that LEAA has substantially failed in its task" and suggested a short, two-year authorization.[14] Yet, Kennedy's bill was less drastic than that proposed by Congressman John Conyers (D-Mich.), chairman of the House Subcommittee on Crime and a vocal critic of LEAA. Conyers's bill provided only a one-year extension, with intensive congressional oversight so major program changes could then be recommended.

Even the most guarded assessment of the war on crime, expressed by a senior GAO official, was negative. Admitting that since Congress had never *clearly* stated that LEAA's primary purpose was *to reduce crime* and since LEAA's contribution was only 5 percent of the total, he agreed it might be "unreasonable to say the LEAA program had failed because the crime rate has increased. But is it unreasonable," he asked, "for people to question whether government in general has failed because the crime rate continues to increase? We think not."[15] And he added that eight years of LEAA programs had brought us no closer to understanding the causes or cures of crime.

Congressional debates, however, did not reflect to any great extent the basic argument about whether LEAA's inability to reduce crime meant the national government should or should not properly have a role or just what that role should be. Instead, most of the amendments debated were still primarily housekeeping details—in particular, earmarking formulas for various programs. Though the suggestion of abolishing LEAA might be bandied about in various press or task force reports, Congress was much more attuned to the political realities of managing an entitlement program.

Disagreement between LEAA supporters and skeptics coalesced primarily in the difference between the House and Senate authorizations. The Senate opted for the administration's five-year authorization, easily defeating a proposal for a short-term authorization made by critic Sen. Joseph Biden (D-Del.). In contrast, the House gave LEAA notice it was on trial status and recommended a short, one-year extension. The conference committee accepted a compromise of three years, an exact repetition of the outcome of the 1973 legislation and a victory for LEAA.

Congressman Conyers tried to add language making it clear that the purpose of the block grant was not only to improve the criminal justice system but to "reduce and prevent crime," but this language was defeated in conference. Sen. Edward Kennedy also claimed his bill would make this clear, but his bill's language to this effect was only indirect.[16] Evaluation was again stressed by both houses: states were now to incorporate uniform evaluation procedures into their plans, and the LEAA administrator must evaluate the likely impact of programs before approving state plans.

Beyond compromising on the reauthorization period and agreeing on the need for more evaluation, Congress applied most of its attention to debating further categorization, each aspect of the criminal justice system having its own particular champion. The cost-conscious Ford administration had recommended against any funding for the 1974 Juvenile Justice Act and now wanted to remove the provision that required states to spend as much money on juvenile justice as they had in 1972. But Bayh's maintenance-of-effort provision survived, although the formula was changed to a percentage (19.15 percent of the amount spent in 1972). Another category that won out in the House, and was agreed to in conference, was an office of community anti-crime programs, the particular concern of Conyers. Conyers was from Detroit and, as an ardent spokesman for the black community and critic of LEAA's early emphasis on police programs, had sponsored the idea of community involvement for several years. There was also general agreement that state judiciaries should be strengthened and court processes streamlined. Much of a bill proposed by Edward Kennedy was adopted: judicial planning committees would draw up judicial plans to be incorporated in the comprehensive state plans, state planning agencies would include members of the judiciary, and state plans must provide "adequate funds for court programs." The Senate also went along with the administration's proposal to set aside discretionary money for the Impact Cities program (in spite of the fact that the program, begun with an eye on the 1972 election, was already being abandoned as a failure two years later and had received extremely sharp criticism).[17] But the House did not accept this further categorization, and it did not pass.

President Ford signed the Crime Control Act of 1976 into law in mid-October 1976 at the height of the presidential campaign. The three-year extension was a decided victory for LEAA. Even though the new authorization was tempered by more categorization and the knowledge that actual appropriations would probably be decreased, for an agency with no clear record of success in reducing crime, the reauthorization was still a major show of support. LEAA at least had a safety jacket of three more years.

CRIME AND THE 1976 ELECTION

By 1976 policymakers were not alone in being tired of the unsuccessful national war on crime. Nearly everyone's attention span had run its course. For both the public and politicians, the issue was great-ly muted in the 1976 presidential election. Thoroughly disillusioned by Watergate, which had come so close on the heels of the Vietnam debacle, the American public was highly skeptical about government in general. Its mistrust could only be reinforced if it watched the steadily spiraling FBI crime rates and remembered the big, empty slo-gans of the "law and order" presidency and the "war on poverty." A national Gallup survey in May 1976 indicated the crime problem as the country's most serious public concern. A Roper Organization poll in June showed crime was Americans' second greatest concern after economic issues, such as inflation and unemployment. But the latter poll also revealed that a majority of Americans would choose a presi-dential candidate on the basis of personal qualities rather than his stand on the issues.[18] After Watergate and Vietnam, presidential integrity and honesty were perceived as the main concern—a concern that dove-tailed with the strengths and strategies of the two major candidates.

In the sense that 1976 was less of an issues election, it was histori-cally more typical than the relatively more clear-cut choices of 1964 (Johnson v. Goldwater) or 1972 (Nixon v. McGovern). What the Republicans learned in '64, the Democrats had learned in '72, and in '76 advisors in both parties sought to tone down the issues and seek the center. Ford was counseled to use a rose-garden strategy or to emphasize looking and being presidential; this aloof position was con-ducive to ambiguous campaign rhetoric. Carter's campaign was charac-terized as coalitional rather than issue oriented, and it generally allowed him to be skillful at the "art of ambiguity."

With the gloomy specter of Richard Nixon haunting the campaign, to promise any great improvement in crime statistics was unnecessarily risky. A sense of betrayal at having voted for a president who prom-ised law and order but then broke the law himself, a sense of injustice at watching convicted national officials get light sentences only height-ened the public's justifiable disbelief in the national war on crime. Po-litical scientist Walter Dean Burnham estimated that as many as half of the voters were convinced "politicians can't cope with crime."[19] Knowledgeable policy experts kept deescalating expectations, warning that the war on crime could not be won by LEAA programs alone. One put it bluntly when he said the intent of the 1968 legislation had been crime reduction and that in this, LEAA had failed. "We have learned little about reducing the incidence of crime, and have no reason to believe that significant reduction will be secured in the near future."[20]

The clearest links between candidates and domestic issues were with primary candidates Republican Ronald Reagan and Democrat Morris Udall (D-Ariz.). Reagan, former governor of California, carried the

Goldwater-Nixon torch and talked a much stronger anticrime rhetoric than Ford. He said that the "criminal justice system has failed the American public by sheltering criminals from prosecution." "What is the cause of crime in America?" he asked. "If one should listen to the Congress of the U.S., its most vocal voices, you will hear the old refrain, 'Poverty is the root cause of crime.' But time *has* proven these people wrong—dead wrong in too many cases."[21] The Ford camp, however, was only too willing to swallow any ideological differences with the right. The struggle for the Republican nomination went to the convention in Kansas City; although it was decided before the first ballot, there was a large Reagan swell that would stay intact and grow during the next four years. On the Democratic side, Udall had promised early in the campaign that if elected he would fight crime with an array of federal programs costing as much as $3 or $4 billion. However, Jimmy Carter, former governor of Georgia, had the Democratic nomination sewn up by the end of the primary season.

In the 1976 election season, *all* the presidential candidates basically agreed on a tougher approach to crime, echoing local politicians across the country about the need to make sure crime didn't pay. Black urban leaders, recognizing that their constituents were especially affected by crime, addressed the issue in their own campaigns in increasing numbers. "The same people who used to campaign against strong law and order measures, perceiving them as a racial thing, now are actively petitioning City Hall for more police protection and stiffer penalties," commented Newark, New Jersey, mayor Kenneth Gibson.[22] Policymakers in many states were increasing the severity of punishments as a deterrent to crime. (Some observers, such as Justice Macklin Fleming of the Los Angeles Court of Appeals, were critical of this cycle of putting harsher penalties on the books because they felt it meant these harsher laws were less strictly enforced.[23]) Liberals and conservatives alike, President Ford, Sen. Edward Kennedy, candidate Jimmy Carter, and Ronald Reagan, joined in supporting such concepts as mandatory minimum sentencing, victim compensation, and streamlined court procedures.

President Ford began his campaign with toned-down rhetoric, translating law and order into concern for the rights of victims, emphasizing the president's constitutional duty in search of domestic tranquillity, and cautioning that the federal role was limited. In an address at the University of Michigan, he lauded LEAA's new program on career criminals. In a September news conference, he listed crime as one of five domestic areas his campaign would emphasize and pledged he "would not tolerate the kind of crime rate increases that have taken place over the last three or four years."[24]

Then, in late September, trying to convince southern voters he was more conservative than Carter, Ford delivered a rousing speech that sounded as though it had slipped by his more cautious campaign strategists. Addressing a convention of the International Association of Chiefs of Police in Miami, Florida, Ford promised "safe streets, secure homes, and the dignity and the freedom from fear which is the birthright of every American" and pledged a crusade against crime in the first one hundred days of his new administration.[25] This prompted critics to ask for an accounting of the previous twenty-eight hundred days of the "law and order" administrations elected in 1968 and again in 1972. Ford also took credit for the small deceleration in the national crime rate—the FBI crime index, while still increasing, was up only 3 percent so far in 1976 as compared to 10 percent in 1975. Democratic vice-presidential candidate Sen. Walter F. Mondale of Minnesota immediately retaliated by pointing to the 60 percent increase in crime during the Republicans' eight years in the White House and called LEAA a shambles.

If Ford's campaign image was to be an experienced incumbent, Carter's was to be a compassionate outsider. In an interview Carter stated, "We pride ourselves on having a good, fair criminal justice system. It's not fair. Now wealth is a major factor in whether or not you get justice."[26] And in his position paper on crime he said, "Overall, I think the best way to reduce crime is to reduce unemployment." Candidate Carter also frequently evoked a favorite image of

> a family who has to push an 18 year old man or woman out of the home, maybe a law abiding person, because the welfare payments and the unemployment compensation, Social Security, don't apply to an 18 year old, and when that young person wanders up and down the street for a week, 2 weeks, 3 weeks, without a chance for a job, there's a push toward shoplifting, breaking in automobiles, selling numbers rackets, prostitution, drugs. Poverty is not an excuse for crime. But it's a reason for or a cause of crime.[27]

Yet Carter's position on crime did not appear too strongly liberal because he projected such a multiplicity of images, at times even sounding like a Republican. As one student of elections noted, "Carter could be perceived as a Southerner in Plains, a Democrat in Chicago, and a liberal in Cambridge."[28]

Carter's only major speech on crime came during the late fall, when he felt most under pressure by the Ford strategy of making *him* the issue and when he was rapidly losing popularity points to Ford. In an address to the Detroit Economic Club, in Ford's home state of Michigan, Carter seized the chance to charge the Nixon-Ford administration with failing to reverse rising crime rates and setting an example for violating the law. The city of Detroit, predominantly black, had 17 percent unemployment, and, in particular, black youths were 52 percent unemployed, so Carter took the opportunity to remind voters of his views on the relationship of unemployment to crime. He lambasted LEAA for waste, poor coordination, widespread mismanagement, and making almost no contribution to reducing crime. And then he claimed *he* would stop the waste of millions of dollars of LEAA funds and "provide the leadership that will turn the tide against the scourge of crime."[29] Except in these isolated instances, however, crime as an issue was much less apparent in the '76 campaign than it had been in the past three elections, when it had been used to great political advantage.

The lack of prominence accorded the crime issue fit in nicely with LEAA's own view of itself as an independent, ongoing agency devoted to system improvement, not to be held accountable for actually reducing crime. Just before the election, LEAA administrator Velde predicted the election would not affect the character of the national war on crime. No one took seriously Ford's last-ditch promise of a crusade on crime in his first one hundred days. And if Carter were elected, he could be expected to trim LEAA's budget, but that was not so much different from President Ford, who, after all, had imposed the first budget cuts in LEAA's history. As it turned out, President Carter was also to follow the pattern of his predecessors in letting LEAA languish without strong presidential leadership, allowing leadership positions within LEAA to remain vacant and delaying serious organizational reform of the agency until reauthorizations rolled around again.

CARTER AND KENNEDY TACKLE LEAA

Like presidents before him, newly elected president Carter was slow to do anything about the floundering national war on crime. Reforming LEAA simply wasn't high on his list of things needing to get done. "We got little pressure, very little, from anyone on this issue,"[30] recalled a White House aide. Moreover, Carter aides were rapidly learning that LEAA was a fixture not easily changed. Another aide explained Carter's position this way:

> Carter didn't talk about it much in the campaign, but he and others around him thought it was a kind of natural target—a lot of money spent, yet no decrease in crime. He said he felt it should be cut back, perhaps way back. But if he went and said he wanted a major cutback, or to abolish it, Congress would laugh at us.

Frankly, it's a special interests problem. Take the $500 billion U.S. budget. If it were not for special interests that could be passed. LEAA is not the worst of these programs but it is a major problem. It's become like an entitlement program.[31]

In some circles there was wishful talk of abolishing LEAA. The *Wall Street Journal*, for instance, ran an editorial challenging the new Carter team to show they were strong enough to actually abolish this "useless federal agency." A Justice Department aide, familiar with LEAA and its problems, said Attorney General Griffin Bell indeed wanted at first to close the agency down. But, as this aide reminisced, he had advised his boss, "You've got to face the real world. If you want to abolish it, you're going to lose total control over it."

Even the mechanics of appointing new leadership within LEAA proved difficult. Judge Bell had said in his nomination hearings (for attorney general) that he planned a careful study of LEAA, "what they have been spending the money on, and what they want to spend it on in the future" and promised to put somebody in LEAA who would do just that. The Justice Department boosted acting administrator James Gregg, a veteran LEAA aide, to be permanent administrator, but the Carter staff viewed the agency as full of Nixon people and eventually rejected the idea of a holdover. Bell had trouble finding qualified candidates willing to preside over the possible dismantling of the demoralized agency. He told a story of offering the position to one very good person, who studied LEAA for a week and decided it was impossible to manage. Bell was comfortable with Gregg, who was viewed as a sort of caretaker, so once again, unwittingly following in the footsteps of previous administrations, Carter left the top leadership positions at LEAA vacant for over a year.

The Carter administration found itself once more starting at square one, deferring action on LEAA until it could examine what other possibilities there were. In April 1977 Bell created a study group of three Justice Department and three LEAA officials to evaluate LEAA and rethink its role. "The notion was," recalled one of Bell's assistants, who chaired the study group, "if you weren't sure you even wanted the agency, set up a study. It was at least arguable that we would recommend abolishing the agency. An internal task force was a good idea—it gave us time to review LEAA and educate Judge Bell."[32] The study group was also a way to elicit and assess reactions from the public and from special interest groups.

The study group report, made public in June, zeroed in on the unmet goals of LEAA: real, statewide planning was not taking place, and LEAA was not playing a "national leadership role." The report recommended essentially doing away with both of these goals, by converting LEAA to special revenue sharing. (Revenue sharing, it may be recalled, had been an integral part of Nixon's New Federalism, and several times Nixon had proposed special revenue sharing for LEAA.) Then the report went on to suggest more of the same restrictions that had plagued LEAA from the start; e.g., instead of statewide planning, states must demonstrate a "criminal justice coordinating function." The White House, however, was not pleased with the study group's report and sent it back to Justice to be reexamined. "We felt it was wrong to let the people inside an agency try to prepare a critical look at it," said one White House staffer.[33] In August of 1978 the president also directed his executive branch reorganization staff within the Office of Management and Budget (OMB) to examine the troubled agency. This group felt the most valuable functions of LEAA were research and statistics gathering, rather than grant making. There followed another period of indecision and false starts. Wide-ranging discussions were held between the Justice Department, the domestic policy staff at the White House, and the OMB concerning the prospect of reforming LEAA through an executive reorganization.

Attorney General Bell later quipped about his attitude toward LEAA:

> I have been through three stages with the LEAA. The first one . . . was to transfer funds to the Treasury, and research to a new agency, the National Institute of Justice. The second stage I went through was hoping that the Congress in its wisdom would transfer the program completely out of the Justice Department and give it to somebody else so I would not have to have anything else to do with it. . . . Now I have reached the next stage. I decided I would make the best of it, that I had a duty to try to make it into a better agency and that it was time to stop complaints about it.[34]

In September 1978, in a follow-up action to the study group's report and perhaps as a trial balloon for the idea of abolishing LEAA, Bell closed down the ten regional offices of LEAA. These offices had been set up during Nixon's tenure, in keeping with New Federalism, to review and approve state plans and offer technical assistance to the states. Bell found that LEAA officials in the Atlanta regional office got paid more than 99 percent of all Georgia state officials did and felt that this pay was way out of line. "Bell was looking for trophies to offer the White House—which was looking for cost-cutting leadership in that first year," commented LEAA counsel Tom Madden.[35] Although the move was announced as merely an effort to streamline delivery of funds, it was generally interpreted as a first step in loosening LEAA's control over grants.

These early Carter-administration efforts provoked vehement criticism, much of which was voiced at early hearings held in August by Congressman Conyers. The prestigious bipartisan Advisory Commission on Intergovernmental Relations came out with a detailed study of LEAA and recommended strongly against going to special revenue sharing. The Association of State Planners calculated that closing the regional offices, instead of saving money, would cost an additional $2.2 million. Congresswoman Elizabeth Holtzman (D-N.Y.) sharply criticized the attorney general for the delay in naming an administrator. Congressmen Conyers and Robert McClory (R-Ill.) let it be known they resented the administration's reorganization plans for LEAA because they believed *Congress* should be the authority to reform the troubled agency. And as the Carter administration procrastinated, time was running out, for LEAA was due to come up for reauthorization in September of 1979.

Meanwhile, liberal Sen. Edward Kennedy had become chairman of the Judiciary Committee, and his staff had developed a detailed plan for a major overhaul of LEAA, a plan that also moved in the direction of special revenue sharing. The Kennedy plan was to send 70 percent of LEAA funds directly (by a complicated formula) to states, cities, and counties, with no planning requirements. Instead of state planning agencies, there would be criminal justice coordinating councils, not to plan but to set state priorities. Juvenile justice would be kept at the same percentage, and there would be separate authorizations for community programs. The three parts of LEAA—the grant programs, National Institute of Justice (NIJ), and a new statistics-collecting bureau—would all be subsumed under a new Office of Criminal Justice Assistance, Research, and Statistics (OJARS) in the Justice Department.

The Kennedy bill dealt with the same problems as the Justice Department study group and was a step ahead of the study group in enunciating basic prinicples to improve LEAA. Because Kennedy wanted administration support and Bell was having trouble with his reorganization plans, they agreed their offices would work together on a new bill. LEAA's counsel described the collaboration:

The Fiederowicz [Justice Department], Feinberg [Kennedy's staff], Madden [LEAA] teamwork went very well on the new bill. We, Fiederowicz and Madden, pressed for cutting paperwork and the other objectives of our internal task force, while Ken Feinberg stressed and added the sections on the pass-through to big cities and the overall formula aspects of the bill. We based a lot of this on the Comprehensive Employment and Training Act.

Grant programs such as LEAA usually run the cycle of being quite open or block-like in the beginning—but then adding specifications and the

categories over the years. That's what's exciting about our new bill—
it would open up the grant process again and add substantial new
amounts of flexibility. I think that would be good and really quite
novel as these federal grant problems go.[36]

Finally, in July 1978, more than a year after the initial Justice Department study group was convened, the Carter-Kennedy bill was unveiled
with great fanfare in a White House rose-garden ceremony.

Another major plan, not too dissimilar to the Carter-Kennedy plan,
was introduced in Congress by Congressman Conyers. Conyers's proposal was more specific about the types of projects for which block
grants might be used. But his efforts, although he indeed had had a
politically popular program in his community anticrime program, were
not taken too seriously by some observers. "Rodino [chairman of the
House Judiciary Committee] tolerates Conyers, but if his jumping
and stomping is going to drown this thing then Rodino will step in,"[37]
explained a Carter-administration aide.

Another LEAA skeptic, Sen. Joseph Biden, who chaired subcommittee
hearings in the fall of 1978, considered preparing comprehensive legislation of his own. An aide to Senator Biden complained, "The philosophy behind the Kennedy bill and the original bill is still basically the
same."[38] Biden submitted an important amendment, which later became
part of the final legislation, setting up guidelines about what kinds of
projects could or could not be funded.

Kennedy's efforts were also criticized by those who liked the original bill. Richard Velde, a former LEAA administrator who, at that time,
served as minority counsel for the Senate Judiciary Committee, explained *his* position with a wry smile:

There are three things I like about the Kennedy bill:
A. that there was a bill at all;
B. that it calls for a four year authorization, and
C. that LEAA is retained in some semblance.
Beyond that, there's not much I like about it at all.[39]

Velde felt a central policy-formation role for the new OJARS would
be dangerous and that comprehensive planning should be continued.
Another LEAA spokesman said Velde's influence shouldn't be under-
estimated: "The Carter/Kennedy bill has a slim chance of passing.
Velde will be a strong revisionist on it. He is stubborn and wants a
1968 block-grants kind of bill. One thing about Velde, he is consistent.
He opposes both the Conyers approach and the Kennedy formula."[40]

Behind the many difficulties and the long delay in trying to reform
LEAA lay the old problem of special interests. Complained Attorney
General Bell, "I find that in Washington . . . you can't do anything

here that you want to do. You have to get along with the different interest groups. I believe we ought to have research, statistics, and revenue-sharing. That's what I started out with. But that would not sell, because we already have LEAA."[41] Kennedy solved the problem of special interests by proposing high appropriations—$825 million annually for the next four years. Under the Kennedy formula, states could choose between two methods of funding: a complex formula reflecting the amount of their crime plus the amount of their criminal justice expenditures, or "a hold-harmless" track, in which states would get the same as they were currently getting. But unless appropriations were high, this two-track funding scheme would not work.

Carter's first budgets had continued the overall LEAA cuts initiated by President Ford, and it was only with reluctance that the White House went along with Kennedy's plan for high authorizations. A White House domestic policy aide explained:

> It's now [1978] authorized for $800 million and funded at about $600 million. We would prefer to cut it back. But Kennedy and Rodino [chairmen of the judiciary committees] want it expanded. Kennedy would like it up to $1 billion but will settle for $800 million. Justice has been negotiating with Kennedy. Hell, Kennedy is a highly visible guy and he has been very loyal to the president. We have no interest in taking him on and making a fight over this.[42]

Feelings in the White House changed, however, as Kennedy proved recalcitrant over his health-care plan, came up with an importantly different energy proposal, and, during the 1979 summer, toyed with the idea of challenging Carter for the Democratic nomination in 1980. Carter's 1979 budget had called for another $110 million cut in LEAA. Kennedy promptly denounced the reduction as "unwise, unnecessary, and unfair." But both House and Senate budget committees made yet further reductions in Carter's 1980 proposal, cutting LEAA back to $486 million.

Kennedy secured a variety of sponsors for his bill, including his House counterpart, Rodino, and conservatives Thurmond and Mc-Clory. Sen. Howell Heflin, a conservative Democrat from Alabama, also proved a good friend to LEAA: he chaired the Conference Committee and helped put through the final bill. After extensive argument, in late December 1979 Congress passed the Justice System Improvement Act, which accepted much of Kennedy's plan. LEAA was replaced by four separate entities: a new National Institute of Justice (NIJ); a new Bureau of Justice Statistics (BJS); a scaled-down LEAA, which would administer only the new formula grants; and a new Office of Justice

Assistance, Research, and Statistics (OJARS), which would provide staff support to and "coordinate the activities" of NIJ, BJS, and LEAA. Formula grants, a sort of amalgam between the old block grants and special revenue sharing, were to be given not only to the states but to cities, counties, or combinations of local governments representing populations of over one hundred thousand. The amount going to each state was determined by population or, if appropriations were high enough, by a four-part formula taking into account population, crime rates, tax rates, and criminal justice expenditures. Within each state, the amounts allocated to state agencies or to local governments essentially depended on each level's contribution to the criminal justice expenditures of the state. Statewide planning was abolished, only to be replaced in each state by criminal justice councils that were to develop three-year applications (streamlined plans) for funds. Local governments were encouraged to submit their applications as part of their states' applications. Explicitly spelled out were *twenty-three categories* eligible for funding, including community programs, strengthening police (as measured by arrest rates, victimization rates, clearance rates, or other objective measures), court reforms, reducing the time between arrest and disposition, alternatives to maximum-security confinement for nondangerous offenders, and the perennial favorite, coordination of various components of the criminal justice system.

The reorganization and generous four-year authorization provided under the 1979 Justice Systems Improvement Act became moot, however, as LEAA ran smack into financial ambush in early 1980. At first, LEAA's prospects seemed bright. In January 1980 President Carter's first budget proposals for the next fiscal year recommended, albeit with lukewarm enthusiasm, a slight increase over the previous year's funding—perhaps not enough to keep up with inflation, but still some $409 million for OJARS and LEAA (for administration and formula grants) within an overall budget of $571 million for justice assistance (including the National Institute of Justice, Bureau of Justice Statistics, Office of Juvenile Justice and Delinquency Prevention, and Public Safety Officers' Benefits Program). But with words reminiscent of the "Vietnamization" of the Vietnam War, Carter withdrew his support:

> After nearly a decade and a half of such support [LEAA assistance], state and local authorities are far better equipped, trained and organized to handle their own problems. Given these improvements, the importance of solving crime of national significance, and continued pressure on Federal resources, the administration has started to redirect its programs toward those problems that can best be resolved at the national level.[43]

Congress soon went on a budget-cutting spree in a vain effort to balance the 1981 budget. Members of the newly formed budget committees in both the Senate and the House were especially active in this effort. Sen. Ernest F. Hollings (D-S.C.), chairman of an appropriations subcommittee, was a key mover in urging the end of funding for LEAA. Hollings was a close friend of former attorney general Griffin Bell, and the two of them had been longtime critics of LEAA. In the House, which had always been less than generous to LEAA, the budget committee moved swiftly and recommended eliminating *all* justice assistance. At about the same time Carter had second thoughts about his proposed increase in LEAA spending. In an unusual move the president—who was making a last-ditch effort to balance the 1981 budget—submitted a new budget proposal in March. In this March budget, LEAA and OJARS were to be phased out, receiving only $15 million for administration (but nothing for grant programs), with a total of $117 million for justice assistance.

There ensued a variety of congressional skirmishes over how best to kill LEAA, including amendments to redistribute appropriations among the various justice assistance agencies, a floor amendment to resurrect LEAA grant programs, and a busing rider to LEAA's appropriations bill. Budget committee members pressed for a total elimination of LEAA funding. Senators Thurmond and Heflin were two of the major advocates for continuing LEAA. Over at the House, Robert McClory (R-Ill.) also pressed for preserving LEAA. But many other former LEAA supporters looked the other way. One LEAA aide told us that Congressman Peter Rodino, the powerful chairman of the House Judiciary Committee, simply "took a walk and failed to exercise any influence that might help us survive." Sen. Edward Kennedy was off campaigning for the Democratic nomination for president, and Senator Biden was apparently indifferent to LEAA's plight.

LEAA officials saw the roof crumbling all around them. They knew Carter had never been their friend. Now OBM director James McIntyre and the influential leaders of the budget committees in Congress had joined the ever-more-popular "get-LEAA" movement. Said one LEAA official, "I knew all along that we should have dropped the name LEAA and come up with some new, more appealing name—'LEAA' as a phrase had become so unpopular that it no longer had credibility." But it was far more than just a name that was being rejected.

Lobbyists for the law enforcement profession, and especially for state criminal justice planners, campaigned to salvage at least some funding for LEAA. They contended that the slight gain to be realized by balancing the budget was not worth killing LEAA. "Maintaining public consciousness about crime" was among the reasons LEAA needed to be preserved, they said.[44]

Still it seemed that the only people who cared in 1980 were some of the state and local beneficiaries of LEAA. One longtime observer expressed the feelings of many criminal justice professionals:

> It is true that crime is no longer a national political issue, as it was in the 1960's—principally, I believe, because political leaders and government officials at the national and state levels have wished it away. But crime remains a major, if not the major issue in many of the nation's cities and large urban areas. Indeed, it is not too much to say that crime and the fear of crime are tearing apart some of the nation's largest communities.
>
> For Congress and the Administration to eliminate the Law Enforcement Assistance Administration would amount to a penny-wise, pound-foolish abdication on the part of the Federal Government of its responsibility to provide leadership and funds to make the criminal justice system work.[45]

Yet not all local officials were sorry to see LEAA abolished. One Massachusetts town manager said LEAA never really worked out that well in his area. There was too much red tape, too many forms to fill out, too many plans to be prepared. "I'd give LEAA a 'D' if I was giving grades out. Mind you, it's not the only federal program I'd abolish. Some of the Small Business Administration community grants and others come just as easily or even more quickly to mind. But I'd have to say that LEAA funds were not treated very seriously here and an awful lot of money was simply wasted."[46] A Colorado county commissioner echoed his acceptance of Congress's decision to kill LEAA: "The hoops you had to jump through to get these funds! . . . The arbitrary decisions were very counterproductive to us. For the last two years, LEAA has been an absolute mess down here, and in the rest of the state."[47]

In the end, in mid-December 1980, Congress appropriated only $15 million for the administration of LEAA and OJARS, cutting out all formula grant monies. LEAA and OJARS remained on the books because they had been authorized for four years, but all they could do in 1981 was to process almost $1 billion in grant monies left over from 1979 and 1980 that was still "in the pipeline." But after 1982 it looked as if the pipes would be empty and these offices would cease to exist. The other justice assistance agencies received funding that was reduced but sufficient to maintain some sort of ongoing operations: Juvenile Justice received $100 million; the National Institute of Justice, $25 million; the Bureau of Justice Statistics, $24 million; and Public Safety Officers Benefit, $12 million.[48]

A NEW CYCLE BEGINS?

During its twelve-year lifetime, LEAA evolved from a highly touted experiment in federalism to at best a struggling subsidy-entitlement program. Though being born of compromise is nothing unusual for national programs, the twin goals of the Safe Streets Act—reducing crime and decentralizing authority—consistently defied reformers and policymakers. Critics looking at where the money was going and at constantly accelerating crime rates initiated study after study of the troublesome agency. But looking back, it is apparent that congressional attempts to relegislate the war on crime did not come to grips with any substantive revision of *what the national role should be*. In fact, the more it changed, the more it remained the same. Democrats began to sound like Republicans, supporting a lock-'em-up approach to crime and special revenue sharing for LEAA. Later supporters of LEAA, like its original congressional sponsors, kept trying to change the agency to favor their own constituencies. Old fashions in LEAA programs—riot control and police equipment—would die out, but new fashions would emerge—courts, juvenile justice, and community action. LEAA's initially troublesome administrative troika was eventually replaced with a four-part organization under OJARS, which might have proved just as difficult. And just a few months after LEAA's budget was killed, a new task force on violent crime was being set up by Reagan's attorney general. Ironically, a familiar opponent of LEAA, former attorney general Griffin Bell, would be cochairman of the task force (along with Governor James Thompson of Illinois).

For twelve troubled years LEAA survived numerous political vicissitudes. One president wanted a different program from the beginning, another used it for his own political advantage, a third began cutting its budget, and a fourth just wanted it to go away. LEAA's declining years were marked by a lowering of expectations, continued presidential neglect, and, finally, a fatal congressional cut in funding. Some observers objected that just as we can't abandon cancer research because it hasn't yet discovered a cure for cancer, so we shouldn't abandon federal anticrime assistance just because it hasn't yet licked crime. Political scientist Herbert Kaufman said LEAA represented to many people "President Nixon's law and order machine, trampling on civil rights and beefing up police forces to suppress expressions of dissent as well as criminal activity."[49] In any case the crime issue had receded from national politics, overshadowed for the moment by economic and energy problems.

During the 1980 presidential election campaign, there was no national candidate who dramatized the need for a war on crime or claimed *he* could restore law and order. Incumbent president Carter, troubled by 20-percent inflation and the Iranian kidnapping of U.S. embassy employees, was suspected of having wanted to abolish LEAA all along. Senator Kennedy, in a quick flashback to the elections of 1968 and 1972, began his primary campaign with a swing through the Deep South, where he charged the Carter administration with "silence" and lack of leadership against crime:

> During the past three years the White House has not issued a single major statement on crime and criminal justice. I regard this incredible three-year long period of neglect as a prime example of the sort of abdication of Presidential leadership that is of such concern to the people of this nation and that will be one of the major issues in this campaign.[50]

But Kennedy was hard pressed to advocate more funding because he was constantly chided as a big spender who believed in throwing money at problems—money that was generally wasted. And because of his bid for the Democratic nomination, he was away from the Senate, where the budget execution of LEAA was in progress.

The Republican campaign carried forward many of the traditional hard-line law and order values, but these values were considerably muted by the overriding goal of fiscal restraint. A Reagan white paper said:

> The criminal justice system has failed in large part because of lenient judges, inadequate punishment, and unnecessarily slow and cumbersome court proceedings.
>
> However the answer to the crime problem does not lie in more federal dollars. . . .[51]

The Republican party platform endorsed the death penalty as a deterrent, opposed federal registration of firearms, and promised to "restore the ability of the FBI to act effectively" against illegal drug traffic. The Republican candidate, former California governor Ronald Reagan, who had talked a tough Goldwater line on crime in the past, now sounded much more moderate and reassuring on all the issues. Anyway, Reagan's big appeal was to cut federal spending across the board. Given the choice, he would certainly want to devolve the whole war on crime (along with welfare) back to state and local governments. In this he was entirely consistent, if not entirely specific. Without using crime as an issue, Reagan impressively won the election on such issues as inflation, balancing the budget, national defense, and questions of leadership.

As the 1980s began, national crime rates were still high and frightening. Serious crime had taken a small dip in the late seventies, the FBI index increasing less than 1 percent in 1976 and actually decreasing 3 percent in 1977. (This time crime experts were cautious about interpreting figures, remembering the transient 1972 decrease that had subsequently flared up again. The most common reasons proposed for the 1976–77 downturn had nothing to do with LEAA—a small decrease in the population of fifteen- to twenty-four-year-olds, those most likely to be involved in crime; an improved employment outlook; or even the bitterly cold winter of 1977. Local police chiefs did credit some LEAA programs, such as those for community action, for more police and police training, and for locking up career criminals, but they also cited an "aroused citizenry" and stiffer security measures.) In 1978 the FBI crime index was up again by 1 percent and in 1979 up by another 9 percent. For the first half of 1980 the crime index showed a 10-percent increase over the figure for the same period in 1979. Victimization studies begun by LEAA in 1973 indicated, contrary to FBI figures, that the crime rate had stayed more or less constant, *but* victimization studies showed a *much higher crime rate* to begin with.

Crime as an issue may be resurgent in the 1980s. National magazines have again made violent crime the "cover-story issue." In a speech before the American Bar Association in February 1981, Chief Justice Warren Burger called again for stepped-up national efforts:

> Like it or not, today we are approaching the status of an impotent society, whose capability of maintaining elementary security on the streets, in schools and for the homes of our people is in doubt.

> I put to you this question: is a society redeemed if it provides massive safeguards for accused persons including pretrial freedom for most crimes, defense lawyers at public expense, trials, and appeals, retrials and more appeals—almost without end—and yet fails to provide elementary protection for its law-abiding citizens?

> Our search for justice must not be twisted into an endless quest for technical errors, unrelated to guilt or innocence.[52]

Burger called for a "damage control program" for the criminal justice system and proposed trial within weeks of arrest, a limit of appellate review to "genuine claims of miscarriage of justice and not a quest for error," and the rehabilitation of prisons. Funding of federal, state, and local police has "failed to keep them in balance with double-digit crime inflation," he said.

As this book went to press, the initial response of the Reagan administration was cautious. Attorney General William Smith said in his nomination hearings that crime in the streets would be his department's top priority, and he did set up an eight-person blue-ribbon task force on violent crime. But the Justice Department emphasized that federal leadership against crime must involve better ideas rather than more federal money. In any case, as before, the task force should serve to delay the immediate need for taking action.

In an attempt to counterbalance what it considers to be the Supreme Court's emphasis on the rights of defendants, the Reagan White House is considering a presidential commission of victims of crime. Legislation benefiting victims has been introduced by Sen. Paul Laxalt (R-Nev.), who was chairman of Reagan's campaign. Other participants in reexamining the federal role in combatting street crime can be expected, such as senior White House aide Edwin Meese, III, a former California prosecutor, Donald Santarelli, a former LEAA administrator who advised Reagan's transition team, and Sen. Strom Thurmond, powerful chairman of the Judiciary Committee.

Reagan's aides have made it plain they do not want another LEAA. LEAA, vulnerable and lambasted on every front, became, in the words of one congressional staffer, "like the turtle in our backyard when we were little; we picked it up so many times it finally died." But the threat of violent crime remains frighteningly ever present in the lives of many Americans, and the pressure on the national government to act will doubtless continue to build.

EIGHT

What Went Wrong?

PUTTING THE Safe Streets Act on the books did little to make America's streets safe. Crime remains a severe problem despite all of LEAA's efforts. After twelve years, the criminal justice system was still fragmented, and statewide planning just hadn't worked out. What went wrong?

An answer is found in the frustrated and despairing words of this state planner:

> Neither we nor the federal government know what to do, or know where to begin. We are trying so many things, so many experiments and studies, but *no one really knows what works*. There is just such a massive problem, that it's too big for any one effort, and it's too hard to control things in order to measure the impact of anything. A lot of what is being done now by LEAA is surely wasted. The biggest effort in the beginning was just to get the money out into the field. It is as if the people at the top in Washington held an amoral attitude about program standards—they just wanted to get the money out there into the hands of the police.[1]

Helping states reduce crime was simply a tremendously difficult, forbiddingly complex undertaking. But, *granting the enormity of the task*, why didn't the nearly $8 billion LEAA spent produce *more* results?

From the beginning, the war on crime was compromised by legislative restrictions, structural contraints, and a reluctance on the part of state and local governments to assume full responsibility for program planning and evaluation. Time and again, for instance, LEAA had to mediate between competing local interests and adjudicate between states and cities and among police, courts, corrections, and juvenile and community programs. And with only its ambiguous statutory mandate to consult, LEAA found itself merely servicing local interests, not actively scrutinizing, prodding, and persuading them. But a new federal initiative *always* suffers birth pangs. New programs *always* encounter bureaucratic resistance. Why didn't LEAA, Congress, or the president provide the *leadership needed to make the war on crime work*?

But *would* presidential or congressional leadership have made the difference?

The fatal flaw of the war on crime was that the role of the national government in fighting street crime was never clearly or satisfactorily defined. The crime issue had been nationalized in presidential elections, but when it got down to actually deciding what to do, policymakers kept rediscovering that crime remained a distinctly local matter. LEAA and the block grant were the offspring of congressional compromise on sticky questions of federalism, but compromise did not really resolve the issue: states continued to want more discretion over block grants, Congress continued to want more accountability over national funds, and LEAA was caught in the middle. Arguments over what strings should be attached to national monies continued to obscure the need for systemwide planning and substantive program evaluation. When Congress finally eliminated LEAA from the national budget, policymakers remembered they had always had doubts about a national role in fighting street crime.

Did the budget execution of LEAA mean that the national government was abdicating leadership or just getting out of an area where it never should have been to begin with, or were policymakers—and the public—just cutting their losses, making a strategic retreat in the war on crime? Did the end of the war on crime represent a failure of will or a failure of American ingenuity? What was it about our system that made it so hard to wage a national war on crime? Have we learned enough to do better next time? *Should* there in fact *be* national anticrime assistance?

Four elements—goals, leadership, planning, and evaluation—that frustrated successful implementation of the war on crime are key to a national role in helping to fight crime in the streets.

INCONSISTENT OBJECTIVES

The primary goal of the original Safe Streets legislation was to *reduce crime*. But another goal, *decentralizing authority*, was inherent in Congress's decision to use the block grant mechanism. These two goals fueled a constant tension in the implementation of the war on crime. A persisting dilemma in LEAA was whether to let the states decide their own priorities and design their own projects or whether to make sure that money was being well spent, to take the initiative in prodding the archaic criminal justice system to change—in short, whether and how to provide leadership.

The 1968 act cited as its purposes "to assist State and local governments in reducing the incidence of crime, to increase the effectiveness, fairness, and co-ordination of law enforcement and criminal justice at all levels of government." Public protection and equipment and training for police were mentioned prominently. But in 1968, despite recommendations by the president's crime commission and despite Ramsey Clark's call for innovation, exactly what it meant to *improve and coordinate the criminal justice system* was not well defined and consisted primarily of the notion of statewide planning.

In its first few years, LEAA had a hard time just getting state plans in, reviewing them, and getting grant monies through to the local grantees. Getting the money out became the immediate objective. One police chief said LEAA "tried to pump massive amounts of money into the criminal justice system without having any adequate benchmarks against which to assess programs and their effectiveness. The people running LEAA have never had any clear focus about what they should be doing—no idea of how the criminal justice system must function as a whole."[2] No matter that the state planning agencies were more concerned with meeting changing yearly guidelines than with long-range planning or coordination. No matter that state officials, not ready to assume responsibility for change, allowed federal money to reinforce an already antiquated law enforcement system. No matter that one state after another turned the program into a pork-barrel operation, distributing funds to the loudest interest groups. At least state planning agencies were on the books, state plans were coming in, and money was going out.

When the first early rush of national funds did nothing to reduce crime, then the only positive accomplishment LEAA could claim was the amorphous hope that statewide planning was somehow improving the criminal justice system. System improvement was harder to quantify than crime reduction (especially if one discounted crime reduction as a standard by which to judge progress!), but it was easier to claim results with. LEAA's clientele—police, judges, corrections officials, and juvenile processors—proclaimed loudly that the money they received was useful (even if they couldn't reduce crime).

Administrator Richard Velde emphasized this point of view: "LEAA should not be held responsible for crime reduction objectives. . . . The LEAA is clearly only responsible for system improvement."[3] By the mid-seventies, system improvement had replaced crime reduction as a goal. By the same token, the crime issue was fading, and the political punch of LEAA as a crime-reduction agency was gone. By the late seventies some LEAA officials even found themselves in the curious position of protesting that crime reduction was *indeed* a function of LEAA.[4]

The other major goal of the original Safe Streets Act of 1968 was *decentralizing authority*. Republicans believed in self-regulation and in helping the states, and southerners particularly wanted to avoid national intervention. The New Federalism philosophy was to award national money with as few strings attached as possible, thereby strengthening the states and criminal justice agencies. LEAA was to "set the very broadest parameters for the states to operate within. . . ."

But for LEAA's day-to-day business of reviewing grant applications and setting guidelines, the idea of decentralizing authority was a handicap. Under this philosophy, no one really knew where the money went or what the substantive quality or the effectiveness of LEAA programs was. Concentrating on its role as money processor, LEAA did not insist on tough standards, did not provide badly needed technical advice, and was too slow to think about evaluation. The National Advisory Commission on Criminal Justice Standards and Goals (1971–73) highlighted LEAA's problems—imprecise goals, lack of data and evaluation, and planning focused only on LEAA funds—but its recommendations were never imposed on either LEAA or the states.

To make matters worse, the personal philosophies of different administrators flip-flopped between the two goals of reducing crime and decentralizing authority. Under Jerris Leonard, LEAA's role was to help reduce crime. Under Donald Santarelli, LEAA was to encourage reform, innovation, and coordination. Under Pete Velde, chief responsibility was to be passed to the states and cities, and LEAA eventually was to work itself out of a job.

Left on its own, without presidential direction, LEAA evolved the habit of never vetoing state plans but instead negotiating "special conditions" with states that failed to meet guidelines. Even LEAA officials admitted that some very bad plans were approved. Evaluation was nonexistent—LEAA didn't even require states to gather the data base to do their own evaluations. In retrospect, an early administrator offered this classic perspective:

There have been almost no directions or goals established for LEAA. Further there has been no attempt to measure what LEAA does. And indeed, most shocking of all, there is not even a knowledge of what

LEAA funds are being spent on. Is this a situation Congress would tolerate elsewhere? If the Office of Education could not tell Congress how the public's money is being spent, would Congress continue to increase each year the appropriations? I doubt it.[5]

Congress wasn't very helpful in clarifying LEAA's goals. "Creeping categorization," first for police equipment and riot control, then for high-impact cities, then for corrections, then for juvenile justice, then for courts and community programs, only added to the confusion. Further, the rules and regulations designed to emphasize these various areas of the criminal justice system were plastered all over the legislation until the statutes looked like a child who has pasted himself over with a box of Band-Aids. Matching ratios, percentages of total appropriations, discretionary programs, separate appropriations bills, and the so-oft-repeated injunction "*state plans shall take* [your choice] *adequately into account*" all had to be sorted through before priorities could be discerned.

LEAA guidelines, reflecting these cascading congressional objectives, grew more complex. Red tape burgeoned. States and cities howled in protest. Again LEAA was caught in the middle. As one critical congressman said, you can't have it both ways: "On the one hand Congress chided LEAA for not maintaining strict enough controls. On the other, it rebuked LEAA for not distributing large sums of money to the states more rapidly. But it is obvious the Congress cannot have project-by-project control and also unrestricted fund distribution."[6]

Finally going another step toward decentralizing authority, the 1979 Justice System Improvement Act introduced formula grants. Under formula grants all states and large cities and counties were *entitled* to a share of money determined by a complicated set of formulas. But as an alternative to the troublesome block grant, formula grants were just a rose by another name. Instead of state planning agencies, each state was still required to have a criminal justice council to analyze the state's problems, set priorities, write a three-year statewide application, and review subgrant applications from cities and counties. Although LEAA did not have to approve state applications, the real kicker was that twenty-three specific categories for spending were spelled out in the new legislation. Congress was consistent in its inability to cut LEAA's apron strings completely. Moreover, until the very end, there still were expectations that LEAA could play a leadership role. When Senator Kennedy introduced the Justice System Improvement Act in 1978, he argued:

Despite past LEAA failures I do not believe that we should abandon the potential for leadership that the Federal Law Enforcement Assistance program holds. . . . rather than simply throwing up our hands about the Nation's crime problem and saying—like we do about the weather —while we care, there is not much that we can do, we must reshape and restructure LEAA to fulfill the country's objectives and expectations.[7]

Throughout, the same ambiguity—how to exert policy direction on a national level yet leave discretion to the states and cities—persisted.

Twelve years' worth of confused goals exacted a heavy toll on the national war on crime, debilitating the effectiveness and leadership of LEAA, sapping the will and capacity of the national government to shape anticrime policy. In some respects the 1979 legislation went some distance toward redefining the goals of the war on crime. It separated system support (LEAA-managed formula grants) from system stimulation (NIJ-sponsored research) and from system analysis (BJS-collected statistics)—a healthy delineation of function. The new statistics-gathering bureau was a vitally needed and wisely independent entity.

A QUESTION OF LEADERSHIP?

While Congress criticized, categorized, and reauthorized, presidents, from Johnson to Reagan, as well as their attorneys general, by and large left LEAA alone—very alone. The lack of policy attention from above not only thrust upon LEAA the responsibility for the day-to-day interpretation of conflicting goals but handicapped LEAA by long delays and rapid turnover in the agency's leadership positions. Moreover, LEAA administrators alternately emphasized different priorities: one year it might be hardware, the next innovation; one year crime control, the next simplifying guidelines; one year regionalization, the next auditing by the Washington office. A veteran LEAA official described the agency's yearning for leadership: "LEAA has suffered from a lack of consistency and from a programmatic problem—they do not view the future here. But the main lack has been a person with authority and respect, a first rate criminologist, like Dr. X of the National Institute of Health or the Food and Drug Administration. But LEAA has never commanded that type of respect from Congress or the White House."[8] Personnel experts in the Department of Justice told us LEAA's personnel policies had been "a disaster area."

The history of LEAA's leadership reveals a repeated pattern of vacancies, confusion, and ineffectiveness.

In 1967 the Johnson administration had originally proposed a single director for law enforcement and criminal justice assistance, but Senator McClellan rejected the idea of LEAA's being under the complete or even indirect authority of the then-incumbent attorney general. Aside from personal animus towards Ramsey Clark, the argument that persuaded Congress was that it would be dangerous to vest in one person the power over a potentially multi-billion-dollar operation. McClellan won, and the result was a troika of administrators, no more than two of the same political party. The troika was interpreted by many, including the first administrators, to mean that policy and administrative decisions required unanimity. But, as one of the first associate administrators warned, the troika arrangement was unwieldy, "a crude attempt at political accommodation that simply doesn't work out in practice."[9]

Johnson's nominees reflected his inclination to take an activist role: New York police commissioner Patrick Murphy, who had helped formulate and direct LEAA's precursor, OLEA, and had a reputation in police circles as a liberal; Wesley Pomeroy, a sheriff from California; and Ralph Siu, an operations research specialist from the Department of Defense. These nominations were made at the very end of Johnson's lame-duck presidency and were blocked by Senator McClellan. The administrators were given recess appointments after the Senate adjourned, but it was expected that Nixon would replace them with his own appointees.

In his first few months in office, Nixon appointed as administrator Charles Rogovin, who had been public defender and then district attorney in Philadelphia. Rogovin described himself as a "Democrat" and as a "cop's lawyer." Richard Velde, the son of a conservative Illinois congressman and Senator Hruska's chief aide on the 1968 Safe Streets Act, was named associate administrator. Friction between the two men was felt immediately and only increased when the second associate administrator, Clarence Coster, a hardware-oriented, conservative former police chief from Bloomington, Minnesota, was appointed at the end of the year. Stalemates arose in which Velde and Coster urged support for police equipment purchases while Rogovin pressed for reform and research. Decisions were delayed or deferred. Substantial time was wasted on bureaucratic minutiae. Administrative procedures developed in a haphazard way. Morale suffered. For example, the development of curricula in police science programs, where LEAA was paying for tuition, was stalled for months because Rogovin could not interest his colleagues. Or certain appointments approved by Rogovin were vetoed by the associate administrators. The associate administrators considered Rogovin too liberal, and Rogovin viewed one of them as reactionary: "He is of a mentality exactly like Louis XIV's!"

Critics said Rogovin lacked administrative talents. Rogovin answered that LEAA's troubles stemmed from the lack of policy direction by the

White House or the attorney general, John Mitchell. Rogovin was convinced that setting policy at the top could have resulted in compliance, that presidential encouragement and willingness at the departmental and agency level to set standards would have made a drastically different program.[10] Instead, John Mitchell's disinterest became policy, and the Nixon administration never genuinely decided where it stood in the midst of contradictory objectives. Rogovin, the odd man out, resigned in June of 1970, citing the impossibility of the troika arrangement. He said later he felt his resignation had been partly successful because it had at least brought the issue of the troika to the fore.

In the 1970 reauthorization hearings, the Advisory Commission on Intergovernmental Relations recommended a single director. Democrats, led by Ramsey Clark and House judiciary chairman Emmanuel Celler, concurred, as they had since 1967. Rogovin testified:

> An agency cannot be managed by three chiefs. Three cannot agree on all matters. From my position as Administrator, I was not permitted to provide policy direction, administrative leadership, or even to settle relatively routine questions of implementation, because of the difficulty of obtaining the approval of the two associates. When I attempted to exercise leadership and my two colleagues disagreed, the agency was stalemated.[11]

But Attorney General Mitchell felt the troika should be kept. Congress temporized, approving a modified troika arrangement, without the unanimity requirement. The administrator would serve as executive head, exercising all administrative and substantive policymaking powers, but he needed the concurrence of at least one associate. (It was not until 1973 that Congress finally abolished the troika, agreeing that "the Administrator shall be the head of the agency. One Deputy Administrator shall be designated . . . for Policy Development. The second Deputy Administrator shall be designated for Administration.")

After Rogovin's resignation, LEAA drifted without an administrator for almost a year. At least one candidate who was offered the job turned it down partly because of the unworkable troika arrangement. Finally, in May 1971, Nixon appointed Jerris Leonard, unsuccessful Republican candidate for the Senate from Wisconsin and former head of John Mitchell's Civil Rights Division in the Department of Justice. Leonard was considered, at least in Nixon circles, a moderate liberal. "They could trust Leonard with this politically troublesome agency. There were attacks of conflict of interest and mismanagement in Alabama and California [in the 1971 Monagen hearings] and the general level of management under Velde and Coster cried out for help. Someone was needed to keep it clean, and Leonard was chosen."[12] Leonard was viewed as a personal friend and protégé of John Mitchell's, and it was rumored he might be in line to become deputy attorney general (if Kleindienst should succeed Mitchell) or even FBI director.

"Let's forget this nonsense about improving the criminal justice system," the new administrator, Leonard, said. "Let's concentrate on crime-specific programs, and we'll find that the criminal justice system will improve at the same time."[13] To reduce crime for the Nixon administration, Leonard instituted the Impact Cities program and crime-specific planning, in which LEAA funds were to be related to specific crimes, such as rape or robbery, rather than to police, courts, or corrections. In line with the Nixon administration's New Federalism, Leonard expanded the number of regional offices and gave them the power to review state plans. According to his theory, the LEAA office in Washington would feed evaluations and goals to the regions and states, and the regions would implement the delivery system and provide technical assistance. Leonard also set up the National Advisory Commission on Criminal Justice Standards and Goals, which helped defuse congressional criticism.

In early 1973, when national attention was focusing on Watergate, Leonard was succeeded by Donald Santarelli, the articulate head of the Criminal Division in Mitchell's Justice Department and the person who had been primarily responsible for the controversial no-knock provision of the D.C. crime bill. Contrary to Leonard, Santarelli said it was time to face the fact that "as a crime reduction agency, LEAA had failed" and that it had been a mistake to "sell" LEAA as such. He claimed LEAA's role should be that of a criminal-justice-improvement agency.[14] He stressed increasing the management effectiveness of the agency, created an office of planning and management, rotated regional administrators, and emphasized citizen participation in anticrime programs instead of hardware development for the police.

During the Watergate period, LEAA's credit within the Justice Department rose, especially in contrast to that of the FBI, which was having its own political problems. LEAA began collecting its own crime statistics, the victimization surveys, in an exploratory way rivaling the FBI crime index. Then in June 1974, at a law enforcement conference in Williamsburg, Virginia, Santarelli said government service had been "cheapened" by Watergate, and he even suggested that President Nixon resign. Santarelli, who was then investigated by the FBI, was himself forced to resign—three months before Nixon departed.

In the closing days of the Nixon administration, when the president was totally preoccupied with the impending likelihood of impeachment, associate administrator Velde was nominated to succeed Santarelli as administrator of LEAA. Velde was one of the few people with a long-term association with LEAA, his familiarity stemming from his work with Hruska on the original 1968 Safe Streets Act. He had a record of favoring hardware and corrections and leaning over backwards to avoid "dictating" to the states. Some sources accused him of regarding the original block grant concept as holy writ and of being too much a creature of Congress. Still, he knew more about LEAA than just about anyone, and he was a valuable ambassador to Congress. Velde had only one deputy administrator, Charles Work, who had been assistant U.S. attorney for Washington, D.C., and a division chief in LEAA. The other deputy administrator slot was left empty for over a year.

But now the hands-off, laissez-faire policy of the new administrator, Velde, was viewed by friends of the deposed administrator, Santarelli, as an abdication of leadership, as letting the agency slip back into the habit of responding to special interests instead of setting policy directions. In his own defense, Velde quoted Congress's intention that LEAA have only a limited role and the constant statutory reminder that the chief responsibility for crime rested with states and localities. Within LEAA factionalism and personality clashes developed. Velde would cite the establishment of task forces, the establishment of an office of juvenile justice, and the rapid processing of state plans as signs of progress. His research director, Gerald M. Caplan, who headed LEAA's National Institute of Law Enforcement and Criminal Justice and had been appointed by Santarelli, would give speeches about "losing the war on crime" and urge LEAA to take the lead in setting standards for sentencing and parole.[15] Velde would come back and cut the budget for some of Caplan's research projects.

In 1976, with the election of Jimmy Carter, Velde resigned and, after a brief spell in private law practice, returned to the Senate Judiciary Committee, there to become minority counsel to Sen. Strom Thurmond. The White House, perhaps secretly desirous of abolishing LEAA, delayed until the following spring, appointing two new deputy administrators, Henry McQuade, an Idaho Supreme Court judge, and Paul Wormeli, who had headed LEAA's SEARCH, a project to computerize criminal case histories. Once more LEAA was left without an administrator, this time for over a year.

Attorney General Griffin Bell tried to get several candidates to take the job, but none of the attractive possibilities wanted to preside over an agency that might soon be severely reorganized or even abolished. Suspended, leaderless, without policy direction, in a long period of uncertainty and transition, the agency suffered serious morale problems.

The Carter White House viewed acting director James Gregg as a solid administrator and was content to let him stay on in an acting capacity for over a year. One LEAA aide described the plight of this caretaking leadership: "One strong point was when James Gregg took over. He really set deadlines, held people accountable, and did the best job conceivable under the circumstances. But you need a strong political leader for LEAA, so if his budget is cut he can raise a ruckus over it."[16] Prophetic words.

Finally, in September of 1978, after hesitating almost two years, President Carter nominated Norval Morris, a University of Chicago law professor and noted authority on criminal justice, to head LEAA. Morris's nomination evoked considerable enthusiasm, and many believed he was just what LEAA needed, a respected expert on criminal justice and the law. But Morris had written widely and forcefully on crime, and in a book he coauthored, *The Honest Politician's Guide to Crime Control*, he had advocated stronger gun control laws and decriminalizing such victimless crimes as gambling, drug abuse, and abortion. When nomination hearings began, the National Rifle Association mounted a vehement attack on him. Senator Thurmond led the charge. "Would you commit LEAA funds," the senator quizzed the professor, "to projects and programs designed to pursue the decriminalization of sex crimes, including research studies and discretionary funds?" The professor tried to explain that LEAA policy would not be the same as his personal philosophy. "But are you not Mr. LEAA?" Thurmond wanted to know.[17] In the final days of the Ninety-fifth Congress, conservative senator Jesse Helms (R-N.C.) threatened to filibuster against Morris on the floor. Morris's nomination never got out of committee, and when Congress reconvened in January 1979, Morris withdrew his name from consideration.

Meanwhile, during this time when LEAA was left without an administrator, Attorney General Bell decided to close the regional offices, thus reversing the attempt by former administrator Leonard to decentralize authority for plan review. Three hundred thirty-five positions of LEAA's staff of 790 were affected, and the move caused a furor of complaints. Former administrator Velde called it "the worst thing that's been done" and predicted it would hurt agency morale and efficiency.[18] One regional administrator pointed out to us that at the same time another domestic federal agency was taking exactly the *opposite* action for exactly the *same* reasons. While LEAA's ten regional offices were being *abolished* as "an essential step toward streamlining delivery of funds by cutting red tape and reducing delays," the Urban Mass Transportation Administration was *setting up* field offices in ten regions in order to "cut costs, red tape and delays in making grants."[19]

In any case, the closing of the regional offices was yet another demoralizing blow for LEAA, scorned and neglected by the administration and hearing daily about its own demise or reorganization in congressional hearings.

At last the position of administrator was filled by Henry Dogin, an associate administrator, who had been New York state planning director and then head of the federal regional office in New York and subsequently with the Drug Enforcement Agency. Not until a year after he was appointed did Dogin get a deputy administrator, and then only one, Homer Broome, the black commissioner of the Los Angeles Police Department, who had served twenty-four years on the police force there. Thus, for just about all of Carter's term, LEAA went without clear or sure leadership.

The 1979 legislation, the Justice System Improvement Act, actually went a step backward, beyond the initial troika arrangement, and provided for *four* administrators and directors, one each for the National Institute of Justice, the Bureau of Justice Statistics, a scaled-down LEAA, and the Office of Justice Assistance, Research, and Statistics. "If one thing was going to be difficult," commented an LEAA aide, "it was the management of the four units, each with its own sign-off. The problem with the troika was stalemate, but now each Administrator has specific independent authority, and decisions will be fragmented and uncoordinated."[20] Other observers suggested that the fragmentation of LEAA into various parts (NIJ, BJS, LEAA, OJARS) was a conscious strategy to weaken the agency. Implicit in the 1979 act was the notion that leadership responsibilities had been removed from the grant-administering LEAA, and given over to the National Institute of Justice; this interpretation was subsequently confirmed by Congress's decision to fund the institute and the Bureau of Justice Statistics (however meagerly) but not LEAA.

A 1979 study concluded that throughout its history, LEAA's administrators offered especially weak leadership:

> Although LEAA was designed originally to develop some leadership to improve criminal justice delivery systems in the United States, its directors have perceived that mission too weakly. Instead of leader and initiator, the agency has consistently followed the whims and wishes of a limited constituency, the police.[21]

But it is not surprising that LEAA could not demonstrate sustained leadership within the criminal justice field, could not bring about a coordinated systemwide perspective, when its home offices were guided so sporadically. To say that LEAA was handicapped by the changing format, the rapid succession, and repeated vacancies in its top administration is to understate the matter. Continued congressional compromise and presidential neglect helped make LEAA's struggle to provide leadership an uphill fight all the way.

THE MYTH OF COMPREHENSIVE STATE PLANNING

The lever upon which the block grant hinged was the comprehensive state plan. In theory, the chance to get more funds and the necessity of meeting LEAA guidelines was supposed to prod states to "define, develop, and coordinate programs to improve law enforcement." The state plan was the point at which the national carrot (action grants) and stick (LEAA guidelines) were to be translated into results.

State planning agencies (SPAS) were supposed to do more than just serve as a conduit for funds, more than just decide on projects submitted by local police departments or sheriff's offices, more than just check up on whether certain percentages of funds were passed through to the cities and to the courts. The statutory language declared that state plans should

> incorporate innovations and advanced techniques and contain a comprehensive outline of priorities for the improvement and coordination of all aspects of law enforcement . . . including descriptions of: (A) general needs and problems; (B) existing systems; (C) available resources; (D) organizational systems and administrative machinery for implementing the plan; (E) the direction, scope, and general types of improvements to be made in the future.[22]

This was a large helping of responsibility for the fledgling state planning agencies. Comprehensive state planning was key.

Before 1968, few states had taken the initiative to institute the reforms proposed by either the 1931 Wickersham Commission or the 1967 president's crime commission. States had been offered $25,000 by the early 1965 OLEA act to form state planning commissions, but only twenty-seven had actually done so. At a planning conference in 1966, Deputy Attorney General Ramsey Clark deplored the caliber of people the governors sent: "Very few governors bothered to pick anybody who had any criminal justice or administrative experience, and most who came were political functionaries."[23] Professor Norval Morris recalled a similarly disappointing experience when he was invited to the Justice Department in 1968 to introduce recommendations of the president's crime commission to representatives of cities and states. After his ideas had "fallen thunderously flat on their face," Morris inquired why. "They assured me that federal monies would come and would be used to take the pressure off the maintenance of their current systems, possibly to make them a bit more efficient, but would certainly not be used for the types of experimental ideas I seemed to be talking about."[24] Many governors were reluctant to accept the political risks they foresaw accompanying federal intervention. Some southern states still wanted to avoid federal civil rights laws and police forces dominated by blacks. Although in the past a number of grant-in-aid programs had required planning, there were few models for a system as complex and fragmented as criminal justice.[25] There was as yet no large body of criminal justice planners to staff the new state planning agencies.

Congress had stipulated that the state planning agencies be representative of law enforcement agencies and units of local government. (In later amendments, Congress also included the judiciary, juvenile justice agencies, community organizations, and citizens.) In practice, however, it proved difficult to recruit and keep talented planners, especially when the newcomers discovered the ambiguity and politics involved. "There are some good people around, who do know what to do," pointed out an LEAA official. "A lot of these are former cops, former FBI agents, who know the deficiencies of the system. Even a lot of police chiefs now know that the 'system' doesn't function as a system, and that there is a need for something more than just more police."[26] But, observed another LEAA aide, "for the most part, these people [state planners] were liberal, idealistic, modern, sold on police-community relations stuff, and just the types who would be chewed up by the 'Mafia' of local police chiefs. They soon learned they would be able to have far less leverage in the state than they expected. So we have had a large turnover at the state level."[27] One frustrated SPA staffer recalled that her state's first plan was "absolutely ridiculous" and complained that there was no model, needed statistics were not available, staff turnover was great, and there were too many lawyers—"cool people"—trying to pioneer new ideas but earning instead distrust and suspicion. "Our biggest lesson," she concluded, "was learning that you were working within the system—a system that's already there."[28]

State planning agencies were first of all confronted with the futility of reform efforts that weren't wanted by local officials. Locals tended to withhold participation until they were convinced that programs proposed by state officials would not affect *their* autonomy. State planners were thus unable to assume the initiative on many important issues—efficiency of police operations, provision of equal justice, and changes in internal procedures to improve administration. An Illinois police chief, for example, bluntly explained that his county was reluctant to accept national funds, fearing national domination and regulations. In Georgia, an attempt to replace local jails with regional, multicounty ones failed because every sheriff wanted his own jail—it gave him status, provided free labor for certain projects, and perhaps brought in extra income if his wife cooked for the inmates. Preserving autonomy was even more important than obtaining additional funds from LEAA. In another state, a planning staffer complained bitterly:

> There are judges in this state that come out of the Salem witch hunt days, and several similar police chiefs. If a police chief doesn't want a training program, you can't do anything about it. In one city where we are trying to experiment with a Youth Resources Bureau, the director is an ass, a bigot—and highly connected politically. So it's a terrible waste of LEAA money there.[29]

Some local agencies did not apply for LEAA money because they felt they were "less politically favored" and therefore deliberately excluded. Commenting on the inability of the state planning agency to meet his needs, a circuit court judge complained, "It appears to me the designation 'Indiana Criminal Justice Planning' is a misnomer. I don't know how you 'plan' justice. And, so far as I have read, it does not seem the agency has anything to offer judicial administration." A local prosecutor felt there was too much politics in the whole process:

> My primary reason for not applying relates to my initial and continuing complaint about the Indiana Criminal Justice Planning Agency —a complete lack of communication between the agency and the hinterlands. I personally feel the agency is concerned with doing good where political benefits can be derived—not where justice can be better served.

Others were concerned that agencies not duplicate services and expressed reservations about continuing the costs of programs once those programs were begun.

Inability to raise matching funds was offered by some as an excuse but not considered a major limitation by most. Officials in smaller cities and counties tended more often to cite this reason for not applying. This response from the mayor of a town of seventy-five hundred was typical:

> I personally feel the larger cities are dominating these funds and are in a better position with personnel to file for these funds and seem to have at their disposal an endless source of matching funds available.... I am on the regional board, and I don't see where these cities can have this kind of money at their disposal. . . . We operate on a very close and honest budget. . . .

But one regional administrator felt that any agency, if it really wanted to, could raise the matching funds. In his dealings with local officials, he said, they were not required to put up cash: for training programs, public education, and acquisition of equipment, local agencies could use personnel *time* or even previously acquired *equipment* as the in-kind match. One officer in a large, urban police department was able to convince his city council to appropriate matching funds by showing them that the city could earn ten dollars for every one dollar it spent; his department realized a 1,000-percent return on its investment in just one year!

Well-organized police and prosecutors fought for the first available action funds. Lacking natural constituencies and lobbying experience, courts and corrections were unable to compete significantly at first. State planning agencies quickly became involved in bargaining with police departments and sheriffs. Several experienced planners, interviewed in the early 1970s, told of being under constant pressure from local agencies, especially police departments, for more funds for hardware and less red tape from Washington. One state director, whose state tried to prohibit massive purchases of hardware, commented later, "We made a mistake to be so against hardware in the first two years. The police want it and can use it, and it's the price you pay to get them to work with you." Frequently planners had to *trade equipment for credibility*: "If you're able to give radios and equipment, you can get some community relations and in-service training," observed a savvy police chief.[30]

Even while they were getting the lion's share of the early (and, to be fair, much smaller) LEAA budgets, police wanted and felt they needed more. "I don't quarrel with LEAA, but I wish we were getting more of it. We need it and we are told by equipment companies that it can be spent for more equipment. We need salaries and overtime for training; we need new and more cars; we especially need a new police headquarters," was a typical police chief's attitude in 1971.[31] An observer in another state described the bargaining process this way:

A small community, with five men on the police force, would want five cars, but after questioning could usually be talked down to two or three cars. Or a small force would order 20 gas masks, 20 bullet-proof vests, 20 of everything—get it while the getting is good! Of course, they used the equipment—but not as much as they got.[32]

Police forces continued to press for more. In 1978, in reaction to past congressional earmarking for other parts of the criminal justice system, the International Association of Chiefs of Police held that LEAA had become "bureaucratic and insensitive" and "especially in recent years has not attended to the needs and goals of police agencies."[33]

In many communities planners became embroiled in heated clashes with chiefs of police. Real planning, some planners admitted privately, was impossible because of the immediate political pressures on governors to yield the newly received funds to the police. Moreover, police frequently enjoyed a special relationship with city councils and mayors. The Massachusetts planning agency, which had a reputation for having an idealistic, think-tank mentality, had particular trouble with the police. At one point the state cut off aid to the planning agency partly because the Boston police chief did not get along with the planners. The Boston office, according to one account, was "a horrible scene." Imagine the frustration of the planner who told one of us in 1971, "You're like a professional psychiatrist to whom I can spell out all my problems. Morale here is zero and I'm in the process of giving up. We've no friends any place, no political base, no power. The mayor views his relationship with us only as a source of funds."[34]

Compared to the friendless, novice planning agencies, police were organized, protected by grandfather clauses, vocal, and visible. As the Advisory Commission of Intergovernmental Relations noted in a helpful study of LEAA,

> While elected and criminal justice officials appear to be willing to meet together, discuss common problems, identify ways of addressing them and coordinate their activities, when the issue of "who gets how much?" is raised, the Safe Streets alliance often breaks down. Those who are best organized and most skilled in the art of grantsmanship have tended to prevail at the state level. . . .[35]

For decades, professional interests in law enforcement have been represented by such lobbying groups as the International Association of Chiefs of Police, the National College of District Attorneys, and the American Correctional Association. Indeed, many of these lobbying groups have been generously favored themselves with LEAA grants; this is a questionable practice, to say the least.[36] Only in 1974 did state planners organize, and since then they have lobbied actively for their planning agencies, the block grant approach, less federal domination, and more funds.

Without a power base of their own, state planning agencies soon found themselves in the business of keeping people happy rather than getting a reform job done. Adaptation and compromise became the first priority in order for the state planning agencies themselves to survive. Planning agencies became involved in not only bargaining with the police but conflicts among governors, state legislators, and mayors. Thousands of local jurisdictions were uncomfortable with planning in general and with the embryonic planning agencies in particular. Many local officials doubted that planning served any useful purpose and were openly hostile to state planners' requests for information. In the words of one state planning director, "Planning was a burden that they would just as soon contract out to an outside firm." Local officials who had applied for grants under both OLEA (categorical grants) and LEAA (block grants) generally saw little difference in administrative simplicity. In some cases it was easier to go directly to Washington. Many county agencies seemed especially resistant to outside influence. Block grants were viewed by many locals as nothing more or less than state-dominated categorical programs. They were right. The national policymakers who promulgated the block grant did want to decentralize grant-in-aid authority to the states. Many cities viewed the state planning agencies as threats to their traditional relationships with the federal executive bureaucracies.

Many large cities thought they were not receiving an adequate share of funds since they had the highest crime rates within their states. Although this may have been true, the cities' complaints also had to do with the political consequences of state use of funds. In 1972, for example, the Democratic Chicago/Cook County Criminal Justice Planning Region prepared a report showing that its allocation from the Republican Illinois Law Enforcement Commission had been less than what they would have received if the allocation were based on either the FBI crime index, the violent crime rate, or the population of the county. In response, the state agency pointed out that the Chicago/Cook County figures did not include the indirect support of state corrections and courts, which must process a disproportionate share of Cook County residents. This argument was only one example of the continuing series of city-state controversies. An LEAA aide recalled the maneuverings of the state houses:

> Many governors have called me trying to learn how they could regionalize funds near the central cities—so they could keep the money away from big cities . . . sometimes because they are at odds with big city mayors, sometimes because of differences in parties. Later, of course, many of the governors claim hypocritically that they have tried to get the money to high crime areas—but I can remind them otherwise.[37]

A congressional relations aide for LEAA said half of his business consisted of congressional calls for favors: " 'How can I get LEAA money

for my constituents?' We tell them to go to their State Planning
Agencies."[38] Not surprisingly, the state planning agencies became
viewed as highly political.

Political rivalries at the local level often delayed innovative, and
therefore controversial, projects. Thus, a city official said:

> We are presently preparing a rather ambitious application for funding
> a multicounty regional detention and treatment facility. The delay is
> due to the difficulty of getting the county commissioners to turn over
> land and buildings for the project. If the commissioners reject our
> request, we will then apply to the Criminal Justice Agency for Youth
> Services.

In this case, after months of delay, the application was rejected, and
the local official was forced to apply for funds from a different federal program. A sheriff from a large, industrialized, northern county
complained:

> Members of the [substate] regional board, from the larger metropoli-
> tan area, are unduly critical of the smaller agencies trying to secure
> funds and, in their pompous attempts to interrogate agents of the
> applying governmental unit, completely overlook the reason for their
> being there. I have no quarrel with the regional director, but I find
> certain members of the board lacking in the ability to communicate
> with "little people."

The sheriff had already received two small grants but had recently
been asked by the regional board to resubmit two other grant proposals; he disliked being turned down, whatever the reason. A city
court judge expressed his frustration over delays in his pet project:

> I know what is needed here, but no one has consulted with me on
> how a grant may be obtained for these purposes. They [the substate
> regional office] know who I am but have not taken the time to discuss
> any of the problems we have with me.

The judge had tried to establish a live-in alcoholic rehabilitation center, but the state planning agency, which happened to be of the political party opposite to the judge's, would fund only nonresident centers.

State planning agencies not only became enmeshed in local politics,
but they had to plow through a morass of red tape imposed by the
Washington offices of LEAA. Much of the problem began with bad tim-
ing. The Safe Streets Act of 1968 was passed in June, but it was October before LEAA administrators were named and November before the
first guidelines for planning and action grants were issued, leaving the

new planning agencies only about half a year to prepare their first comprehensive plans. Each year thereafter, as guidelines were refined and changed, partly because of the increasing sophistication of the LEAA Washington office, the creeping categorization imposed by Congress, and other federal laws, deadlines for plans continued to be unrealistically short. In some years, plans were due as little as three months after new guidelines were issued.

LEAA guidelines dealt primarily with procedural requirements—administrative practices and financial control—and LEAA tended to emphasize technical compliance, i.e., making sure the right amount of money went to each pot. State planning agencies were encouraged to divide their block grants into a number of standard functional categories, set up by LEAA; this procedure allowed for accounting of funds to Congress but made for superficial shopping lists of programs instead of a long-range analysis of needs. Guidelines largely ignored criteria for comprehensiveness, program effectiveness, or standardization across the states. (Only in later years did guidelines deal at all with standards and evaluation, and only in 1978 was the importance of a data *base* beginning to be recognized.)

Under all these pressures, state planning agencies, not surprisingly, took the path of least resistance. Planning gradually became viewed as nothing more than an annual ritual to trigger funds, an intricate labyrinth of bureaucratic compliance exercises that had to be traversed in order to get the money. No one planned for more than the 4 or 5 percent of the state's criminal justice budget that was contributed by LEAA. Instead of grants' being based on the seriousness of the crime problem, funds were distributed—and dissipated—in a broad geographical area. Because states were free to redirect funds that were not expended in planned categories—this policy was sanctioned by LEAA "in recognition of the need for maximum flexibility"—there was frequently little articulation between *planned* allocations and *actual* dollar distribution. State plans were often telephone-book length, hard to read, confused, and devoid of usable information.

"Much of what you need to know is difficult to understand in these plans," observed one informant. He gave the example of a state planning agency in Kentucky where the director had a major problem because local towns did not keep records. "It's a great victory if you can get a small town just to keep some records. In a big city change and progress may be on a different scale."[39] An LEAA aide commented on occasional glaring inadequacies:

I suspect not more than a few states have done an adequate job, for example, New York, Illinois, Texas, and Michigan, and I think Massachusetts, too. Heck, New York always has more lawyers in the General Counsel's office of the SPA than we do here. Generally the poor states and the small states and the corrupt states—and where you have all three of these aspects—are the worst. Take Nevada—we had to suggest to them that they have an organized crime component in their plan. They said that thought hadn't occurred to them—can you imagine![40]

And a Justice Department official pointed out other inconsistencies, such as a Vermont plan that spent 320 pages responding to the drug situation whereas the New York state plan had only one page! In the case of the New York plan, the LEAA plan review office even wanted the names of the organized-crime families before they would approve it!

Although statutorily empowered to do so, LEAA never once rejected a state plan as inadequate. There were too many political pressures to get the money out. Also, in a catch-22, the states with the poorest plans were also those most desperately in need of federal assistance. If a state plan did not comply with LEAA guidelines, LEAA would negotiate with the state; if negotiations failed, LEAA still sent out the money but on "special conditions" that the state would correct the deficiencies in its plan in a certain period of time. One senior LEAA official put it this way:

Some states like Alabama, Florida, California, Maryland up to recently, North Dakota, Nevada, and Arizona just haven't followed the intent, and we have been too lenient with them with this nonsense about "special conditions." We really haven't followed the law in that we let the states get around us on this comprehensive plan stuff. One Northeast state came in and said they would comply with our corrections guidelines after we approved their plans with "special conditions" last year—and this year they came back and still haven't done much or even come close.[41]

An occasional few plans were notably successful. Illinois, for example, was considered by some to be the best in 1971:

They have action programs that are very well worked out at the state level. They have done some things on the state-wide system, such as put in a second radio in police cars throughout the state so they can communicate across jurisdictions. They have set up about 1500 innovative programs. They have developed corrections systems improvements. They have developed review processes and are already able to report on implementation.[42]

In the 1978 reauthorization hearings, state planners said that in the "good states," planning *was* impacting the total criminal justice budget, not just the 4 or 5 percent contributed by LEAA. The planners claimed that in some jurisdictions, planning was performing five important functions: providing information about the operation of the criminal justice system, collecting and analyzing crime data, analyzing the budget, measuring productivity and cost effectiveness, and influencing elected officials to "think system."

But in general the quality of state plans was frustrating to LEAA. In 1976 one LEAA official told us, "State planning is a demonstrated failure. Most state planners have no influence." Two years later another LEAA aide called expectations of comprehensive statewide planning "ludicrous," observing that "the federal response to criminal justice problems is structurally deficient. It is *absolutely impossible* for a state level agency to plan for criminal justice."[43] According to Richard Velde, the hands-off LEAA administrator from 1975 to 1977, state plans tended to fall into four categories: reasonably good, like New York and Georgia; a few that waxed "hot and cold," like California and Delaware; a few that were very good, like Massachusetts, Colorado, and Michigan; and those that were terrible, like Tennessee and New Mexico. Already in the mid-seventies some LEAA people were talking about abolishing state planning and substituting federal standards; this change materialized in the 1979 Justice Systems Improvement Act. Real comprehensive state planning was an acknowledged failure.

The 1979 act, though substituting a three-year application for the yearly comprehensive plan and replacing state planning agencies with criminal justice councils, still talked about many of the same functions that planning was expected to accomplish: analyzing the criminal justice problems within the state, establishing priorities, preparing a comprehensive state application, reviewing and coordinating local applications, developing new and improved approaches to criminal justice, fund accounting, auditing, and evaluation. But whether it's called priority setting or system coordination, any form of planning faces formidable obstacles. In a democracy, planning is extremely difficult because diverse interests do not agree about the specific terms of long-range objectives. This was particularly true for Safe Streets programs. In addition, the confusion of administrative and planning roles, the lack of a power base for the state planning agencies, the tremendous political infighting among different levels of government, the detailed procedural guidelines from Washington, and the lack of a data base about the crime problem all served to frustrate planning for safe

streets. Americans are not sure they want to yield to their government
the right to control their future, and that, after all, is what planning
is really about.

PROGRAM EVALUATION

> We couch our studies so as not to be too harsh, but the data are
> very bad. That's one of the things you learn to do around here when
> you work for these outfits—you sort of sink to their level.[44]

> When Thomas Edison . . . was asked about his efforts on the electric
> light bulb, and what kind of progress he was making, he said, "I know
> 3,000 materials that will not work as a filament. . . ."[45]

One of the most frustrating problems of the national war on crime
was the lack of standards and criteria with which to evaluate the success or failure of LEAA-sponsored programs. Baseline data have not been
available and are just beginning to be collected. The New Federalism
philosophy meant cities and states were to do their own evaluation;
LEAA did not enforce the collection of evaluation data or apply standards across the states. All too often, localities were not even able to
define what was actually happening with LEAA money, how far LEAA-
sponsored programs were implemented, or even exactly what procedures had been used *before* LEAA programs were started. One respected
policy analyst, Eleanor Chelimsky, noted that when her firm tried to
evaluate the $160 million High Impact Anti-Crime Program (begun
in 1972 and in trouble by 1974), there were so few data available and
what limited data were available were so unconfirmed that her study
was forced to concentrate on *process* rather than *outcome*, i.e., whether
the money was administered well, *not* whether it helped to reduce
crime.[46] Some researchers believe the final verdict on LEAA is that most
programs cannot be meaningfully or vigorously evaluated because of
lack of data.

Evaluation was an afterthought to the organizational launching of
the federal war on crime and seemed always to be started too late.
LEAA's ambiguous goals made it easy to confuse what exactly evaluation should consist of: *describing the state of the project* or *assessing
its outcome*. For example, in 1972, LEAA's chief auditor explained *his*
obligations by giving this example: concerning a training grant for
police, he could properly ask whether the money was spent for the
stated purpose and how many officers completed training and stayed
in the police force, but he could not ask whether the training was useful or what the opportunity costs were of using money for this and

not something else.[47] Criminologists Norval Morris and Gordon Hawkins offered this lament: "Although something labeled 'evaluation' is done, the product of that process is a bizarre blend of encomiastic description, selected factual information, and unsubstantiated assertion, which has the objectivity of a sales brochure."[48]

For evaluation to be successful, funds and protocol for it must be built into the initial plan of a program. Only then can *before* and *after* be compared. But consider, for example, the impossibility of evaluation in this typical local station house: "The statistics are all inaccurate. We haven't even turned any in this year because the old lady who served as our secretary and took care of the books retired. But no one ever paid any attention to serious record keeping anyway." Instead of the experimental, hypothesis-testing perspective needed in evaluation, most block grant participants simply wanted to get the most for their towns or police forces, advocated their own pet projects, or were concerned only with the efficient distribution of funds.

Much of the failure to evaluate was because of neglect on the part of LEAA. From the first, eager to get the money flowing, LEAA refrained from sanctioning states for poor plans and avoided setting national standards for plans. Only when facing up to severe congressional criticism in 1972 did LEAA make the embarrassing discovery that the Washington office itself had no information on the impact of programs it was sponsoring. In response, LEAA administrator Leonard beefed up LEAA's auditors. But Leonard himself was a staunch New Federalist, and his audits were more concerned with *where* the money went than *how well* it was spent.

A highly critical series of reports from the General Accounting Office again stressed the continuing inadequacy of evaluation, and in the 1973 amendments, Congress stipulated that the National Institute for Law Enforcement and Criminal Justice (LEAA's research arm) undertake evaluation of LEAA programs. In response, institute director Gerald Caplan (under LEAA administrator Santarelli) set up the Office of Evaluation to do evaluation for the whole of LEAA. But the institute was already overburdened with mandates—to run training programs, to disseminate information, to provide technical assistance to state planning agencies, in addition to sponsoring research on the causes of crime and developing new techniques to fight crime—and was already handicapped by pressures for action-oriented research products and instant solutions, its relatively small budget, and its lack of independent budget authority. With the addition of evaluation functions, the institute was being asked to carry a tremendous share of the burden of making LEAA effective.

Numerous studies continued to criticize LEAA for not developing operational standards for planning and evaluating and for not pushing for uniform data-collection and reporting systems. LEAA's response was that these were state responsibilities. Finally, in the 1976 amendments, Congress urged the institute, "in consultation with State planning agencies, [to] develop criteria and procedures for the . . . evaluation of programs and projects."

The institute's attempts at evaluation were mixed. A $2 million experiment aimed at building up the capacity of states and localities to evaluate their own programs failed because so few model plans were submitted. Some interesting basic research on the methodology of evaluation, such as modeling the effects of change on one area of the criminal justice system on the other areas, has been undertaken. And as part of a planned, long-term evaluation of LEAA programs by topic, some "phase I" studies, admittedly nonrigorous state-of-the-art reviews, were made.[49] How symptomatic that after some ten or twelve years of being in operation and facing imminent demise, LEAA finally got around to phase I of evaluation!

In another area, data collection, LEAA should be credited with real initiative, although progress here has also been slow and piecemeal. In the early 1970s, LEAA's Statistics Division (of the National Criminal Justice Information and Statistics Service) began making victimization surveys, utilizing Census Bureau interviews to ask representative samples of the population whether they had been the victims of crime in the past year. This approach, known as the National Crime Survey, was an attempt to get a truer picture of the amount of real crime than the FBI's Uniform Crime Report, which was compiled from local police records of arrests. Victimization surveys, published annually since 1973, have their own problems of reliability—how to validate responses, how to narrow the geographical areas of sampling. But they are undoubtedly an improvement and will be continued and refined by the new Bureau of Justice Statistics. Another effort at data colection was project SEARCH, or System for the Electronic Analysis and Retrieval of Criminal Histories, begun by LEAA in 1969.[50] This project met with intense controversy over the issue of privacy. Responsibility for the computerized file of criminal case histories was eventually given to the FBI.

As fundamental as data management is for *evaluation*, it can also be a *source* of new policy initiatives. According to LEAA, one of the more successful innovations was PROMIS, or Prosecutor's Management Information System. Developed in 1969 by the U.S. Attorney's Office in Washington, D.C., PROMIS was a computerized record-keeping system designed to help prosecutors schedule their overwhelming case loads and identify quickly those cases involving serious crime or habitual offenders. The PROMIS data revealed that 7 percent of those arrested accounted for 25 percent of those processed by the system. Other research showed that as few as 10 percent of all arrested criminals accounted for 60 percent of all the recorded crime. Thus, a picture built up of "career criminals," who make crime a profitable business. Career criminals are not only hardened professionals, more likely to hurt their victims and to shoot to avoid arrest, but they commit a disproportionate number of serious crimes and also skillfully manipulate court procedures, such as plea bargaining and delaying tactics, to avoid prison sentences. The assumption was that incapacitating career criminals early and locking them up for a long time might do more to reduce crime than trying to rehabilitate or deter them.

In October 1973 Charles Work left the Washington, D.C., U.S. Attorney's Office to become deputy administrator of LEAA, where he pushed and developed PROMIS as a national program. In May 1975 the program got underway with $4.5 million in discretionary grants for twenty-one cities and the state of Rhode Island. By his own description, Work "marketed the program carefully. We set up guidelines in LEAA. We picked carefully the recipients of the funds. . . . We were asking the prosecutors to set some priorities."[51] LEAA considered the criminal program successful, "beyond our greatest expectations," and "the best-used money of any of the LEAA funds."

But other observers were less sanguine. In an independent and hard-hitting on-site assessment of the Washington, D.C., PROMIS, the district attorney in Denver, Colorado, Dale Tooley, explained why he rejected LEAA funds for a PROMIS system for his state:

> The PROMIS system is supposed to provide ready information on which better decisions can be made. In fact, it provides virtually no information to those who handle cases in the office. We selected three cases at random. . . . For example, the robbery case computer print-out incorrectly listed one of the charges in the case, inaccurately reported the place of the offense, listed the wrong judge to whom the case was assigned, failed to list the defense counsel (although that was reflected in the file), listed the trial date as being a month earlier than it in fact was and failed to list a continued date for proceedings in the case. Fortunately, these errors of the PROMIS system did not adversely affect the prosecution of the case, because the deputies in the office responsible for prosecuting the case paid no attention to the data processing print-out, because such print-outs were so often incorrect.[52]

Other data-collection projects sponsored by LEAA were aimed at evaluating broad criminal justice policy decisions and getting down to the question of *what works* and *what doesn't*. An institute-sponsored evaluation of a new Massachusetts gun control law showed that whereas the number of gun assaults decreased, the number of assaults with other weapons increased. PROMIS data have been used to identify that small percentage (about 15 percent) of police who somehow account for more than half of all convictions. The study of career criminals also led to an evaluation of mandatory-minimum sentencing, an idea that gained great popularity in the late seventies. A majority of states have adopted mandatory-minimum sentencing, and it is viewed not only as a means of making sure crime doesn't pay—providing harsher, more certain sentences—but also as a means of equalizing justice—removing disparities in sentencing that currently exist. But a 1977 RAND Corporation study sponsored by LEAA showed that although mandatory sentences can reduce crime by incapacitating offenders, the increase in the prison population might be unacceptably large:

> The most efficient policy, in the sense of producing the highest crime reduction and lowest increase in prison population, appears to be a policy of sentencing all convicted felons to 1.2 years of prison. But it reduces the crime rate by 20 percent while raising the prison population 85 percent.[53]

The reason presumably is that the current crime rate is influenced by judges who already discriminate successfully between first-time juvenile offenders and those criminals who are likely repeaters and pose serious risks to the community.

Victimization surveys and such experiments as PROMIS represent LEAA's coming to grips with the lack of an adequate data base, a lack everyone had bemoaned for years. In this area LEAA was beginning to make significant contributions.

One reason for the difficulty of evaluation in LEAA programs was the unwillingness, at the local level, to adopt an experimental attitude, to view evaluation as a tool to be used in decision making, not as a threat or a nuisance. Research breakthroughs simply did not provide sufficiently attractive models to encourage local officials to deal in scientific measures instead of political intuition.

DISCUSSION

The federal war on crime was based on two assumptions: that money would make a difference and that planning would produce coordination. Unfortunately these assumptions were not completely valid. James Gregg, the OMB examiner for LEAA who later became acting administrator of LEAA, explained it this way:

> There just has not been the right attitude or the sophistication at the

state and local level to warrant too much money too fast. Personnel systems in law enforcement are still very rigid and conservative, and there is very little lateral transfer. I feel it is very important to recognize that it is not money alone that will solve these types of things.[54]

Just spending more money, studies of other federal social programs have shown, without fundamentally changing the way participant agencies go about their business will not produce results. Reform and innovation were particularly hard to come by in the entrenched criminal justice agencies. Here, for example, are three views of the inertia in police departments:

A police lieutenant: There is no planning, no information system, no executive leadership. There's the problem of our chief. He's fearful of experiments. Doesn't even like the idea of using private cars, plain clothes or different levels of manpower in proportion to the peak crime days or hours in the week.

A police-community relations administrator: Though we can get support for improved community relations from our chief and from many of the younger officers, what is needed most is training programs for *the middle management*—those officers who have been on board for 15 to 20 years. I've already had this turned down, even though the people at the top of the department support me. So our chief problem isn't money; it's the people we have in our own department.

A juvenile delinquency specialist: Our police department has a rigid, old, militarylike chief, straight, honest, uptight about any change. The department is run by the chief; it's a one-man show; the mayor is afraid of the chief and the law and order issue. LEAA won't make any difference here; serious planning, and evaluation are a waste if the chief isn't for it.

Most of the Safe Streets funds ended up being spent for "more of the same," although some small and heartening areas of innovation were successful. One of the nation's most thoughtful students of anti-crime policy summed it up this way in 1975: "Nearly ten years ago I wrote that the billions of dollars the Federal Government was then preparing to spend on crime control would be wasted and indeed might even make matters worse if they were merely pumped into the existing criminal justice system. They were and they have."[55]

Then too, most important, *accountability* was never successfully fixed in the national war on crime. The block grant was unique in that local police chiefs, prosecutors, judges, correctional officers, and juvenile delinquency agencies exercised substantial influence over national funds, *without* being accountable to congressional oversight. National funds effectively insulated criminal justice agencies even further from state elected officials. A study of intergovernmental relations has shown that "state agencies which are funded by federal grants are relatively autonomous decision-making units—operating with little oversight by state or federal officials. . . . As the amount and complexity of federal funding increases, so does the likelihood that administrators will lobby independently for funds, reprogram or reallocate appropriations and use supplementals to finance existing programs."[56] This was especially true in the case of criminal justice, where a long tradition of independent police departments, courthouses, and corrections bureaus was underscored by the philosophy of New Federalism and the political weakness of the state planning agencies. LEAA, beset by confused goals, changing leadership, the failure of planning, and near-nonexistent evaluation, was not able to demand accountability or stand accountable itself.

NINE

The War on Unsafe Streets: Lessons and Prospects

THE PAST SEVERAL years have witnessed a dramatic rise in the number of people who say that crime is increasing in their neighborhoods. Public support for harsher punishments and the death penalty has reached record high levels. In the early 1980s, well over half of the American people say they are afraid to walk home alone at night. Increasing numbers of the elderly are prisoners of fear even at high noon. More and more Americans say they have little or no confidence in the ability of the police to protect them from violent crime. We read about teenagers who have set on fire not only buildings but human victims—merely for the sake of excitement. "It's absolutely a war zone down there," said a visitor about the crime wave in Atlanta, a city that had one of the highest per capita crime rates in recent years. In an average week there are four hundred murders in the U.S. In four or five years, some experts predict, every household will be victimized!

High crime rates affect more than our safety; they are expensive. Police, courts, and correctional facilities are more costly than ever. Moreover, businesses in crime-ridden areas have closed down or have had to relocate. The poor, as always, are hardest hit—not only do they suffer the highest crime, but they have to travel farther or lose their jobs when businesses relocate and, as consumers, have to pay more when businesses hire private security.

In the spring of 1980 a race riot in Miami, sparked by the acquittal of four white policemen accused of beating to death a black insurance salesman, claimed fifteen lives, injured three hundred, and raised fears that the 1980s would witness again the violent urban disorders that so frightened America in the late 1960s. Grave problems of unequal opportunity and unequal justice persist in America.

Plainly, people are angry and tired of crime and violence. They see their neighborhoods terrorized, businesses forced to close, their cities threatened by fear and disorder. Almost two million offenders were locked up or under some form of parole in one recent year—that's five times the population of Wyoming, or 1 in every 110 Americans! But it's not enough. Save for a couple of temporary and questionable dips in 1972 and 1976, the FBI crime index climbed relentlessly upward in every year of the nation's campaign to make the streets safe and shows every inclination to climb yet higher. The Department of Justice's victimization survey data, while apparently stable, are so much higher than the FBI crime index that they are on a different scale altogether and no more reassuring. More than 5 of every 100 Americans today are victims of serious crime in any one year. Moreover, criminologists say we have to wait until the population of sixteen- to twenty-year-olds decreases before crime will decline, and then, when this population swells in another generation, we may expect yet another increase in crime.

Crime control remains a high priority. As late as 1978, even in the wake of such fiscally conservative movements as Howard Jarvis's Proposition 13 in California, the proposed constitutional amendment for a balanced budget, and the Kemp-Roth tax-cut proposal, a majority of Americans still wanted the federal government to spend more money fighting crime.[1] But people are increasingly resigned to the reality of unsafe streets. Americans are learning, unhappily, to live with crime. They stay home more, buy more locks and burglar alarms, and carry whistles and Mace; joggers carry cash so disappointed muggers won't beat them up. Citizens in numerous towns have formed vigilante patrols. But today's police chiefs, judges, FBI directors, presidents, former LEAA administrators—even political candidates—no longer claim to be able to prevent or reduce crime.

Did the national war on crime at least improve the capabilities of the criminal justice system? Old LEAA partisans, such as godfather Sen. Roman Hruska, thought so:

> LEAA has already achieved one major accomplishment which no amount of criticism can ever take from it. It has established for the first time in our two centuries of existence as a nation, a true criminal justice system, in which the various components are working together.[2]

A list of key research results put out by LEAA in a 1978 briefing shows a partial accounting of the kinds of improvements that were attempted (figure 5). Others, however, strongly dispute this achievement by LEAA. Robert McKay, respected former dean of the New York University Law School, said "the criminal justice system in the United States is a failure. It is in disarray at every level. It neither controls crime nor punishes criminals. The money spent by the LEAA in the 'war on crime' has had no perceptible effect (unless it can be argued that crime would have been even more prevalent without LEAA)."[3] The public certainly is disillusioned and disheartened. A 1981 Harris poll reported that at least 79 percent of Americans feel our system of law enforcement does not discourage criminal activity.

FIGURE 5. Key Research Results Claimed by LEAA

JURY OPERATIONS:

- Jury pools can be cut 20 to 25% while still maintaining adequate trial coverage
- Nationwide, savings could total $50 million annually
- Some courts already using the new methods, with New York County reporting $1.2 million annual savings
- Jury reform programs beginning in 18 court systems with institute funding.

POLICE RESPONSE TIME:

- Citizens fail to report most crimes immediately
- Reporting delays diminish impact of rapid police response time
- Findings have implications for manpower allocation, communications technology, and crime reporting patterns.

CRIMINAL INVESTIGATIONS:

- Victim/witness key to solving most crimes
- Information from crime scene more important than "leads" developed later on
- Screening procedures developed to help police decide whether case can be productively pursued
- Improved investigative procedures to be tested in five jurisdictions.

LIGHTWEIGHT BODY ARMOR:

- Inconspicuous, can be worn routinely
- Field tested in 15 major cities
- Credited with saving the lives of 3 officers and preventing serious injury to another 10

SENTENCING GUIDELINES:

- Designed to reduce disparity within a jurisdiction
- Guideline sentences cover 85 percent of cases
- Denver now using guideline system
- Guidelines being developed in Chicago, Newark, and Phoenix

POLICE PERFORMANCE MEASURES:

- Arrest data and reported crime figures inadequate measures
- New system uses a variety of "indicators" to assess a department's productivity
- Sound performance evaluation methods increasingly crucial in light of budgetary pressures
- Testing to begin soon in four cities.

Source: LEAA *General Briefing*, mimeographed handout, 1978.

There is no doubt that there have been some successful LEAA programs. For example, a list of key research results put out by LEAA in a 1978 briefing shows a partial accounting of the kinds of improvements that were attempted (figure 5). There remains a great need for systematic and rigorous measurement of the impact of LEAA programs in the field. But politics, unlike science, does not wait for complete and controlled evidence, and the political verdict on LEAA is in. Why was our political system unable to deal with crime in the streets? Was the national war on crime a victim of misplaced optimism? Or was it a failure of politics, a failure of structure, of will? Just what should the federal role in fighting crime be? Should politics and crime ever be separated? Does our society have to tolerate high levels of crime in order to keep its freedoms? What are the lessons we can profitably learn from the "other" war we lost, the national war on crime?

WHAT WORKS/WHAT DOESN'T?

The American people are used to having grand goals. In 1968, at the start of the national war on crime, America had won world wars and stopped polio and was putting men on the moon. Why shouldn't we also be able to stop crime? A new priesthood of social engineers and action intellectuals set the mood of optimism. The limits of ad hoc and piecemeal social intervention were as yet only dimly perceived. Advice that urged restraint or moderated aspirations was not regarded as advice at all. Inaction was inconceivable.

Yet the missing cornerstone on which such confidence was precariously balanced was *knowledge*—knowledge about how to stop crime, about what works and what does not. We simply did not know enough to start a heavily funded crash program, and we ended up funding our fears, not serious research and experiments. As one LEAA official said, "The reason we don't do better in curbing crime is that *we don't know how*. Why crime goes up, or equally important, why it goes down, as it did around the country in 1972, is poorly understood." And most disturbing, substantial ignorance persists today.

Two urbanologists put it this way: "Confidence in our ability to frame solutions has declined as understanding of problems has grown. As explanations have become more tentative, so the proposals put forth these days are more modest than the programs launched with such high expectations in the 1960's. One can say—at least about the domestic sphere of government action—that we now know more than we did, but, deprived of our hubris, are less confident in our ability to shape a future as we will."[4]

Many of the reports of the president's 1967 crime commission gave advice and made suggestions that seemed promising. But some were misleading. James Q. Wilson wrote of the commission's Task Force on Juvenile Delinquency, "The report represents a high-water mark of the misplaced optimism of the 1960's about what government was able to accomplish. There was no reason to believe, then or now, that we know how to improve the family or that more money spent on schools or housing would lead to reductions in delinquency."[5] Wilson also said LEAA did not develop new knowledge about crime control or prevention.

Mostly what we have learned through the LEAA experiment is what *doesn't* work. The list of what *doesn't* seem to reduce crime includes, surprisingly enough, such long-touted police reforms as saturation patrolling,[6] quicker response times,[7] advanced technology,[8] and college education for police.[9] With help from LEAA studies, optimistic notions about rehabilitation have been discredited, as have those about parole, the death penalty as a deterrent, and preventive detention.[10] Sociologist Marvin Wolfgang testified in January of 1978 that "the weight of empirical evidence indicates that no current preventative, deterrent, or rehabilitative intervention scheme has the desired effect of reducing crime."[11]

Let us be more specific about one of these LEAA programs that did not work as intended. Enormous amounts of block grant and other funds were spent on educational programs aimed at upgrading the quality of law enforcement officers—especially policemen. Typically, police were encourged to take courses at nearby community colleges or other institutions of higher education. Their tuition and other costs were paid for. They were strongly encouraged to participate. But, in practice, many police officers seized this as an opportunity to upgrade themselves more as a means *to get out of police work* than as a means to improve their effectiveness in police work and crime prevention. Teachers and directors of these programs have told us that the programs were a major flop. Said one educator based in Sacramento, California, "Ninety percent of the police who came through our programs in California promptly left their jobs soon after they completed their LEAA-funded educational programs. Most of them merely took advantage of these opportunities to get themselves qualified for higher-paying and safer jobs." It is little wonder that LEAA closed this program down—even before LEAA was shut down itself. Note, however, that the program's goal was well intended. Better-educated police, logically enough, would make better and more sensitive police officers. In some communities the program doubtless worked to achieve this objective. Elsewhere, however, there were significant unintended consequences.

There is a new agreement, emerging in part from LEAA projects, that judges and jailers just cannot handle the volume of criminals they are presented with. We should make courts more efficient, as attempted by the PROMIS and career criminal programs; we should keep out of prison those who do not have to be there, such as drunks, addicts, genuine first-offender juveniles; we should make it easier for witnesses to cooperate; we should treat as adults those juveniles who commit serious crimes. The notion of mandatory-minimum sentences has gained support, as a means of both correcting the disparities in sentencing that currently exist and incapacitating repeaters. America already has on the books some of the harshest sentences in the Western world, but these sentences do not serve as a deterrent because, with plea bargaining necessary to prevent a total collapse of our overcrowded courts and prisons, only a small fraction of those criminals apprehended ever serve significant sentences. We have learned that *if we want to make sure crime does not pay, we have to make punishment swift and certain*. In addition, convicted criminals should be made to compensate their victims for economic, mental, and emotional losses. The personal responsibility of crime must not be lessened by our impersonal system of laws.

Today it is easier to buy a handgun in most American cities than it is to obtain a library card. Conservative critics still insist our laws should be directed toward the criminal use of firearms rather than toward restricting the legitimate use of firearms by law-abiding citizens. But ask any inner-city quick-food-store clerk or gas station attendant, such as the young Boston man who told us of being regularly held up, *nearly once a week*: "Tonight I was robbed of $42.00 just half an hour ago. There were two of them, and they both had guns sticking into me. It's a little nerve-wracking to have them yell at you that what you have given them is not enough, especially with guns in your ribs!" In Japan, crimes involving handguns are rare. Why? Because under Japanese law the only persons allowed to carry handguns are law enforcement officials. Merely banning Saturday-night specials is not enough. The number of all kinds of handguns in private use must be reduced to a minimum. Fifty percent of all murders in the U.S. are committed with handguns. Baltimore police bought fifteen thousand guns from citizens in 1974; handgun murders promptly fell 24 percent the next year and 35 percent the next. Some states provide stiff, mandatory sentences for illegally carrying guns. Still, studies find handguns are manufactured and exported by other states with no restrictions. We would do well to study the rationale and effectiveness of Japanese and British gun-ownership regulations. Plainly, a serious national policy on firearms control is needed here.[12]

Crime, as we have learned, is not the kind of problem amenable to dramatic breakthroughs. Rather, "it is a problem we will be picking away at for a long time to come, and with luck, there should be a little bit of progress here and a little bit there. Cumulatively it may add up to the kind of knowledge and programs that will have a major impact on our crime problem."[13]

But the most important lesson learned from our twelve-year war on unsafe streets is that the ability of the national government to control crime is substantially less than almost everyone thought or was led to expect. There is a new disbelief and even resentment, nurtured by presidential manipulation of the crime issue, about promises and rhetoric; there is a new and possibly healthy skepticism, emerging in part from the LEAA failures, about the ability of government to solve such societal problems as crime. Unless this skepticism is put to good use, however, unless we get down to what must be done next, unless we are willing to face the price of solutions, the results will be only cynicism and further defeat.

MANIPULATION OF THE CRIME ISSUE

Crime in the streets, it should be added, should never have developed at all as an issue in *national* poliitcs. The primary constitutional responsibility for crime prevention and control has always rested with the states and localities, and the national government does *not* have a large, direct stake in most areas of law enforcement and criminal justice. Federal law enforcement officials constitute a small proportion of total police forces, and most are highly specialized, such as agents in narcotics or border patrol. Decisions by inferior courts are subject to appeal to the federal system, but such appeals are rare, and in practice the local bench can afford to be relatively independent.

But by the mid-sixties, many people felt the states had failed in their responsibility for crime control. With civil rights enforcement and urban riot control by national guardsmen, federal peace keeping was dramatically exhibited from Little Rock to Detroit for the first time in a generation. The character of the criminal justice system, with its overwhelming emphasis on local control, might have been a reason for federal inaction, but inaction was unacceptable to the public, alarmed and fearful about crime, to national legislators, and to the increasingly harried chief executive, Lyndon Johnson. Even those who, without knowing what strategies would work, believed the national government needed more time also recognized that the extent of the crime problem was changing old beliefs and, with them, the virtues of restraint.

Presidents obviously could not prevent or stop crime, nor could they alone do much about it. Political scientist Richard Neustadt wrote, "What Presidents do every day is make decisions that are mostly thrust upon them, the deadlines all too often outside their control, on options mostly framed by others, about issues crammed with technical complexities and uncertain outcomes. The technicalities may be no less mysterious to Presidents than the uncertainties yet they must choose, even if only to defer."[14] Yet presidents and would-be presidents used the crime issue for short-term political advantage. Crime in the streets as a national issue was *manufactured* and milked by presidential candidates, who began a sorry stream of symbolic politics rather than attending to practicalities and management in the war on crime. Too often presidents and would-be presidents failed to emphasize the complexity of the problem in relation to the limited resources of government. Too often presidents and would-be presidents fanned public outrage and focused it onto false expectations for their own benefits. That the public was and still is genuinely and deeply fearful of crime does not legitimize the manipulation of this fear that occurred in the elections of 1964, 1968, and 1972. Only in the mid-seventies did issues of management and fiscal accountability, or perhaps the pervading public cynicism engendered by Vietnam and Watergate, or perhaps merely the public's waning attention span, begin to temper the political rhetoric about crime.

In 1964 presidential candidate Barry Goldwater first capitalized on the nation's concern about crime, labeling the Democratic president and his attorney general personally culpable for increasing lawlessness in America. Here the issue of solving the sociological causes of crime versus the immediate need to get tough on criminals was first brought up for national debate. President Johnson offered us his antipoverty and social services programs—his dreams of a Great Society—and, when they fell into disrepute, sought a categorical grant program to serve as a catalyst for the war on crime. In the final days of his lame-duck presidency, his proposal ran into such congressional, gubernatorial, and interest group opposition that it was radically recast into the block grant form.

In 1968, continuing to exploit the crime issue, candidate Richard Nixon blamed the Democratic administration for the 50-percent increase in crime since 1964. The attorney general was again a prime target—Nixon claimed Ramsey Clark had practically encouraged crime. President Nixon appointed conservatives to the Supreme Court, prodded the District of Columbia police, sponsored preventive detention and no-knock legislation, and tried to fashion a more responsive federal drug campaign, but he seriously neglected the basically Republican response to crime, LEAA. In retrospect, it is clear that Nixon went to considerable lengths to portray himself as a hard-liner on crime, even though he and most of his staff realized this was primarily symbolic politics. Under the block grant, so vigorously championed by Republicans in Congress, states and localities preserved the status quo in their criminal justice agencies—along with the same old escalating crime statistics.

In 1972, Nixon and Attorney General Mitchell claimed for themselves a remarkable record on crime, though in the end, of course, the president abused the integrity of his office and lost the good will of the American people. Meanwhile LEAA still languished. By 1976, the old crime rhetoric had gone out with a bang—Watergate—and a whimper—President Ford's budget cuts in LEAA. Candidate Jimmy Carter promised to reduce unemployment, to cut the bureaucracy, to balance the federal budget, and never, never to lie to us, but he did not promise (much) to reduce crime. Instead, as president, Carter promptly continued to neglect LEAA and reduce its budget. A growing force of congressional and interest group members said *sociological causes of crime must be considered irrelevant to the politics of crime control*, and Congress cut LEAA's budget further. Finally, LEAA was shut down as the urge for a new symbol, a balanced budget, overwhelmed Congress. But President Reagan, freed from LEAA, immediately set up a new task force to find out what the federal government should do about crime in the streets.

Thus, in the space of five elections (1964–80), *crime as an issue* went from being exploited to being ignored, from being a profitable vote getter to being nothing but trouble, from being an explosive emotional symbol to being something that everyone was glad to be rid of. *Crime*, however, continued to flourish.

A SYSTEMIC WEAKNESS

The war on crime was also a failure to plan and a failure to appreciate the limits of federalism. The architects of LEAA gambled on the willingness of state political leaders to see that LEAA monies were invested wisely. We now know that few states seriously accepted the challenge, some states did a deplorable job, and most did what can only be called a mediocre or uneven job. However much all levels of government agreed on the need to make our streets safe, disagreement followed on specific policies and programs. Disorganization was almost guaranteed by trying to accommodate the varied preferences and abilities of the nearly forty thousand separate political jurisdictions throughout the nation that had some responsibility for law enforcement and criminal justice. Our political system was designed, of course, to accentuate checks and balances, promote limited government, and accommodate diverse perceptions of the common good. Yet diversity, even as it basically reflects liberty, exacts a costly price in efficiency.

As one state after another turned LEAA monies into a pork-barrel operation, funds were distributed to the strongest and loudest interest groups or to too many groups in too many geographical areas. The political incentives inherent in that mode of distribution led to a neglect of experimentation, innovation, and evaluation and made it nearly impossible to concentrate funds, to test for or to demonstrate impact. LEAA was altered only slowly, even after it was seen to be ineffective. The reason relates to the dynamics and staying power of programs— the pork-barrel nature of LEAA was a plus for both legislators and LEAA when measured by political criteria. The sizable amounts of money given out by LEAA created new vested interests, such as the state planning agencies, and reinforced many old interests, such as police, that had a high stake in preserving the agency's essential character.

Not only were LEAA funds a generous pork barrel, but everyone seemed to have a piece of the action when it came to how LEAA was to be managed and even what it was supposed to do. Presidential and congressional interests often diverged, and the injection of local views intensified the conflict over LEAA's objectives. These confusions, disagreements, and rivalries were evident from the policy-initiation through the policy-implementation stages, and they weakened LEAA's capacity to provide leadership for state and local governments.

A certain sympathy is in order for LEAA, facing, as it did, the handicaps of inconsistent objectives, creeping categorization, leadership vacuum and personnel turnover, and the difficulties of getting states to plan and evaluate. Sincere and able people did try hard to make LEAA programs work. As one gentle secretary, who had worked for ten years in LEAA, chided us sweetly, "Now I hope you won't write about all those myths!" And in the words of Sen. Roman Hruska:

> even in those cases where there was less than full agreement on the use of LEAA funds, my own close study of the matter persuades me that the fault, if any, lies not with LEAA but necessarily with local police, courts, and corrections officials who actually are in charge of administering and operating the law enforcement activities.[15]

Indeed, few federal assistance programs could have withstood the intensive scrutiny applied to LEAA. We asked a series of Department of Health, Education, and Welfare officials in the late 1970s whether their programs could withstand investigations as comprehensive as the studies covering LEAA. Most said no. During the same years, for example, the Department of Justice suffered virtually the same losses in its fight on drugs and on organized crime and gun control, although each of these programs received noticeably less public criticism than did LEAA. (For instance, in an assessment similar to those of LEAA, the General Accounting Office found in 1977 that even after spending $800 million over a ten-year period, even with all the publicity given the federal strike forces, the national war on organized crime was faltering. Not only was organized crime flourishing, but it was taking over legitimate businesses, and the federal campaign "lacked coherent strategy, clear organization, and even a workable definition of its adversary.")

LEAA was a new type of program for the Department of Justice, the first of its kind to be associated with distributing such large amounts of money. And yet, in comparison with state and local budgets, LEAA's contributions were a drop in the bucket. To expect great changes from 4 or 5 percent additional input was perhaps unrealistic. And even if LEAA did not show enough leadership in sponsoring research or fostering experimentation and evaluation, it may well have provided needed support to some financially distressed cities and police departments, courts, and prisons. An executive director of the International Association of Chiefs of Police, not exactly an unbiased source, said LEAA provided "considerable benefits to law enforcement and the public." Asked about LEAA's failure to make an impact on the crime rate, he reasoned, "We've spent many, many more billions of dollars and still have welfare."[16]

For now, in an era when it is cheaper to send a youngster to Har-

vard than to San Quentin, when President Reagan is slashing the domestic budget, and when LEAA grant monies have been completely cut
off, the future of national anticrime assistance looks grim. Perhaps we
should consider the venerable proposition that we, the public, got the
kind of anticrime policy we deserved—one that reflected our own
doubts and uncertainties about the causes of crime and about how
much we were willing to pay to "solve" crime. In this broadest sense,
could it be that the policy failures of LEAA were failures of the American people as well? And how much crime will America tolerate before
we demand action again?

VALUES IN CONFLICT

After the first rush of great expectations for LEAA had worn off,
there began to be heard official interpretations that blamed LEAA's
failure to reduce crime on *society's tolerance of crime*. Attorney General Edward Levi, who headed the Department of Justice under President Ford, complained, "We have a country which is very tolerant
and has been willing to take a degree of lawlessness which is rather
surprising. I suppose what one has to say is that the main problem is
the willingness of the country to accept that rate. . . ."[17] Strangely, for
a country that is so fearful of crime, over half of all street crimes are
not even reported. Some people may be reluctant to get involved with
the police, some may fear retaliation, and others are cynical because
they have cooperated in the past only to see criminals win immediate
release. Many believe the police are not able to do much to stop crime.
A high percentage of prosecutions fail for lack of witnesses, even
while police continually stress that more citizen concern and coopera-
tion is key.

Sociologists and psychologists often say America has had a long history of violence, from Wounded Knee to the Wild West, from the
Civil War to Birmingham, from the Ludlow mine massacre to the
Atlanta child murders of 1981. Today violence has become so widespread in our society, from abused children to battered wives, from
blackboard jungles to gang warfare, from Charles Manson to Son of
Sam, that its use is apparently legitimized as a solution to human difficulties. Children who learn violence at home are immunized—and de-
humanized—by it. Violence on television, even on children's programs,
continues unabated. "Broadcasters and program producers . . . work
to feed the insatiate consumptive needs of the videotube for atten-
tion-getting scripts under conditions driving them to use violence almost as an exclamation point before the commercial breaks."[18]

But even if Americans have experienced much violence, is it really fair to say they *tolerate* crime? Opinion polls show time and again the public's intense fear of crime and its consistent desire for a governmental response. Isn't the real question whether Americans are *willing to pay the price* to solve the crime problem in their country? Or even whether they clearly perceive *what the price is?*

If America truly lacks the will to solve its crime problem—and this remains to be seen—it is because unrecognized and conflicting values dissipate our national motivation. At least three major areas of value conflict have figured as a recurring motif in the failure of national crime control policy: (1) ensuring domestic tranquillity versus preserving civil liberties, (2) undertaking national planning versus maintaining local control, and (3) changing our social institutions versus relying on government to do the job. These values all relate to designing and managing federal policy; those values involved in making a person a criminal are the subject of many other and fascinating studies.[19] Each question here is a variation of "what is the proper role of government?", not "what causes crime?" Yet the question of crime causation lies like a sphinx at the crux of crime control policy, not only because of our susceptibility to Newtonian logic, but also because the answer may ultimately lie in which values one *chooses* to believe in.

The politics of the war on crime began in the mid-sixties with this quandary: are the injustices of society at the root of crime, or are criminals just plain evil? At that time we had Ramsey Clark and Lyndon Johnson as the champions of the social justice school and Barry Goldwater, George Wallace, and Richard Nixon as the get-tough heroes. Later, in the mid-seventies, Jimmy Carter joined the social justice school, claiming, albeit softly, that unemployment is the chief cause of crime. The get-tough persuasion was represented by Ronald Reagan and some students of criminal justice policy. Many contemporary criminologists stress there are no "root causes" of crime, that ghetto life and criminal friends may just set the stage for what remains the individual's decision whether to commit a crime. The public itself has become more hard-line about the need to punish and deter. Still, other social scientists point to continuing inequalities in modern American life as responsible for crime. One psychiatrist, for example, pinpoints the disaffection behind today's proliferation of violence:

I would say our difficulty, really, is the "American Dream." By that I mean the feeling that everyone can be prosperous and happy because no other country in the world offers the opportunity that America does. For those who don't achieve riches and happiness, it means frustration, and this can make a person hateful, vengeful, and driven by a need to act aggressively, to take short cuts.[20]

Theft is seen by some analysts as a way of getting back what has been denied to the unemployed, black, ghetto teenager.[21] Others say the larger questions, such as equality in the delivery of criminal justice services to minorities, were ignored by LEAA.[22] The debate between social justice and getting tough continues.

Plainly, ideas from both the "get-tough" and the "social justice" approaches to crime prevention must be heeded. Unless our society unsympathetically punishes criminals of all kinds—white collar crimes as well as street crimes—crime, cheating, and corruption will continue to pay in America. Still, there is a real danger in dismissing the relationship between crime and poverty. Sadly, it is the poor themselves who are the most frequent victims of crime. We must be careful that by rationalizing away our obligation to get at the "root causes" of crime we do not make justice and safety the right of only those who can afford them.

These various philosophies have been divided into those which emphasize the institutional causes of crime—poverty, unemployment, racism—and those which depend on personal qualities to explain crime—greed, laziness, disrespect for the law.[23] The same tension between institutional and personal solutions enters the discussion of what is the proper role of government in fighting crime. How much power should the government have in order to prevent and control crime?

America has an impressively strong tradition of civil liberties. Not for America the minimal crime rates of the Soviet Union, explained to us by a high-ranking law professor in Moscow. Criminals, he said, are aware of the nature of the obstacles to their crimes; if these obstacles are made high enough, then they simply will not commit crime.[24] The Soviet Union makes these obstacles high indeed. Not for us the hypothetical situation presented by LEAA's Gerald Caplan:

> It is imaginable to have a general curfew for everyone of all ages, from 9 p.m. to 6 a.m. It is imaginable to establish "check points" every few blocks in central city areas, through which all vehicular traffic must pass and undergo inspection. All these devices have been used, often successfully, to control "deviant" behavior in other countries. While they might be equally successful here, they are not the kind of experiments we think ought to be considered.[25]

Americans prize their individual freedoms and liberties so much that they guarantee even criminal defendants more due process protections than does any other nation; the possibility that an innocent person will be convicted is reduced to a near minimum. The Supreme Court strengthened the rights of defendants during the 1960s, but not without certain side effects in our criminal justice system. For example, the Exclusionary Rule, which provides that improperly obtained evidence shall not be used in a trial, often means that rather than a criminal's or erring law enforcement official's being punished, both go free. Moreover, because of the number of procedural motions that can be filed by the defendant, trials are delayed, courts overcrowded, and lower and lower plea bargains accepted. Yet the possibility that those in power will overstep their bounds is abhorrent. Police brutality, for example, is unfortunately still real. A unique lawsuit by the Department of Justice charged brutality against the entire Philadelphia police force in 1979. And in 1980 a bitter race riot in Miami was provoked by an accusation of police brutality.

"Along with the civil right to vote, go to school, and have a job is the right not to be mugged, robbed, or assaulted," asserted Sen. Edward Kennedy in explaining his position on crime.[26] (The right not to be mugged is not, of course, in the Constitution—one must translate from the God-given rights of life, liberty, and the pursuit of happiness. Our system merely proposes to treat the offender properly should an offense occur, but it does not guarantee the citizen protection from that offense before it happens.) The obligation of a government to society, to protect the person, the property, and the freedom of movement of its citizens, weighs against the state's obligation to protect against the abuse of its own power at the expense of individual citizens, to protect the rights of the accused. Basically, it all comes down to the rights of society versus the rights of the individual. Unless we are willing to spend many billions of dollars more to solve the crime problem—and we apparently are not—we will have to face up to this dilemma of society versus the individual or face more and more crime.

Not only do we Americans cherish our wide range of individual liberties, but, from our national beginnings, we have harbored an intense suspicion of central government. A national police force is anathema. We are so little predisposed to centralized planning and management that in a sense we have grown to consider inefficiency and confusion the very hallmarks of democracy. Time and again, as noted in the above chapters on LEAA's legislative history, the compromise formulas between federal and local authorities did not work. Two major positions have been taken on the question of where authority should reside. One holds that local governments can best administer justice; the other argues that the national government must set policy and enforce standards.

Those who call for maximum local control say state and local governments are closer to the people, more accessible, and better able to understand and solve unique local problems. Theorists and practitioners who hold these views believe power should be widely distributed in order to protect individuals from the arbitrary actions of a strong central government. Watergate only strengthened their belief. Federalism also ensures that groups denied representation in a unitary, or centralized, system of government will have greater access to multiple centers of decision-making authority. One proponent of a noncentralized form of government points out that as cities have become inincreasingly urbanized, the sheer growth in population has replaced geographic distance as a barrier to political participation. "Because of the mediating effects of federalism, Americans are still not as far removed from their political institutions as might be expected in a political system embracing over 200 million people."[27]

Advocates of more central direction, or tighter standards and more uniform policy implementation, argue that improved technology, rapid transportation, and instant communication have removed the original purposes of federalism. Federalism, they say, is too slow, too inefficient, too tolerant of inequalities. Overlapping jurisdictions prevent efficient delivery of services and thus restrict the opportunities of the disadvantaged. The civil rights struggles in the South in the 1960s are cited as evidence of the federal system's tolerance of injustices and the need to use the national government to protect minorities from local abuses of power. Others believe the problem is less abuse of national power than inaction:

> Capricious or arbitrary action is not as serious a problem in national government as it is in local governments . . . where political institutions are often too weak or disorganized to challenge the bureaucracy. The problem in Washington is more often one of persuading the bureaucracy to act when it knows from experience that doing as little as possible reaps the greatest benefits.[28]

Moreover, the structure of decentralized power cannot match the advantages of organized corporate power, with its generous campaign contributions, effective lobbying, and overrepresentation on decision-making councils. Finally, federalism is said to militate against the ideal of equality—for example, by allowing local courts to inflict widely different punishments for the same crime.

Value conflicts about federalism were not satisfactorily resolved when policymakers were trying to decide, in 1968, whether and how the national government should get involved in what was, after all, a local responsibility, namely, street crime. Today, when the balance has swung in favor of less federal involvement and an eloquent spokesman for decentralization presides in the White House, uncertainty persists. A study by the Council on Municipal Performance, a nonprofit research organization in New York, showed that state and local governments were refusing to accept auditing standards for general-revenue-sharing funds and, further, that many local officials did not feel the same accountability for general-revenue-sharing funds as for local taxes.[29] Accountability, never fixed by the block grant, was certainly not fixed by formula grants either and will continue to be a problem for any national anticrime assistance.

Another conflict in values stems from our recent recognition that government alone cannot stop crime. During the Nixon administration, presidential counselor Daniel Patrick Moynihan once said the social factors that produce crime cannot be solved by government legislation or regulation. Either the "private subsystems of authority"—family, neighborhood, church, and school—would dispose an individual to be law-abiding, or they would not. This theme has been echoed resoundingly—government alone cannot end the crime wave. "We cannot rely solely on the law enforcement officer or the criminal justice system. The police officer can do little to alleviate isolated poverty in a land of wealth; he cannot insure the integrity of businessmen bent on defrauding the public; nor can he strengthen the unity of families shattered by indifference. These and myriad other problems must be solved by all of society."[30] And again, "We have learned that the conditions that really make a difference in crime control lie largely outside governmental authority—in such areas as child rearing, family stability, and transmission of values."[31]

Poverty and unemployment may be fairly within the purview of government, but the evidence linking them with crime is mixed. Of course there is a connection—there is certainly more crime in our poorest neighborhoods and during periods of increased joblessness—but criminologists have not found a one-to-one relationship: most poor people are honest, and criminals do not necessarily turn to crime because they cannot find a job. Moreover, the 1970s FBI crime indexes swelled during a time when, according to informed observers, the relative economic position of minorities improved.

Other large-scale social and demographic phenomena involved in crime are clearly outside the influence of government. Disruptions in the 1960s and 1970s, including the coming to adolescence of the children of the post–World War II baby boom, mass migration of poor whites and blacks to densely populated central cities, and, of course, the war in Vietnam, have apparently encouraged crime. During the 1960s we added over thirteen million persons between the ages of fourteen and twenty-four to the population, and this is the age group that is vastly overrepresented among both lawbreakers and the unemployed. James Q. Wilson once wryly observed, "The largest reductions in crime would be made if we could change men into women and convert all persons who are sixteen to twenty-five years of age into persons who are thirty to thirty-nine."[32] When the children of the children of the baby boom reach the fifteen- to twenty-four-year age group, in the 1990s, they will probably produce another surge in crime rates. Dramatic growth in the consumer economy has meant more things are available to steal. Even the oil shortage, inflation, and bad winters or hot summers are cited as reasons for high crime.

Several conclusions follow from the premise that government alone cannot stop crime. One possibility is that citizens need to take more responsibility for their own environment; this idea was behind LEAA's Community Anti-Crime Program. Despite skepticism about the effectiveness of this program, it has political appeal. And, quite apart from national and state programs, more and more neighborhood organizations have sprung into action with various neighborhood "crime" or "neighborhood watch" activities, taking upon themselves the responsibility of regulating unwanted intruders in their housing areas. With the ending of national funds, we are likely to see more of this kind of local initiative. Other possibilities are that we will just have to fight crime without attacking it at its roots or that we will simply wait it out until the population bulge of youthful offenders passes. Both of these latter possibilities summon grim specters, of repressive, hard-line policies or of the increasing isolation of those who can afford protection from the unpatrolled combat zones of the cities. Judge David Bazelon described the dangers he perceives in separating crime causation from crime control: "I fear that if we shift from concern for the individual to mechanical principles of fairness, we may cease trying to learn as much as possible about the circumstances of life that may have brought the particular offender to the bar of justice."[33]

Sadly, Americans seem to have little faith in alternative institutions to replace the faith they have lost in government. Families, schools, churches, and mass media are all suffering from either decomposition or fragmentation or are simply failing to offer leadership in this area. School bond issues are turned down regularly; television violence is still profitable to advertisers. Americans today do not look as though they really want to invest in their institutions. And yet we will have to build and nurture more mediating and dispute-resolving institutions if we are going to make our way in our increasingly fragmented and tension-ridden society. It is ironic and disheartening that at the very time we are more than ever prepared to admit that government alone cannot solve crime, we seem indifferent to tackling the job of improving our social and neighborhood institutions. If we are not willing to do so, we will just have to live with high levels of crime.

CRIME AND POLITICS

"Losing the War on Crime" was the title of an address by a senior LEAA official a few years ago. It is worth quoting in some detail:

First, we have more crime than any other place in the world, more this year than last, and much, much more than we had in 1964 when Senator Goldwater became the first Presidential candidate to argue that the Federal government must do something about crime in the streets.

Second, most of the increase occurred in the midst of high employment and unprecedented affluence and during a period when the Federal government launched a new, multi-billion dollar anti-crime program.

Third, despite the persistent, often clarion, calls for "law and order," no significant strengthening of the punitive or deterrence features of the criminal justice system took place during the past decade.

Fourth, efforts to understand better the underlying causes of crime have progressed little. Even among serious observers, the attachment to particular explanations has been promiscuous, one theory yielding to another in quick succession.

Fifth, today virtually no one—scholars, practitioners and politicians alike—dares to advance a program which promises to reduce crime substantially in the near future.[34]

In the face of this stinging critique, who would dare suggest a significant role for LEAA? This same official suggests three targets: improving fairness, effecting economies in the administration of justice, and reducing the costs of crime to individual victims. Others say the real question is how to make sure crime does not pay. Although LEAA helped expose inadequacies, we seem locked into a system that has a far-from-adequate number of courts, prosecutors, defense counsels, and correctional facilities. In a study of the Massachusetts court structure, a committee headed by Archibald Cox put it nicely: "Prompt trial is essential to effective law enforcement. Without it, the penalties for crime cease to deter. The elimination of delay between arrest and trial would markedly reduce the number of crimes, especially crimes threatening the personal security of typical citizens. . . ."[35] Mandatory-minimum sentences, a widely praised reform nowadays, will plainly add to prison overcrowding. Our prison population has jumped some 15 to 20 percent in the past couple of years already. Yet state budgets in many cases are cutting back on this very expenditure. Construction costs per inmate range from $30,000 to $50,000 and higher. As one observer noted, the choice may be between "pay the bill and lock 'em up" or "don't pay the bill and let 'em loose."

The national role in fighting crime in the streets is, and will doubtless remain, a small one. Any prudent national crime control policy will need better data, more experiments, better evaluation, and more focused research. Such a policy should concentrate on juvenile justice and continue to work towards certainty of sentencing. More money is needed for systematic research and development of crime prevention strategies. The national government should be much more in the business of designing, testing, and publicizing crime prevention strategies than of pouring out money and organizing conferences. It should continue to improve crime statistics, develop evaluation methods, and run pilot research programs. A more scientific approach will not necessarily reduce crime but could enable us to understand who is helped or hurt by different strategies and how much various strategies cost.

These days it is fashionable to talk of the *limits* of government. But the limits of government are a pallid excuse for the political exploitation of the crime issue, the mismanagement of LEAA, and the ineffective national leadership that characterized so much of the war on crime.

Twelve years, however, is a short time for what should have been viewed as a long-term campaign. Focus and stamina, over the long haul, have been cardinal ingredients in almost all policy successes. If we have learned to be skeptical about presidential promises, if we have learned government alone cannot solve the crime problem, if we have learned there is a price, inexact but high, that must be paid if we are to make sure crime doesn't pay, then we have profited by this defeat. *Politics will not—and should not—be separated from crime control policy* while the solutions are still uncertain and *while there still are conflicting values to be addressed.* But politics that amounts to fact-free rhetoric, politics that does not make frank reference to value conflicts, can be dangerous. We now know it was dangerous to play to the public's fears, to oversell LEAA as a "war" on crime, to claim successes in time for the next election. It will be dangerous *not* to examine the causes of crime, *not* to debate where accountability should be placed, and *not* to lay down straight what the cost of crime control is.

In his second address to Congress, Abraham Lincoln put it this way:

> The dogmas of the quiet past are inadequate to the stormy present. The occasion is piled high with difficulty and we must rise with the occasion. As our case is new, so we must think anew. We must disenthrall ourselves, and then we shall save our country.

NOTES

Preface

1. William Proxmire, "Advice from a Budget-Cutter," *Today*, 4 April 1980, p. 8.

1. THE POLITICS OF CRIME IN AMERICA

1. *The Figgie Report on Fear of Crime: America Afraid*. A-T-O Inc., 16 September 1980. See also Gallup polls quoted in *U.S. News and World Report*, 21 January 1980, p. 49, and in the *Denver Post*, 1 March 1981.
2. Milton Eisenhower, *The President is Calling* (Garden City, N.Y.: Doubleday, 1974), p. 452.
3. Lyndon B. Johnson, *The Vantage Point* (New York: Holt, Rinehart and Winston, 1971), p. 160.
4. Richard Hofstadter and Michael Wallace, eds., *American Violence: A Documentary History* (New York: Random House, 1971), pp. 30–31.
5. Donald Cressey, "The State of Criminal Statistics," *National Probation and Parole Association Journal* 3 (1957): 232.
6. Hans Zeisel, "The Future of Law Enforcement Statistics: A Summary View," *Federal Statistics: A Report of the President's Commission on Federal Statistics*, 2 (1971): 541.
7. Daniel Bell, "The Myth of Crime Waves," *The End of Ideology* (New York: Collier Books, 1960), p. 151.
8. Albert D. Biderman, "Social Indicators and Goals," in *Social Indicators*, ed. Raymond A. Bauer (Cambridge, Mass.: MIT Press, 1966), p. 115.
9. James Q. Wilson, "Crime and the Criminologists," *Commentary*, July 1974, p. 51.

2. PLACING THE CRIME ISSUE ON THE NATIONAL AGENDA

1. Theodore Sorensen, *Kennedy* (New York: Bantam, 1966), pp. 528, 530. See also Arthur M. Schlesinger, *Robert Kennedy and His Times* (New York: Ballantine, 1979), especially chapters 14–16.

2. Sorensen, *Kennedy*. See also the especially useful memoir of one of John F. Kennedy's early civil rights advisors, Harris Wofford, *Of Kennedys and Kings* (New York: Farrar, Straus & Giroux, 1980).

3. Howard Zinn, *SNCC: The New Abolitionists* (Boston: Beacon Press, 1965).

4. Kennedy said, on 20 May 1963, "I would also hope that any person, whether a citizen of Alabama or a visitor there, would refrain from further outbreaks. I hope that state and local officials in Alabama will meet their responsibilities." *Public Papers of the Presidents* (Washington, D.C.: U.S. Government Printing Office, 1962), p. 391.

5. Kennedy, television message, 11 June 1963, *Public Papers of the Presidents* (Washington, D.C.: U.S. Government Printing Office, 1964), p. 469.

6. Gallup poll released 20 June 1961.

7. Gallup polls released 16 July 1963, 6 June 1964, and 12 November 1964.

8. Sorensen, *Kennedy*, p. 534.

9. David Lawrence, "What's Become of 'Law and Order'?", *U.S. News and World Report*, 26 August 1963, p. 104.

10. "Use of Confession in Trial Is Curbed," *New York Times*, 23 June 1964.

11. Ibid.

12. "Crime in the U.S.—Is It Getting Out of Hand?" *U.S. News and World Report*, 5 August 1963, p. 41.

13. Ibid., p. 40.

14. Lincoln Steffens, *Autobiography* (New York: Harcourt, Brace and World, 1931), p. 285.

15. David Lawrence, "The War Against Crime," *U.S. News and World Report*, 29 June 1964, p. 112.

16. "Speech to GOP Convention," *New York Times*, 15 July 1964.

17. "Goldwater's Acceptance Speech to GOP Convention," *New York Times*, 17 July 1964.

18. Ibid.

19. Arthur Krock, "Street Crime and Rioting as a National Issue," *New York Times*, 21 July 1964.

20. "Johnson News Conference," *New York Times*, 19 July 1964.

21. "Goldwater at Illinois State Fair," *Chicago Tribune*, 20 August 1964.

22. "Goldwater Says He'd Curb Court," *New York Times*, 16 September 1964. Also Theodore White, *The Making of the President: 1964* (New York: Atheneum Publishers, 1965), pp. 367–68.

23. "Wilkins Says Goldwater Victory Might Bring About Police State," *New York Times*, 7 September 1964.

24. "Three Democratic Worries," *Commonweal*, 18 September 1964, pp. 624–25.

25. "Humphrey in South Dakota, Vows Better Deal for Farmers," *New York Times*, 12 September 1964.

26. "Katzenbach Links Street Riots to Crime Rise, Not Rights Drive," *New York Times*, 19 September 1964.

27. "The Curious Campaign—Point by Point," *Newsweek*, 19 October 1964, pp. 27–28.

28. "Goldwater in Final Speech at Civic Auditorium in San Francisco," *New York Times*, 3 November 1964.

29. "Interview with Barry Goldwater," *U.S. News and World Report*, 21 December 1964, pp. 46–49.

30. Barry Goldwater, campaign speech at Al Lang Field, St. Petersburg, Florida, 15 September 1964, p. 4, mimeographed.

31. Lyndon B. Johnson, 16 October 1964, in Dayton, Ohio, *Public Papers of the Presidents* (Washington, D.C.: U.S. Government Printing Office, 1964), p. 1371.

3. A FIRST PRESIDENTIAL RESPONSE

1. "Bar Leader Finds High Court Too Lenient in Criminal Cases," *New York Times*, 30 January 1965.

2. Nicholas Katzenbach, Introduction to Richard Harris, *The Fear of Crime* (New York: Praeger, 1968), p. 7.

3. Gerald Caplan, "Reflections on the Nationalization of Crime, 1964–1968," *Law and the Social Order*, no. 3 (1973), p. 590.

4. Herbert Hoover, inaugural address, 4 March 1929, *Public Papers of the Presidents* (Washington, D.C.: U.S. Government Printing Office, 1974), p. 2.

5. "President Forms Panel to Study Crime Problems," *New York Times*, 27 July 1965.

6. Statement by Nicholas Katzenbach before the Subcommittee on Administrative Practice and Procedure of the Committee on the Judiciary, U.S. Senate, 26 May 1971.

7. Lyndon B. Johnson, "Statement by the President following the Signing of Law Enforcement Assistance Bills," 22 September 1965, *Public Papers of the Presidents* (Washington, D.C.: U.S. Government Printing Office, 1966), p. 103.

8. Interview, Washington, D.C., 1971.

9. Nicholas Katzenbach, statement, Hearings on S. 1792 and S. 1825, before a subcommittee of the Committee on the Judiciary, U.S. Senate, 25 July 1965, p. 7.

10. Public Law 89–197, 22 September 1965, sec. 7.

11. Lyndon B. Johnson, "Statement by the President Following the Signing of Law Enforcement Assistance Bills," *Public Papers of the Presidents* (Washington, D.C.: U.S. Government Printing Office, 1966), p. 1012.

12. Interview, Washington, D.C., 1971.

13. Lyndon B. Johnson, "Remarks on Crime Control at the Signing of the District of Columbia Appropriations Bill," 16 July 1965, *Public Papers of the Presidents* (Washington, D.C.: U.S. Government Printing Office, 1966), pp. 759, 761.

14. Georgetown University Law Center, Institute of Criminal Law and Procedure, "Summary of the Study and Evaluation and Recommendations for Future Programming in the Criminal Justice Field—Study and Evaluation of Projects and Programs Funded under the Law Enforcement Assistance Act of 1965," mimeographed (Washington, D.C.: LEAA, March 1971), pp. 25–26, 42.

15. "Lawlessness in U.S.—Warning from a Top Jurist," *U.S. News and World Report*, 5 July 1965, p. 60.

16. "A Shift in the Wind in Washington," *U.S. News and World Report*, 6 September 1965, p. 27.

17. "Eisenhower's Views on the Breakdown in Law and Order," *U.S. News and World Report*, 13 September 1965, p. 20.

18. J. Skelly Wright, "Crime in the Streets and the New McCarthyism," *New Republic*, 9 October 1965, p. 10.

19. J. Edgar Hoover, "The Faith of Freedom," *Vital Speeches of the Day*, 15 November 1965, p. 71.

20. "GOP Links Crime to City 'Machines,'" *New York Times*, 20 December 1965.

21. "Johnson Presses Anti-crime Drive," *New York Times*, 10 March 1966.

22. *Miranda* v. *Arizona*, 384 U.S. 436 (1966). See also "High Court Takes Confession Cases," *New York Times*, 23 November 1965.

23. "Leary Says Court Decision Will Hurt 'Law and Order,'" *New York Times*, 15 July 1966.

24. Arthur Krock, "In the Nation: The Wall between Crime and Punishment," *New York Times*, 14 June 1966.

25. Richard Nixon, "If Mob Rule Takes Hold in U.S.—A Warning from Richard Nixon," *U.S. News and World Report*, 15 August 1966, p. 64.

26. "GOP Will Press Racial Disorders as Election Issue," *New York Times*, 4 October 1966.

27. At the Sixtieth Annual Meeting of the National Association of Attorneys General in Cleveland, the consensus was that "confession rates have remained stable even in states where the *Escobedo* ruling has been extended to require the police to warn suspects of their rights."

28. John T. Elliff, *Crime, Dissent and the Attorney General* (Beverly Hills, Cal.: Sage Publications, 1971), p. 49.

29. For a perceptive discussion of some of the internal divisions and politics of the crime commission see Lloyd E. Ohlin, "Report on the President's Commission on Law Enforcement and Administration of Justice," *Sociology and Public Policy: The Case of Presidential Commissions*, ed. Mirra Komarovsky (New York: Elsevier, 1975), pp. 93–115.

30. United States Government, a report by the President's Commission on Law Enforcement and Administration of Justice, *The Challenge of Crime in a Free Society* (Washington, D.C.: U.S. Government Printing Office; New York: Avon, 1968) (the commission is cited hereafter as the president's crime commission). See also James Q. Wilson, "A Reader's Guide to the Crime Commission Reports," *The Public Interest*, no. 9 (Fall 1967), p. 74.

31. James Vorenberg, the former executive director of the crime commission, reflecting on the commission's work five years later, concluded that the strong sense of optimism the commission had to the effect that something could be done about the crime problem was premature. He cites 1968 as a bad year for criminal justice, noting that Richard Nixon's charges that the Supreme Court was the primary cause of crime provided police officials, prosecutors, legislators, and the general public with an easy explanation for the enormous increases in crime in the late 1960s. "This relieved some of the pressure for change, a process which criminal justice officials were finding painful and more difficult than expected." He also observes that "five years later crime is unquestionably a far worse problem for the country than it was then and our system of criminal justice—the police, courts, and corrections agencies—seem less capable of coping with

it." James Vorenberg, "The War on Crime: The First Five Years," *Atlantic Monthly*, May 1972, pp. 63–69.

32. Nicholas Katzenbach, statement before the Subcommittee on Administrative Practice and Procedure, Committee on the Judiciary, U.S. Senate, 26 May 1971, mimeographed.

33. Harry McPherson, *A Political Education* (Boston: Mass.: Atlantic-Little Brown, 1972), pp. 382–83.

34. *President's Task Force on Crime* (December 1967), mimeographed. Copy on file, Lyndon B. Johnson Presidential Library, Austin, Texas.

35. Lyndon B. Johnson, *The Vantage Point* (New York: Holt, Rinehart and Winston, 1971), p. 355.

4. LEGISLATING FOR THE WAR ON CRIME

1. The commission report was published eight months later. United States Government. *The Report of the National Advisory Commission on Civil Disorders* (Washington: U.S. Government Printing Office, March 1968).

2. Lyndon B. Johnson, "State of the Union Address," *New York Times*, 11 January 1967.

3. United States Government, a report by the President's Commission on Law Enforcement and Administration of Justice, *The Challenge of Crime in a Free Society* (Washington, D.C.: U.S. Government Printing Office; New York, Avon, 1968). The recommendations are contained on pp. 293–301 in the Government Printing Office (GPO) edition and pp. 650–64 of the Avon paper edition. Page numbers of notes following refer to the GPO edition.

4. Ibid., pp. 15 and 291.

5. Gerald R. Ford, as quoted in "Johnson's Crime Message," *New Republic*, 18 February 1967, p. 10.

6. "Johnson Sets Strategy for a War on Crime," *Business Week*, 11 February 1967, p. 82.

7. "Johnson's Program on Crime Delights Some Criminologists," *New York Times*, 12 February 1967.

8. Ibid.

9. "Johnson's Crime Message," *New Republic*, 18 February 1967, p. 10.

10. Sen. John McClellan, *Hearings: Controlling Crime Through More Effective Law Enforcement*, Subcommittee on Criminal Laws and Procedures of the Committee on the Judiciary, U.S. Senate, 7 March 1967, p. 153.

11. Report from the Committee on the Judiciary, Omnibus Crime Control and Safe Streets Act of 1967, U.S. Senate, Report No. 1097, 29 April 1968, pp. 220, 221.

12. Interview with Ramsey Clark, Washington, D.C., 7 December 1971.

13. Ibid.

14. U.S., Congress, House, *Congressional Record* (3 August 1967), p. 21201.

15. Warren Christopher, deputy attorney general, press release, 29 August 1967, pp. 1, 2. Copy on file, Lyndon B. Johnson Presidential Library, Department of Justice files, Austin, Texas.

16. Interview, Washington, D.C., 1971.

17. "Crime Time," *Newsweek*, 3 June 1968, p. 36.

18. Senate hearings, 1967, p. 840. (See n. 10.)

19. Interview, Washington, D.C., 1971.

20. Senate Report 1097, p. 37.

21. U.S., Congress, Senate, Committee on the Judiciary, hearings before Subcommittee on Criminal Laws and Procedures, *Controlling Crime Through More Effective Law Enforcement*, 7 March 1967, pp. 384–85.

22. Lyndon B. Johnson, "Remarks at the Swearing in of Ramsey Clark as Attorney General," 10 March 1967, *Public Papers of the Presidents* (Washington, D.C.: U.S. Government Printing Office, 1968), pp. 312–14.

23. Bobby Baker, with Larry King, *Wheeling and Dealing: Confessions of a Capitol Hill Operator* (New York: Norton & Co., 1978), pp. 265–66.

24. Interview, Washington, D.C., 1971.

25. See Harry McPherson, *A Political Education* (Boston: Atlantic-Little Brown, 1972), p. 280. This particular quote comes, however, from a memo, "For the President," 14 June 1968.

26. See "Target: The Supreme Court," *New York Times*, 15 May 1968. See also "Cruel Hoax: Veto Called For," *New York Times*, 7 June, 1968, sec. 2, p. 38.

27. Quoted in Richard Harris, *The Fear of Crime* (New York: Praeger, 1968), p. 99.

28. Ford, quoted in *New York Times*, "Johnson's Inaction on Anticrime Bill Criticized by Ford," 14 June 1968.

29. Ramsey Clark, personal files, Lyndon B. Johnson Presidential Library, Austin, Texas.

30. McPherson, *Political Education*, p. 279.

5. LAW AND ORDER IN THE 1968 ELECTIONS

1. "Poll Finds Crime Top Fear at Home," *New York Times*, 28 February 1968.

2. "63% in Gallup Poll Thinks Courts Are Too Lenient on Criminals," *New York Times*, 3 March 1968.

3. Gallup poll data released in 1964–66, summarized in part in a 19 July 1966 release, indicated this response to the following query: "Do you think the Administration is pushing integration too fast, or not fast enough?" "Too fast 30% February, 1964; 34% April 1965; 40% August 1965; 46% July 1966; and 52% July 1966."

4. Richard M. Nixon, "Toward Freedom from Fear," mimeographed, campaign statement issued in New York, New York, 8 May 1968.

5. Lyndon B. Johnson, "Letter to the Majority Leader of the Senate on Crime Control and Safe Streets Bill, 9 May 1968," *Public Papers of the Presidents* (Washington, D.C.: U.S. Government Printing Office, 1969), pp. 585–86.

6. A good account of Johnson's foreign policy problem in early 1968 in Herbert Y. Schandler, *The Unmaking of a President: Lyndon Johnson and Vietnam* (Princeton, N.J.: Princeton University Press, 1977).

7. "GOP Unit Scores Johnson on Crime," *New York Times*, 23 April 1968.

8. Alexander M. Bickel, "Crime, Courts and the Old Nixon," *New Republic*, 15 June 1968, p. 9.

9. "Negro Rights Leader Says Nixon Plays on Prejudice," *New York Times*, 10 July 1968.

10. Edward W. Knappman, ed., *Presidential Election 1968* (New York: Facts on File, 1970), p. 51.

11. James Reston, "Political Pollution: The Myths about the Candidates," *New York Times*, 18 August 1968.

12. Hubert H. Humphrey, Remarks at the Democratic National Convention, mimeographed, Chicago, Illinois, August 1968.

13. "Nixon Comments on Law and Order," *New York Times*, 5 September 1968.

14. "Politics: Agnew Opens His Campaign," *New York Times*, 5 September 1968.

15. "O'Brien Attacks Role of Agnew," *New York Times*, 12 September 1968.

16. "Agnew Deplores Demonstration," *New York Times*, 14 September 1968.

17. "81% in a Poll See Law Breakdown," *New York Times*, 10 September 1968. "Poll Finds Most View GOP As Better Able to Handle Issues," *New York Times*, 8 September 1968. "Poll Finds Nixon Holds Lead on Issue of Law and Order," *New York Times*, 13 September 1968.

18. Quoted in Ralph H. Phelps, "Humphrey's Dilemma," *New York Times*, 13 September 1968.

19. "Wallace Diagnoses High Court as 'Sick'," *New York Times*, 10 July 1968. For an analysis of the George Wallace role in American politics, see Daniel A. Mazmanian, *Third Parties in American Elections* (Washington, D.C.: Brookings Institution, 1974), especially chapter 1.

20. "Humphrey Links Wallace to Fear," *New York Times*, 2 October 1968.

21. Tom Wicker, "In the Nation: But Who Will Guard the Guards?", *New York Times*, 15 October 1968.

22. Hearings before the Subcommittee on Administrative Practice and Procedures of the Committee on the Judiciary, *Presidential Commissions*, U.S. Senate, 27 May 1970, pp. 166, 168–69.

23. James Q. Wilson, "Crime and the Liberal Audience," *Commentary*, January 1971, p. 71. See also Richard Scammon and Ben J. Wattenberg, *The Real Majority* (New York: Coward McCann, 1970).

24. See, for example, Gordon Tullock, "Does Punishment Deter Crime?", *The Public Interest*, Summer 1974, pp. 103–11, and Isaac Ehrlich, "The Deterrent Effect of Capital Punishment: A Question of Life and Death," *American Economic Review*, June 1975, pp. 397–417.

25. John W. Dean III, *Blind Ambition* (New York: Pocket, 1977), pp. 389–90.

26. Richard M. Nixon, acceptance speech, Republican National Convention, Miami Beach, Florida, July 1968, mimeographed.

6. LAUNCHING THE WAR ON CRIME

1. Advisory Commission on Intergovernmental Relations, *Safe Streets Reconsidered: The Block Grant Experience 1968–1975* (Washington, D.C.: ACIR, 1977), p. A-55.

2. James Q. Wilson, interview, Cambridge, Massachusetts, 12 April 1977.

3. Advisory Commission on Intergovernmental Relations: *Block Grants: A Comparative Analysis* (Washington, D.C.: ACIR, 1977), p. A-60.

4. James L. Sundquist, *Making Federalism Work* (Washington, D.C.: Brookings Institution, 1969), p. 266.

5. Richard P. Nathan, et al., *Monitoring Revenue Sharing* (Washington, D.C.: Brookings Institution, 1975).

6. Richard W. Velde, associate administrator of LEAA, in speech to SPA directors, Denver, Colorado, 3 August 1970, mimeographed.

7. Nixon's speech on crime in the District of Columbia, November 1970, quoted in *Congressional Quarterly: Crime and the Law*, 1971, p. 27.

8. Committee on the Judiciary, U.S. Senate, unpublished report of the proceedings on the nomination of Charles H. Rogovin and Richard W. Velde, 12 March 1969.

9. Joseph Kraft, "President in Blue," *Washington Post*, 3 June 1971; also Edward Jay Epstein, *Agency of Fear* (New York: G. P. Putnam's Sons, 1977).

10. *Congressional Quarterly: Crime and the Law.*

11. Hearings before Subcommittee 5 of the Committee on the Judiciary, U.S. House of Representatives, testimony of Ramsey Clark, Former Attorney General of the U.S., 18 February 1970.

12. Ibid., testimony of John N. Mitchell, 12 March 1970.

13. Hearings before Committee on the Judiciary, U.S. Senate, testimony of Richard W. Velde, associate administrator, LEAA, 7 July 1970.

14. Ibid., remarks of Sen. Roman L. Hruska, 24 June 1970.

15. Ibid., remarks of Sen. Edward M. Kennedy, 30 July 1970.

16. Minority views of Messrs. Bayh, Hart, and Kennedy, on report from the Committee on the Judiciary, Senate, on the Omnibus Crime Control Act of 1970, No. 91–1253, Calendar No. 1270, 29 September 1970.

17. The House, for example, did not approve the Nixon administration's proposal to waive state-to-city pass-through requirements but continued to require that states pass through to cities and localities 75 percent of LEAA monies. The Senate, on the other hand, came up with a new formula that was more favorable to the states, namely, that states should pass through to cities a portion of LEAA funds that was the same as the local share of total state-local law enforcement expenditure. Given the greater financial difficulties of the cities, as well as their overwhelming crime burdens, this was seen as an attempt to disenfranchise urban areas. The Senate version prevailed in conference. As another example, the House bill would have replaced the troika administration of LEAA with a single administrator, whereas the Senate retained the troika but added more vague language about who was really in charge. Again the Senate version was accepted.

18. For example, grants were provided to establish Criminal Justice Coordinating Councils to help cities with populations of over two hundred fifty thousand write plans for law enforcement and criminal justice projects. More vague wording was written in to ensure that the comprehensive state plans would provide "adequate assistance" to areas with both high crime and high law enforcement activity. Although this requirement was a direct response to the challenge of the National League of Cities, Congress did not set a specific dollar amount or percentage formula to be given to high crime areas.

19. *Time*, 18 October 1971, p. 34.

20. Hearings before the Subcommittee on Legal and Monetary Affairs of the Committee on Government Operations, U.S. House of Representatives, testimony of Bill Baxley, attorney general of the state of Alabama, 20 July 1971.

21. Ibid., testimony of Charles H. Rogovin, former administrator, LEAA, 5 October 1971.

22. Interviews with White House staff, Washington, D.C., winter 1971.

23. Jerry Wilson, *Police Report* (Boston: Little, Brown, 1975), p. 68

24. Interview with former White House aide Geoffrey Sheppard, 8 May 1977.

25. Interview with Richard Velde, associate administrator, LEAA, 10 June 1971.

26. "The Attorney General and Crime," *Washington Post*, 11 September 1971.

27. Joseph Kraft, "President in Blue," *Washington Post*, 3 June 1971.

28. David Seidman and Michael Couzens, "Getting the Crime Rate Down: Political Pressure and Crime Reporting," *Law and Society Review* 8 (1974): 457–94.

29. "Attorney General and Crime."

30. Interview with LEAA officials, 1972.

31. Ibid.

32. Interview with Daniel L. Skoler, head of a division in LEAA, 4 May 1971.

33. Twentieth Century Fund Task Force on the Law Enforcement Assistance Administration, *Law Enforcement: The Federal Role*, background paper by Victor S. Navasky (New York: McGraw Hill Book Co., 1976).

34. Quoted in Edward Jay Epstein, *Agency of Fear* (New York: G. P. Putnam's Sons, 1977), pp. 225–26.

35. Ibid.

36. *Law Enforcement*.

37. Epstein, *Agency*.

38. Richard Nixon, radio text, 14 March 1973.

39. Quoted in Judith Axler Turner, "Congress Holds Past Criticism in Check as It Considers Revenue-Sharing Role for LEAA," *National Journal*, 31 March 1973.

40. Interview with Paul Woodward, LEAA general counsel, 7 June 1971.

41. Interview with Richard Velde, associate administrator of LEAA, 10 June 1971.

42. Quoted in Richard S. Frank, "LEAA Moves to Improve Its Performance as a Pioneer in Revenue-Sharing Technique," *National Journal*, 29 January 1972.

43. Charles L. Owen, executive director of the Kentucky Crime Commission, in testimony before Subcommittee 5, House Committee on the Judiciary, LEAA, 1973.

44. James V. Stanton, testimony before Subcommittee 5, House Committee of the Judiciary, LEAA, 1973.

45. Clark Hoyt, "Anti-crime Funds Mishandled," *Detroit Free Press*, November 1972.

46. Joint explanatory statement of the Committee of Conference on the

Senate Amendment to H.R. 8152, 93rd Cong., 1st sess.

47. Congressman Peter Rodino, on the conference committee report, *Legislative Record*, 26 July 1973.

48. Cities of over two hundred fifty thousand in population could submit annual plans to SPAS, and planning grants were authorized for interstate metropolitan regional planning units. Matching requirements were simplified and reduced to 90 percent federal to 10 percent hard cash local, with the state supplying half of the nonfederal share. Citizen, community, and professional organizations could now participate in state planning agencies and in regional planning units (RPUS); however, the majority of RPU members were to be elected officials.

49. Theodore H. White, *Breach of Faith: The Fall of Richard Nixon* (New York: Atheneum Publishers, 1975), p. 323.

50. Michael D. Reagan, *The New Federalism* (New York: Oxford University Press, 1972), pp. 130–31.

51. Eleanor Chelimsky, *A Primary Source Examination of the Law Enforcement Assistance Administration, and Some Reflections on Crime Control Policy* (Washington, D.C.: MITRE Corp., 1974).

52. Aaron Wildavsky, "Government and the People," in *Perspectives on the Presidency*, ed. Aaron Wildavsky (Boston: Little, Brown, 1975), p. 52.

7. THE DECLINE OF LEAA

1. Charles E. Silberman, *Criminal Violence, Criminal Justice* (New York: Random House, 1978).

2. Henry S. Dogin, LEAA administrator, quoted in *Boston Globe*, 23 November 1978.

3. Gerald Ford, speech at the University of Jacksonville, Jacksonville, Florida, 16 December 1971, quoted in *President Ford: The Man and His Record*, *Congressional Quarterly*, August 1974.

4. Ronald J. Ostrow, "Nation's Serious Crime Up 17 Percent," *Honolulu Advertiser*, 31 March 1975; Thomas T. Moore, "U.S. Crime Worse than Figures Show," *San Francisco Examiner and Chronicle*, 3 March 1974, and *U.S. News and World Report*, 4 August 1975.

5. Interview with Walter Fiederowicz, associate deputy attorney general, Washington, D.C., 13 November 1978.

6. *New York Times*, 6 September 1975.

7. Comptroller general's GAO report to Congress, *Difficulties of Assessing Results of Law Enforcement Assistance Administration Projects to Reduce Crime* (Washington, D.C.: U.S. Government Printing Office, 19 March 1974).

8. Interview, Washington, D.C., December 1976. This person wished to remain anonymous because her company received substantial evaluation contracts from LEAA.

9. Fiederowicz interview.

10. Richard E. Cohen, "Renewal of LEAA Likely despite Doubts on Crime Impact," *National Journal*, 20 September 1975.

11. Ibid.

12. Statement of Sen. Roman L. Hruska, *Congressional Record*, 29 July 1975.

13. Testimony of Attorney General Edward H. Levi before the Senate

Subcommittee on Criminal Laws and Procedures of the Senate, *Amendments to LEAA*, 2 October 1975.

14. Opening remarks by Sen. Edward F. Kennedy, *Amendments to LEAA*, 2 October 1975.

15. Testimony of Victor Lowe, director of the Government Division of the General Accounting Office, before the Subcommittee on Crime of the House of Representatives, "LEAA," 19 February 1976.

16. Kennedy's bill, S. 3043 in the 94th Congress, stated, "Congress finds that the financial and technical resources of the Federal Government should be used to provide constructive leadership and direction to State and Local governments in combating the serious problem of crime. . . ."

17. Eleanor Chelimsky, *High Impact Anti-Crime Program*, vol. 1 (Washington, D.C.: MITRE Corp., 1976).

18. Roper Organization poll, May 1976, reported in *New York Times*, 4 June 1976.

19. Quoted in Dena Kleiman, "Crime May Not Be the Best of All Issues," *New York Times*, 17 April 1977.

20. Gerald Caplan, " 'Losing' the War on Crime," mimeographed. (Address given at the Los Angeles Town Hall, Los Angeles, 9 December 1975).

21. *New York Times*, 24 May 1976.

22. Quoted in Timothy D. Schellhardt, "States Crack Down on Crime with a Host of Stiff New Measures," *Wall Street Journal*, 24 June 1976.

23. Macklin Fleming, *Of Crimes and Rights* (New York: W. W. Norton, 1978).

24. President Ford, address at the University of Michigan, quoted in *New York Times*, 7 September 1976.

25. President Ford, address before the International Association of Chiefs of Police in Miami, Florida, 27 September 1976.

26. Radio interview with Bill Moyers on the 1976 campaign, Public Broadcasting Systems, 6 May 1976.

27. Jimmy Carter, speech at Portland, Oregon, rally, 27 September 1976, quoted in *The Presidential Campaign 1976*, vol. 1, pt. 2 (Washington D.C.: U.S. Government Printing Office, 1978).

28. Gary R. Orren, "Candidate Style and Voter Alignment in 1976," *Emerging Coalitions in American Politics*, ed. Seymour Martin Lipset (San Francisco: Institute of Contemporary Studies, 1978).

29. Jimmy Carter, address to the Economic Club of Detroit, Michigan, 15 October 1976, quoted in *The Presidential Campaign 1976*.

30. Interview with Margaret McKenna, deputy counsel to the President, Washington, D.C., 20 July 1978.

31. Interview with David Rubenstein, deputy director of domestic policy, Washington, D.C., 20 July 1978.

32. Fiederowicz interview.

33. Rubenstein interview.

34. Testimony of Attorney General Griffin Bell before the Subcommittee on Crime of the House of Representatives, *Restructuring the Law Enforcement Assistance Administration*, 1 March 1978.

35. Interview with Thomas Madden, LEAA counsel, Washington, D.C., 13 November 1978.

36. Ibid.

37. Interview with an administration aide, Washington, D.C., 13 November 1978.

38. Interview with Tom Connally, legislative aide to Sen. Joseph R. Biden, Washington, D.C., 13 November 1978.

39. Interview with Richard Velde, Senate Judiciary Committee minority counsel, Washington, D.C., 13 November 1978.

40. Madden interview.

41. Testimony of Attorney General Griffin Bell before the Subcommittee on Criminal Laws and Procedures of the Senate, *Federal Assistance to State and Local Criminal Justice Agencies*, 16 August 1978.

42. Rubenstein interview.

43. *The United States Budget in Brief, Fiscal Year, 1981* (Washington, D.C.: Executive Office of the President, 1980), p. 56.

44. Telephone conversation with Tom Parker, executive director of the Criminal Justice Association, 7 May 1980.

45. Patrick V. Murphy, president, Police Foundation, "A Federal Problem Called Crime" (letter to the editor), *New York Times*, 23 April 1980.

46. Interview, May 1980.

47. El Paso County Commissioner Chuck Heim, quoted in *Colorado Springs Sun*, 29 May 1980.

48. Telephone interview with Stephen T. Boyle, director of congressional liaison, OJARS, 18 March 1981, and in-house memoranda from Boyle, 28 May, 27 June, 2 July, and 24 December 1980.

49. Herbert Kaufman, quoted in "LEAA Going Out of Business after 12 Years," *Cleveland Plain Dealer*, 13 October 1980.

50. Quoted in B. Drummond Ayres, Jr., "Kennedy, in Deep South, Charges President with Neglect on Crime," *New York Times*, 10 November 1979.

51. "Official Reagan/Republican Positions on Crime and Justice," mimeographed, 31 January 1980.

52. Quoted in "Excerpts from Burger Texas Speech," *New York Times*, 9 February 1981, and in "Burger Urges More Funds to Battle 'Crime Inflation,'" *Rocky Mountain News*, 9 February 1981.

8. WHAT WENT WRONG?

1. A state planning director in an anonymous interview, 1971.

2. Police Chief James Parsons of Birmingham, Alabama, quoted in John M. Goshko, "Strife within Crime Agency May Force Shakeup by Ford," *Washington Post*, 21 September 1975.

3. Richard W. Velde, "A Response to Newspaper Reports Concerning a Report by the Center for National Security Studies," statement in the *Congressional Record*, Senate, 25 May 1976.

4. James E. Hagerty, "Criminal Justice: Toward a New Federal Role," *Public Administration Review*, March–April 1978, pp. 173–76.

5. Charles H. Rogovin, Statement before the House Subcommittee on Legal and Monetary Affairs of the Committee on Government Operations, 5 October 1971.

6. Congressman William Steiger, quoted in Eleanor Chelimsky, *A Primary-Source Examination of the LEAA, and Some Reflections on Crime Control Policy* (Washington, D.C.: MITRE Corp., May 1974).

7. Statement of Sen. Edward Kennedy, *Congressional Record*, Senate, 10 July 1978.

8. Interview with Perry Rivkin, associate administrator, LEAA, Washington, D.C., 2 February 1978.

9. Wesley Pomeroy, quoted in *National Journal*, 25 April 1970.

10. Interview with Charles Rogovin, president, the Police Foundation, 1 November 1971.

11. Charles Rogovin, testimony in Senate hearings, 1970.

12. Interview with Ron Ostrow, *LA Times* Washington News Bureau, 7 May 1971.

13. Jerris Leonard, quoted in Richard S. Frank, "LEAA Moves to Improve its Performance as a Pioneer in Revenue-Sharing Techniques," *National Journal*, 29 January 1972.

14. Santarelli, quoted in John M. Goshko, "Strife," and in Victor S. Navasky, *Law Enforcement: The Federal Role: Report of the Twentieth Century Fund Task Force on the* LEAA (New York: McGraw-Hill Book Co.), 1976.

15. Gerald M. Caplan, " 'Losing' the War on Crime" (Address given at the Los Angeles Town Hall, 9 December 1975), and interview with James Vorenberg, Harvard Law School, 26 May 1977.

16. Interview with Timothy West, Office of Congressional Liaison, LEAA, Washington, D.C., 13 November 1978.

17. Unpublished Senate confirmation hearings on Norval Morris for LEAA administrator, September 1978.

18. Interview with Richard Velde, minority counsel to the Senate Judiciary Committee, Washington, D.C., 13 November 1978.

19. Joseph L. Mulvey, regional administrator, LEAA Denver Regional Office, pointed out quotes by Peter Flaherty, deputy attorney general, in the *Washington Post*, June 1977, and by Richard S. Page, administrator of the Urban Mass Transportation Administration, in the *New York Times*, 4 April 1978.

20. Telephone conversation with Helen Lessen, General Counsel's Office, LEAA, 7 May 1980.

21. Luis P. Salas and Ralph G. Lewis, "The Law Enforcement Assistance Administration and Minority Communities," *Journal of Police Science and Administration* (1979): 399.

22. Omnibus Crime Control and Safe Streets Act of 1968.

23. Interview with Ramsey Clark, Washington, D.C., 7 December 1971.

24. Norval Morris in *Federal Probation*, June 1968.

25. Daniel Skoler, "Comprehensive Criminal Justice Planning—A New Challenge," *Crime and Delinquency*, July 1968.

26. Interview with Gerald Caplan, director of the National Institute for Criminal Justice and Law Enforcement, Washington, D.C., 1971.

27. Interview with Daniel Skoler, former deputy director, Office of Law Enforcement Assistance, Washington, D.C., 4 May 1971.

28. Interview with Sandra Braemenk, assistant to the director, Office of Justice Administration, Boston, Massachusetts, November 1970.

29. Interview with Massachusetts SPA staff member, Boston, Massachusetts, November 1970.

30. Interview with Police Chief Stafford, Jacksonville, Illinois, 1971.

31. Interview with Deputy Chief of Police Hanlon, Worcester, Massachusetts, 1971.

32. Interview with Mr. Morgan and Mr. Bremer, consultants at the Institute of Government, University of Georgia, Athens, 24 February 1972.

33. Testimony of Glen D. King, executive director, International Association of Chiefs of Police, before the Subcommittee on Criminal Laws and Procedures of the Senate Judiciary Committee, 23 August 1978.

34. Interview with George Kuper, finance administrator, Office of Justice Administration, Boston, Massachusetts, 1971.

35. Carl W. Stenberg, "The Safe Streets Act: Seven Years Later," *Perspective*, winter 1976, p. 9.

36. From 1969 to 1977, LEAA provided over $63 million to these groups: National District Attorneys Association; National Center for State Courts; American Bar Association; International Association for Chiefs of Police; National Sheriffs' Association; National Council on Crime and Delinquency; National Conference of State Criminal Justice Planning Administrators; National College of District Attorneys; National League of Cities; National Legal Aid and Defender Association; Council of State Governments; American Correctional Association; National Association of Attorneys General; International City Management Association; National Council of Juvenile Court Judges; National Association of Counties; National Governors' Conference; National Association of Pretrial Services Agencies. Source: LEAA *Annual Reports, 1969–77*, 28 July 1977. While conducting interviews at LEAA in November 1978, we met a lobbyist for state planners who was very much at home in LEAA offices. Since the interests of some of these groups, such as state planners, may coincide with the interests of LEAA—for example, in claiming success for the block grant and requesting higher congressional appropriations with fewer federal strings—a certain amount of mutual back scratching occurred.

37. Interview with Paul Woodward, LEAA general counsel, Washington, D.C., 7 June 1971.

38. West interview.

39. Conversation with Douglas Harmon, American University, Washington, D.C., 1971.

40. Woodward interview.

41. Ibid.

42. Interview with Richard Velde, LEAA associate administrator, Washington, D.C., 10 June 1971.

43. Hagerty, "Criminal Justice."

44. Interview with a technical staff associate for a private research and evaluation corporation, Washington, D.C., December 1976.

45. Testimony of Mayor Tom Moody, of Columbus, Ohio, president of the National League of Cities, before the Subcommittee on Criminal Laws and Procedures of the Senate Judiciary Committee, 16 August 1978.

46. Eleanor Chelimsky, *The Need for Better Data to Support Crime Control Policy* (Washington, D.C.: MITRE Corp., 1976).

47. Interview with Robert G. Goffus, chief of Audit Branch, LEAA, Washington, D.C., 18 January 1972.

48. Norval Morris and Gordon Hawkins, *Letter to the President on Crime Control* (Chicago: University of Chicago Press, 1977), p. 4. Morris, the dean of the University of Chicago's Law School, and his colleague offer a provocative set of recommendations for presidential leadership in the area of crime control.

49. Susan O. White and Samuel Krislov, eds., *Understanding Crime: An*

Evaluation of the National Institute of Law Enforcement and Criminal Justice (Washington, D.C.: Committee on Research on Law Enforcement and Criminal Justice, National Research Council, National Academy of Sciences, 1977).

50. Gordon Karl Zenk, *Project* SEARCH: *The Struggle for Control of Criminal Information in America* (Westport, Conn.: 1979).

51. Testimony of Charles R. Work before the Subcommittee on Criminal Laws and Procedures of the Senate Judiciary Committee, 27 September 1978.

52. Letter from Dale Tooley, district attorney for Colorado, to Charles D. Weller, Denver Anti-Crime Council, 9 April 1973.

53. Joan Pettersilia and Peter W. Greenwood, *Mandatory Prison Sentences: Their Projected Effects on Crime and Prison Populations* (Santa Monica, Cal.: RAND Corp., 1977).

54. Interview with James Gregg, Office of Management and Budget examiner for LEAA, Washington, D.C., 1971.

55. James Q. Wilson, "Crime, Punishment and Reformation," in *The Americans: 1976*, ed. Irving Kristol and Paul Weaver (Lexington, Mass.: Lexington Books, 1976).

56. George E. Hale and Marian L. Palley, "Intergovernmental Relations and the Decision-Making Process" (Paper delivered at the Annual Meeting of the American Political Science Association, Washington, D.C., 1–4 September 1977). See also by the same authors, *The Politics of Federal Grants* (Washington, D.C., Congressional Quarterly Press, 1981).

9. THE WAR ON UNSAFE STREETS: LESSONS AND PROSPECTS

1. Gallup poll, quoted in *U.S. News and World Report*, 21 January 1980, p. 49; Yankelovitch poll, October 1978, reported in *Time*, 23 October 1978; Louis Harris survey, reported in *Boston Globe*, 3 July 1978.

2. Senator Hruska, *Congressional Record*, (30 September 1976), p. S 17320–S 17321.

3. Robert McKay, "It's Time to Rehabilitate the Sentencing Process," *Judicature*, December 1976, reprinted in *Congressional Record* (10 March 1977) S 3966–Sec. 7.

4. William Gorham and Nathan Glazer, eds., "The Introduction and Overview," in *The Urban Predicament* (Washington, D.C.: Urban Institute, 1976), p. 2.

5. James Q. Wilson, "Crime, Punishment and Reformation," in *The Americans: 1976*, ed. Irving Kristol and Paul Weaver (Lexington, Mass.: Lexington Books, 1976), p. 100.

6. Studies by the Police Foundation and the RAND Corporation, quoted in Frances W. Sargent, "Getting the Most from Our Police," *Boston Globe*, 21 February 1977.

7. Gerald M. Caplan, "Why Government Alone Can't End the Crime Wave," *U.S. News and World Report*, 11 April 1977, p. 82.

8. Ibid., but see also Caplan's earlier statement that "advanced technology probably offers the best hope of holding down crime in the near future," quoted in Alan Otten, "Crime Fighting," *Wall Street Journal*, 16 January 1975.

9. Study by the National Advisory Commission on Higher Education for Police Officers, quoted in *Boston Globe*, 27 November 1978.

10. Arlen J. Large, "Preventive Detention, One Year Later," *Wall Street Journal*, 4 February 1972.

11. Edwin McDowell, "House Panel on Violent Crime Finds Experts Are Short on Solutions," *New York Times*, 15 January 1978.

12. On the inadequacy of present efforts see Franklin E. Zimring, "Firearms and Federal Law: The Gun Control Act of 1968," *Journal of Legal Studies*, January 1975, pp. 133–98.

13. Gerald M. Caplan, director of the National Institute of Law Enforcement and Criminal Justice, "Why Government Alone Can't End the Crime Wave," *U.S. News and World Report*, 11 April 1977, p. 82.

14. Richard Neustadt, *Presidential Power: The Politics of Leadership, With Reflections on Johnson and Nixon* (New York: John Wiley, 1976), p. 34. See also Thomas E. Cronin, *The State of the Presidency*, 2d ed. (Boston: Little, Brown, 1980).

15. Senator Hruska, *Congressional Record*, 30 September 1976.

16. Quoted in "Justice Report/Renewal of LEAA Likely despite Doubts on Crime Impact," *National Journal*, 20 September 1975, p. 1330.

17. Edward H. Levi, interview, *U.S. News and World Report*, 30 June 1975, p. 32.

18. Douglass Cater and Stephen Strickland, *TV Violence and the Child* (New York: Russell Sage Foundation, 1975), p. 131.

19. See, for example, Murray A. Straus, Richard Gelles, and Suzanne Steinmetz, *Behind Closed Doors: A Survey of Family Violence in America* (New York: Doubleday, 1979); Graeme R. Newman, ed., "Crime and Justice in America: 1776–1976," *Annals of the American Academy of Political and Social Science*, January 1976, especially, pp. 1–30; Charles E. Silberman, *Criminal Violence, Criminal Justice* (New York: Random House, 1979); Robert P. Rhodes, *The Insoluble Problems of Crime* (New York: John Wiley, 1977).

20. "Comeback of Violence in America," interview with Dr. David Abrahamsen, *U.S. News and World Report*, 22 October 1973.

21. Lynn A. Curtis, "The Conservative New Criminology," *Society* 14 (1977): 8, 12–15.

22. Luis P. Salas and Ralph G. Lewis, "The Law Enforcement Assistance Administration and Minority Communities," *Journal of Police Science and Administration* 7 (1979).

23. Frank Zimring and Gordon Hawkins, "Ideology and Euphoria in Crime Control," mimeographed (Chicago: University of Chicago Law School, n.d.).

24. Interview with Boris S. Nikiforov, Moscow, February 1977.

25. Gerald M. Caplan, " 'Losing' the War on Crime," mimeographed. (Address given at the Los Angeles Town Hall, 9 December 1975), pp. 6 and 13.

26. Quoted in David Farrell, "Sen. Kennedy's Thoughts on Crime," *Boston Sunday Globe*, 24 July 1977.

27. Daniel J. Elazar, "The United States as a Federal Nation: Some Recent Developments," April 1976, mimeographed, p. 54. See also his *American Federalism: A View from the States* (New York: Crowell, 1964).

28. A. Lee Fritschler, *Smoking and Politics: Policymaking in the Federal*

Bureaucracy (Englewood Cliffs, N.J.: Prentice-Hall, 1975).

29. Quoted in "Lax Funds—Sharing Audits Hit," *Denver Post*, 28 July 1979.

30. Richard Starnes, "Product of Law Enforcement Industry Proves Elusive," *Rocky Mountain News* (Denver), 23 July 1974.

31. Caplan, " 'Losing' the War."

32. James Q. Wilson, "Crime and Law Enforcement," in *Agenda for the Nation*, ed. Kermit Gordon (Washington, D.C.: Brookings Institution, 1968), pp. 182–83.

33. Judge David Bazelon, "Criminals Are the Final Result of 'Our Failing Social Justice System,' " *Center Magazine*, July–August 1977, p. 30.

34. Caplan, " 'Losing' the War."

35. "Summary of Report on the State of Massachusetts Courts," mimeographed, Governor's Select Committee on Judicial Needs, Chairman Archibald Cox, December 1976, p. 1.

BIBLIOGRAPHY

BOOKS

Abt, Clark, ed. *The Evaluation of Social Programs*. Beverly Hills: Sage, 1976.

Baker, Ralph, and Meyer, Fred A., Jr. *Evaluating Alternative Law Enforcement Policies*. Lexington, Mass.: Lexington Books, 1979.

Banfield, Edward C. *The Unheavenly City*. Boston: Little, Brown, 1968.

Bardach, Eugene. *The Implementation Game*. Cambridge, Mass.: MIT Press, 1977.

Bauer, Raymond A. *Social Indicators*. Cambridge, Mass.: MIT Press, 1966.

Becker, Theodore. *The Impact of Supreme Court Decisions*. New York: Oxford University Press, 1969.

Bell, Daniel. *The End of Ideology*. New York: Collier Books, 1960.

Bent, Alan Edward. *The Politics of Law Enforcement*. Lexington, Mass.: D. C. Heath & Co., 1974.

Blumberg, Abraham S. *Criminal Justice: Issues and Ironies*. New York: New Viewpoints, 1979.

Bragaw, Louis K. *Managing a Federal Agency: The Hidden Stimulus*. Baltimore: Johns Hopkins University Press, 1980.

Campbell, J. S. *Law and Order Reconsidered*. New York: Praeger, 1971.

Casper, Jonathan. *American Criminal Justice*. Englewood Cliffs, N.J.: Prentice-Hall, 1972.

Christenson, Reo M. *Challenge and Decision: Political Issues of Our Time*. New York: Harper and Row, 1976.

Cipes, Robert M. *The Crime War*. New York: The New American Library, 1968.

Cronin, Thomas E. *The State of the Presidency*. 2d ed. Boston: Little, Brown, 1980.

Derthick, Martha. *New Towns In-Town: Why a Federal Program Failed*. Washington, D.C.: Urban Institute, 1972.

————. *Uncontrollable Spending for Social Service Grants*. Washington, D.C.: Brookings Institution, 1975.

DeWolf, L. Harold. *What Americans Should Do About Crime*. New York: Harper & Row, 1976.

200

Donovan, John C. *The Politics of Poverty.* 2d ed. Indianapolis: Pegasus, 1973.

Douglas, Jack D. *Crime and Justice in American Society.* Indianapolis: Bobbs-Merrill, Inc., 1971.

Dunsire, Andrew. *Implementation in a Bureaucracy.* New York: St. Martins Press, 1979.

Elazar, Daniel J. *American Federalism: A View from the States.* New York: Thomas Crowell, 1964.

Elliff, John T. *Crime, Dissent and the Attorney General.* Beverly Hills, Cal.: Sage Publications, 1971.

Epstein, Edward Jay. *Agency of Fear.* New York: G. P. Putnam's Sons, 1972.

Feeley, Malcolm M., and Sarat, Austin D. *The Policy Dilemma: Federal Crime Policy and the Law Enforcement Assistance Administration, 1968–1978.* Minneapolis: University of Minnesota Press, 1980.

Fleming, Macklin. *Of Crimes and Rights.* New York: W. W. Norton, 1978.

Fritschler, A. Lee. *Smoking and Politics: Policymaking in the Federal Bureaucracy.* Englewood Cliffs, N.J.: Prentice-Hall, 1975.

Gorham, William, and Glazer, Nathan, eds. *The Urban Predicament.* Washington, D.C.: Urban Institute, 1976.

Hargrove, Erwin C. *The Missing Link: The Study of the Implementation of Social Policy.* Washington, D.C.: Urban Institute, 1975.

Harris, Richard. *The Fear of Crime.* New York: Praeger, 1968.

―――. *Justice, The Crisis of Law: Order and Freedom in America.* New York: Avon Books, 1969.

Haveman, Robert H., ed. *A Decade of Federal Antipoverty Programs.* New York: Academic Press, 1979.

Hofstadter, Richard, and Wallace, Michael, eds. *American Violence: A Documentary History.* New York: Random House, 1971.

Inciardi, James A. *Reflectionism Crime: An Introduction to Criminology and Criminal Justice.* New York: Holt, Rinehart and Winston, 1978.

Jacob, Herbert. *Justice in America.* Boston: Little, Brown, 1965.

―――. *Crime and Justice in Urban America.* Englewood Cliffs, N.J.: Prentice-Hall, 1980.

Jacob, Herbert, ed. *The Potential for Reform of Criminal Justice.* Sage Criminal Justice Systems Annuals, vol. 3. Beverly Hills, Cal.: Sage Publications, 1974.

Johnson, Lyndon B. *The Vantage Point.* New York: Holt, Rinehart and Winston, 1971.

Komarovsky, Mirra, ed. *Sociology and Public Policy: The Case of Presidential Commissions.* New York: Elsevier, 1975.

Kristol, Irving, and Weaver, Paul, eds. *The Americans: 1976.* New York: Lexington Books, 1976.

Larson, James S. *Why Government Programs Fail: Improving Policy Implementation.* New York: Praeger Publishers, 1980.

Levin, Martin. *Politics and Criminal Courts.* Chicago: University of Chicago Press, 1977.

Levitan, Sar A., and Wurzburg, Gregory. *Evaluating Federal Social Programs: An Uncertain Art.* Kalamazoo, Mich.: Upjohn Institute, 1979.

McPherson, Harry. *A Political Education*. Boston: Atlantic-Little, Brown, 1972.

Marmor, Theodore. *The Politics of Medicare*. Chicago: Aldine, 1973.

Morris, Norval. *The Future of Imprisonment*. Chicago: University of Chicago Press, 1974.

Morris, Norval, and Hawkins, Gordon. *The Honest Politician's Guide to Crime Control*. Chicago: University of Chicago Press, 1970.

————. *Letter to the President on Crime Control*. Chicago: University of Chicago Press, 1977.

Murphy, Patrick V. *Commissioner: A View from the Top of American Law Enforcement*. New York: Simon & Schuster, 1977.

Nachimias, David, ed. *Public Policy Evaluation*. Madison, Wis.: University of Wisconsin Press, 1978.

————. *The Practice of Policy Evaluation*. Madison, Wis.: University of Wisconsin Press, 1980.

Nakamura, Robert T., and Smallwood, Frank. *The Politics of Policy Implementation*. New York: St. Martin's Press, 1980.

Nathan, Richard P., and Adams, C. F. *Revenue Sharing: The Second Round*. Washington, D.C.: Brookings Institution, 1977.

Nathan, Richard P.; Manuel, Allen D.; Calkins, Susannah E.; and Associates. *Monitoring Revenue Sharing*. Washington: Brookings Institution, 1975.

Nelson, Richard R., and Yates, Douglas T. *Innovation and Implementation in Public Organizations*. Lexington, Mass.: Lexington Books, 1977.

Neubauer, David W. *Criminal Justice in Middle America*. Morristown, N.J.: General Learning Press, 1974.

Neustadt, Richard. *Presidential Power: The Politics of Leadership with Reflections on Johnson and Nixon*. New York: John Wiley, 1976.

Newman, Graham R., ed. *Crime and Justice in America: 1776–1976. Annals of the American Academy of Political and Social Science*, January 1976.

Niederhoffer, Arthur. *Behind the Shield: The Police in Urban Society*. New York: Anchor Books, 1969.

Palumbo, Dennis, ed. *Evaluating and Optimizing Public Policy*. Urbana, Ill.: Policy Studies, 1980.

Pound, Roscoe. *Criminal Justice in America*. New York: Da Capo Press, 1972.

Pressman, Jeffery, and Wildavsky, Aaron. *Implementation*. Berkeley, Cal.: University of California Press, 1973.

Radin, Beryl A. *Implementation, Change and the Federal Bureaucracy*. New York: Teachers College Press, Columbia University, 1977.

Radzinowicz, Leon, and King, Joan. *The Growth of Crime: The International Experience*. New York: Basic Books, Inc., 1977.

Reagan, Michael D. *The New Federalism*. New York: Oxford University Press, 1975.

Rhodes, Robert P. *The Insoluble Problems of Crime*. New York: John Wiley, 1977.

Rodgers, Harrell R., Jr., and Bullock, Charles S., III. *Law and Social Change: Civil Rights Laws and Their Consequences*. New York: McGraw Hill, 1972.

Scammon, Richard, and Wattenberg, Ben J. *The Real Majority*. New York: Coward McCann, 1970.

Seymour, Whitney North, Jr. *Why Justice Fails.* New York: William Morrow, 1973.

Sherrill, Robert. *The Saturday Night Special.* New York: Charterhouse, 1973.

Silberman, Charles E. *Criminal Violence, Criminal Justice.* New York: Random House, 1978.

Skolnick, Jerome H. *Justice without Trial: Law Enforcement in a Democratic Society.* 2d ed. New York: John Wiley, 1975.

Straus, Murray A.; Gelles, Richard; and Steinmetz, Suzanne. *Behind Closed Doors: A Survey of Family Violence.* New York: Doubleday, 1979.

Sundquist, James L. *Making Federalism Work.* Washington: Brookings Institution, 1969.

Van Horn, Carl E. *Policy Implementation in the Federal System.* Lexington, Mass.: Lexington Books, 1979.

White, Theodore H. *The Making of the President: 1964.* New York: Atheneum, 1965.

―――. *Breach of Faith: The Fall of Richard Nixon.* New York: Atheneum Publishers, 1975.

Williams, Walter. *Government by Agency: Lessons from the Grants-in-aid Experience.* New York: Academic Press, 1980.

Williams, Walter, and Elmore, Richard, eds. *Social Program Implementation.* New York: Academic Press, 1976.

Wilson, James Q. *Varieties of Police Behavior: The Management of Law and Order in Eight Communities.* New York: Basic Books, 1968.

―――. *Thinking About Crime.* New York: Basic Books, 1975.

Wilson, Jerry. *Police Report.* Boston: Little, Brown, 1975.

Zenk, Gordon Karl. *Project* SEARCH: *The Struggle for Control of Criminal Information in America.* Westport, Conn.: Greenwood Press, 1979.

Zimring, Franklin E., and Hawkins, Gordon J. *Deterrence: The Legal Threat in Crime Control.* Chicago: University of Chicago Press, 1973.

SELECTED ARTICLES

Bazelon, David L. "Criminals Are the Final Result of Our Failing Social Justice System." *The Center Magazine,* July–August 1977.

Bickel, Alexander M. "Crime, Courts, and the Old Nixon." *New Republic,* 15 June 1968.

Caplan, Gerald. "Reflections on the Nationalization of Crime, 1964–1968." *Law and the Social Order* 5 (1973).

―――. " 'Losing' the War on Crime." Mimeographed address given at Los Angeles Town Hall, Los Angeles, 9 December 1975.

Cohen, Richard E. "Renewal of LEAA Likely Despite Doubts on Crime Impact." *National Journal,* 20 September 1975.

―――. "The Nation's Crime Fighting Agency Is Fighting for Its Survival." *National Journal,* 7 May 1977.

Cressey, Donald. "The State of Criminal Statistics." *National Probation and Parole Association Journal* 3 (1957).

Curtis, Lynn A. "The Conservative New Criminology." *Transaction, Social Science, and Modern Society* 14 (1977).

Frank, Richard S. "LEAA Moves to Improve Its Performance as a Pioneer in Revenue-Sharing Technique." *National Journal,* 29 January 1972.

Hagerty, James E. "Criminal Justice: Toward a New Federal Role." *Public Administration Review*, March–April 1978.

Hale, George E., and Palley, Marian L. "Intergovernmental Relations and the Decision-Making Process." Paper delivered at the Annual Meeting of the American Political Science Association, Washington, D.C., 1–4 September 1977.

Oaks, Dallin. "Studying the Exclusionary Rule in Search and Seizure." *University of Chicago Law Review* 37 (1970).

Salas, Luis P., and Lewis, Ralph G. "The Law Enforcement Assistance Administration and Minority Communities." *Journal of Police Science and Administration* 7 (1979).

Seidman, David, and Couzens, Michael. "Crime, Crime Statistics, and the Great American Anti-Crime Crusade: Police Misreporting of Crime and Political Pressures." Paper delivered at the Annual Meeting of the American Political Science Association, New York City, September 1972.

Silver, Isidore. "Crime and Conventional Wisdom." *Transaction, Social Science, and Modern Society* 14 (1977).

Skoler, Daniel. "Comprehensive Criminal Justice Planning—A New Challenge." *Crime and Delinquency*, July 1968.

Stenberg, Carl W. "The Safe Streets Act: Seven Years Later." *Intergovernmental Perspective*, Winter 1976.

Taylor, Robert E. "Shutting Down the LEAA." *Wall Street Journal*, 2 December 1980.

Turner, Judith Axler. "Congress Holds Past Criticism in Check as It Considers Revenue-Sharing Role for LEAA." *National Journal*, 31 March 1973.

Vorenberg, James. "The War on Crime: The First Five Years." *Atlantic Monthly*, May 1972.

Wilson, James Q. "A Reader's Guide to the Crime Commission Reports." *Public Interest*, no. 9 (1967).

———. "Crime and the Criminologists." *Commentary*, January 1971.

———. "Lock 'Em Up and Other Thoughts About Crime." *New York Times Magazine*, 9 March 1975.

———. "Crime and Punishment in England." *Public Interest*, Spring 1976.

Zeisel, Hans. "The Future of Law Enforcement Statistics: A Summary View." In *Federal Statistics: A Report of the President's Commission on Federal Statistics*, vol. 2, 1971.

Zimring, Franklin, and Hawkins, Gordon. "Ideology and Euphoria in Crime Control." Mimeographed. Chicago: University of Chicago Law School, n.d.

SELECTED REPORTS AND DISSERTATIONS

Advisory Commission on Intergovernmental Relations. *Making the Safe Streets Act Work: An Intergovernmental Challenge*. Washington, D.C.: ACIR, September 1970.

———. *State-Local Relations in the Criminal Justice System*. Washington, D.C.: ACIR, August 1971.

———. *Safe Streets Reconsidered: The Block Grant Experience, 1968–1975*. Washington, D.C.: ACIR, January 1977.

———. *Block Grants: A Comparative Analysis*. Washington, D.C.: ACIR, October 1977.

Bureau of Justice Statistics, U.S. Department of Justice. *Criminal Victimization in the U.S.: A Description of Trends from 1973 to 1977.* Washington, D.C.: U.S. Government Printing Office, 1979.

————. *Intimate Victims: A Study of Violence Among Friends and Relatives.* Washington, D.C.: U.S. Government Printing Office, 1980.

Calder, James D. "Presidents and Crime Control: Some Limitations on Executive Policy Making." Ph.D. dissertation, Claremont Graduate School, 1978.

Chelimsky, Eleanor. *A Primary Source Examination of the* LEAA, *and Some Reflections on Crime Control Policy.* Washington, D.C.: MITRE Corp., May 1974.

————. *High Impact Anti-Crime Program.* Washington, D.C.: MITRE Corp., January 1976.

————. *The Need for Better Data to Support Crime Control Policy.* Washington, D.C.: MITRE Corp., July 1976.

Comptroller General's Report to the Congress: Difficulties of Assessing Results of Law Enforcement Assistance Administration Projects to Reduce Crime. Washington, D.C.: General Accounting Office, 19 March 1974.

Congress. *How Federal Programs to Coordinate Programs to Mitigate Juvenile Delinquency Have Proven Ineffective.* Washington, D.C.: Government Accounting Office, 25 April 1975.

Congressional Budget Office. *Federally Assisted Programs Impacting on State and Local Governments.* Washington, D.C.: CBO, Winter 1980.

Crime and the Law. Congressional Quarterly, 1971.

Federal Bureau of Investigation and Hoover, J. Edgar, or Kelley, Clarence. *Crime in the United States: Uniform Crime Reports.* Washington, D.C.: FBI, 1960–80.

Garofalo, James. *Local Victim Surveys: A Review of the Issues.* Washington, D.C.: National Criminal Justice Information and Statistics Service, 1977.

Graham, Hugh Davis, and Gurr, Ted Robert. *Violence in America: Historical and Comparative Perspective: A Report to the National Commission on the Causes and Prevention of Violence.* Washington, D.C.: U.S. Government Printing Office, 1969.

Institute of Criminal Law and Procedure, Georgetown University Law Center, "Study and Evaluation of Projects and Programs Funded Under the Law Enforcement Assistance Act of 1965." Mimeographed. Washington, D.C.: ICLP, March 1971.

Institute for Law and Social Research. (1) PROMIS Research Project: Highlights of Interim Findings and Implications; (2) Expanding the Perspective of Crime Data: Performance Implications for Policy Makers: (3) Curbing the Repeat Offender: A Strategy for Prosecutors. Mimeographed. Washington, D.C.: ILSR, 1977.

Law Enforcement Assistance Administration. National Criminal Justice Information and Statistics Service. *Criminal Victimization in the United States.* Annual volumes. Washington, D.C.: LEAA, 1973–present.

Mahoney, Barry. "The Politics of the Safe Streets Act, 1965–1974: A Case Study in Evolving Federalism and the National Legislative Process." Ph.D. dissertation, Columbia University, 1976.

National Advisory Commission on Civil Disorders. *The Report of the*

National Advisory Commission on Civil Disorders. Washington, D.C.: U.S. Government Printing Office, March 1968.

National Advisory Commission on Criminal Justice Standards and Goals. *A National Strategy to Reduce Crime.* Washington, D.C.: U.S. Government Printing Office, 1973.

National Commission on Law Observance and Enforcement. *Reports* (Wickersham reports). Washington, D.C.: U.S. Government Printing Office, 1931; Montclair, N.J.: Patterson Smith Reprint Series, 1968.

National Commission on the Causes and Prevention of Violence. *To Establish Justice, To Insure Domestic Tranquility.* Washington, D.C.: U.S. Government Printing Office, 1969.

————. *Law and Order Reconsidered: Report of the Task Force on Law and Law Enforcement.* Washington, D.C.: U.S. Government Printing Office, 1970.

National Research Council. *Understanding Crime: An Evaluation of the National Institute of Law Enforcement and Criminal Justice.* Washington, D.C.: NRC, 1977.

O'Connell, Lawrence W., and White, Susan O. "Politics and Evaluation in LEAA: The New England States." Mimeographed. Paper delivered at the American Political Science Association, New Orleans, 4–8 September 1973.

President Ford: The Man and His Record. Congressional Quarterly, 1974.

President's Commission on Law Enforcement and Administration of Justice. *The Challenge of Crime in a Free Society.* Washington, D.C.: U.S. Government Printing Office, 1967; New York: Avon, 1968.

"Reforming the Criminal Justice System." Special issue of *Current History,* July–August 1976.

Sherman, Lawrence W., and the National Commission on Higher Education for Police Officers. *The Quality of Police Education.* San Francisco: Jossey-Bass, Inc., Publishers, 1978.

Twentieth Century Fund Task Force on the Law Enforcement Assistance Administration. *Law Enforcement: The Federal Role,* background paper by Victor S. Navasky. New York: McGraw Hill Book Co., 1976.

White, Susan O., and Kislov, Samuel, eds. *Understanding Crime: An Evaluation of the National Institute of Law Enforcement and Criminal Justice.* Washington, D.C.: Committee on Research on Law Enforcement and Criminal Justice, National Research Council, National Academy of Sciences, 1977.

SELECTED HEARINGS

U.S., Congress, House, Committee on the Judiciary, Subcommittee 5. *Anti-Crime Program: Hearing.* 98th Cong., 1st sess., March–April 1967.

U.S., Congress, Senate, Committee on the Judiciary, Subcommittee on Criminal Laws and Procedures. *Controlling Crime through More Effective Law Enforcement.* 90th Cong., 1st sess., March–May, July 1967.

U.S., Congress, House, Committee on Government Operations, Subcommittee on Legal and Monetary Affairs. *Hearings on LEAA Performance.* 92d Cong., 1st sess., 20 July 1971, 5 October 1971.

U.S., Congress, Senate, Subcommittee on Delinquency. *Hearings on the*

Juvenile Justice and Delinquency Prevention Act of 1974. Washington, D.C.: U.S. Government Printing Office, 1974.

U.S., Congress, Senate, Committee on the Judiciary, Subcommittee on Criminal Laws and Procedures. *Amendments to Title 1 (LEAA) of the Omnibus Crime Control and Safe Streets Act.* 94th Cong., 2d sess., October–December 1975, March 1976.

U.S., Congress, Senate, Committee on the Judiciary. *Hearings on the Nomination of Griffin B. Bell.* 95th Cong., 1st sess., 11–14, 17–19 January 1977.

U.S., Congress, House, Committee on the Judiciary, Subcommittee on Crime. *Restructuring the Law Enforcement Assistance Administration.* 95th Cong., 1st and 2d sess., August, October 1977; March 1978.

U.S., Congress, Senate, Committee on the Judiciary, Subcommittee on Criminal Laws and Procedures. *Federal Assistance to State and Local Criminal Justice Agencies.* 95th Cong., 2d sess., 16, 23 August 1978.

INDEX